"Stanley Loomis has done full justice to a much-maligned woman. He has done more; he has written a very remarkable book. There is not a dull page in it; his prose is polished, urbane, often evocative, always intelligent. His knowledge and understanding of the eighteenth century are equal to his love for it . . . Madame Du Barry's life up to Louis XV's death is told with brilliance and an admirable sense for comedy. Her later years are, fittingly enough, related in a more mellow, nostalgic key, but it is in this period of her life . . . that her image reaches us with the greatest immediacy. Her touching love affair with the Duc de Brissac is treated with the delicacy of a man of the world; the final nightmare, with indignation and dramatic impact. Entertained at first, then moved, the reader, after the admirable final paragraph, is left pensive. Few books are published of which this could be said."

—*Saturday Review*

DU BARRY

A Biography

•

STANLEY LOOMIS

PYRAMID BOOKS • NEW YORK

DU BARRY

A PYRAMID BOOK
Published by arrangement with J. B. Lippincott Company

PRINTING HISTORY

Lippincott edition published April, 1959
Third printing, 1959
Pyramid edition published November, 1965

Library of Congress Catalog Card Number 59-7780

Printed in the United States of America

PYRAMID BOOKS are published by Pyramid Publications, Inc.
444 Madison Avenue, New York, N. Y. 10022, U.S.A.

Contents

PART I

Chapter 1

IN THAT LONG and curious procession of women known as "the left-hand Queens of France," Jeanne, Comtesse du Barry, came last. The French Revolution, which destroyed so many ancient continuities, destroyed too the flamboyant tradition of the *maîtresse en titre,* the Royal Mistress. Because she died on the guillotine Madame du Barry might be seen as expiating the crimes and follies of her predecessors. The fact that the "Scarlet Lady" who was dragged to the scaffold was, in truth, an amiable, middle-aged woman, many years retired from the "glorious dishonor" which made her name a scandal is either ignored or not known. Even today the woman behind the name du Barry and the story of her life remain obscured by lurid legend. Only Madame de Pompadour, her predecessor at Versailles, shares du Barry's celebrity, but the Marquise de Pompadour, thanks to the fascination she has held for biographers, survives as a woman and a personality. So much, indeed, has been written about Madame de Pompadour that the casual reader of biography might be left with the impression that Louis XV soon followed her to the grave and that little of interest or consequence followed her exit from the stage of Versailles. To those familiar with the neglected history of the *ancien régime* the death of Madame de Pompadour would be viewed not as an end but rather as a beginning.

The reign of favor that followed Pompadour's passing introduced to history a life which began in the obscurity of the provinces, then rose from the streets of Paris to a position of eminence among the most dazzling in the civilized world. The death of Louis XV sent the Comtesse du Barry back into obscurity from which she was again to be drawn by the mighty drama of the French Revolution. Curious in itself, her story comprehends the decline and fall of a civilization, a "way of life," a political heritage. The landscape against which her life must be depicted is the landscape of history. Although the wider prospect is often closed to view by the narrower but nearer event, the distant shapes and contours are the landmarks of pre-Revolution France. She was, almost completely, the creature of her age. As such her biography has a dimension of interest that is deeper than an account of the life of Madame du Barry. It is not, for example, at Vaucouleurs where she was born that her life may properly be said to begin, but rather at the palace of Versailles where Fate for some years had been weaving a tapestry of strange design and color.

Madame de Pompadour died on April 15 of 1764. She was little more than forty, but the cruel claw of ambition on one side and that of anxiety on the other had torn her frail constitution apart. "My sufferings," she once was heard to complain, "are like those of Christ of yore."

Pompadour's had been the paradox of some great concert pianist born with insufficient fingers, for this woman who is one of history's most celebrated courtesans was, in fact, frigid. To warm a temperament that by nature was cool, to stir a sensuality that at best was sluggish, she had recourse to curious aphrodisiacs and exotic diets. At breakfast she drank truffle and celery soup washed down by hot chocolate which had been laced by triple vanilla and ambergris. But the very fear that she would not be able to do that which she must made her, in its effect, the less able to do it. The diet made her stout; the worry gave her wrinkles, those first wrinkles that are terrible to all beautiful women, but to a Favorite of the King of France presage not merely the ruin of her beauty but of her fortune.

At last, at the moment when in the eyes of the ever-calculating courtiers she seemed most likely to fall, she retired as Mistress, remaining at Versailles as procuress and—so it was explained to the Pope—"confidential advisor" to Louis XV. It was an extraordinary arrangement, but the Marquise de Pompadour was an extraordinary woman. Henceforth her term of favor was to depend on mind and wit alone, on the power of her charm to bewitch, on her incomparable ability to delight, distract and amuse a world-weary and aging satyr.

Reading the memoirs of the time it is not difficult to picture those endless supper parties, those night-long fêtes at Choisy, at Fontainebleau, at Marly, Bellevue and Versailles with the bright smiles, the never relaxed vivacity, the always-tinkling laughter of their presiding hostess. But from the Marquise's lady-in-waiting, Madame du Hausset, we catch a glimpse of the show after the curtain has fallen: weeping, insomnia, headaches and palpitations, the shrieking nerves of a woman close to collapse. In January of the year the Marquise died her friend Madame de la Ferté found the poor creature almost raving: "She complained of sleeplessness and indigestion, and of feeling as if she were suffocating. She told me how grieved she was by the deplorable state of the kingdom, assuring me that only affection for the King kept her at his side. She spoke of how much happier she would have been living peacefully at Menars, but the King could not spare her. In opening her heart she became passionate and eloquent beyond anything I have ever seen in her. She seemed distraught, almost raving, and never in my life have I heard a clearer sermon on the unhappiness which is the outcome of ambition: I saw her at once so profoundly unhappy, so arrogant, so wildly excited, and in spite of her great power, so utterly helpless that when I left her after an hour I felt that death was now her only hope."

It is said that her years of favor cost France close to eighty million dollars, an estimate that does not include the cost of the Seven Years War and of her various other excursions into statecraft. She was clever, capable and gifted with many talents, but ambition obliged her to play a rôle for which she was not suited. Pride, not lust was her sin; the wages of that sin were paid her with a pitiless precision.

Breath had scarcely left the body when it was flung onto a litter and hurriedly whisked from the palace by a back door to be taken to Pompadour's house in the town. Etiquette, which was unable to bar death from Versailles, at least could decree that his victims be removed immediately. On April 17 Louis pulled aside the curtains of his study overlooking the Cour de Marbre and stepped onto the balcony. A cold rain beat down in gust-driven sheets against the courtyard, but as the King stood there in the thickening light of late afternoon, peering toward the Church of Notre-Dame de Versailles, his head was uncovered. He watched the little procession pass before the palace gates and then turn up the avenue that leads toward Paris where by Pompadour's desire her body was to be entombed in the vault of the Capuchin church. He stood so until the hooves of the horses clattering over the cobbles could be heard no more. Then he went inside.

"The poor Marquise," he said dully, "is having bad

weather for her trip to Paris." Two tears streamed down His Majesty's cheeks.

She had been his mistress for fourteen years; his friend for twenty.

Louis XV was fifty-four. He could look back on such a life as has been given very few mortals, crowned or uncrowned, to enjoy. At five he had succeeded to the oldest and mightiest throne in Europe. As though it were not enough that he should inherit almost inconceivable wealth and power the gods, to make their gift seem quite flawless, added personal beauty, intelligence, and sensibility. When he assumed the sceptre at thirteen years of age his reign began with the radiant promise of a spring morning that dispelled the wintry gloom and cold of the long reign that had passed. Adored by his subjects, aped by his courtiers, Louis entered history like a young knight mounted on a white charger. He left it an object of contempt and hatred; despised by his subjects, deplored by posterity.

It is possible that the only gift the gods need ever bestow is strength of character. Without it those other more obvious gifts are meaningless if not downright dangerous; with it the other gifts may sometimes be acquired through the usual means: hard work. His lack of character brought Louis—and with him France—to a condition close to ruin. "He was endowed," wrote that professional observer of men the Chevalier d'Éon, "with great penetration, great judgment and a profound knowledge of men and of things. All he lacked was the strength of character to control his ministers and ambassadors as a king should. In the midst of his own court he possessed less power than a prison official. With incredible weakness he permitted his disloyal servants to triumph over the faithful and he always did more for his open enemies than for his true friends."

Indolence, diffidence and an ever-restraining sense of personal unworthiness, these soon made themselves evident. "He rises at eleven," wrote a diarist of the time, "and leads a useless life. From his frivolous distractions he occasionally steals an hour of work; the sessions with his Ministers cannot be called work, for he lets them do everything, merely listening and repeating what they say like a parrot. He is still a child." The King was thirty years of age when this description was written. Not until his reign was half over did Louis become something more than a mere puppet of Ministers or of women more strongly willed than himself: during his minority there had been the Regent, then for nearly twenty years his Minister, the gentle Cardinal Fleury, who while he wielded power mildly, clutched it firmly. Death alone succeeded in unloosing the ninety-year-old Cardinal's tenacious grasp. Louis was by then well down the path that led to the quagmire of sloth and sensuality in which, at such cost to his people and his House, he was finally to flounder.

Of the five mistresses who lent their lustre to his reign, the first three were the de Nesle sisters; and each in descending order was worse than the other. The first, Madame de Mailly, made up in vivacity of manner for what so conspicuously she lacked in beauty of person. Foreigners who saw Madame de Mailly were shocked. It seemed to them that the descendant of Saint-Louis owed it to his station in life to select for a mistress a woman more attractive than Madame de Mailly. But all his life it was charm, the delight of female companionship and conversation that the lonely Louis XV would seek to find in women. Madame de Mailly was at heart a good woman, assuming her station with gentle gravity, loving the King as the modest La Vallière had loved his forbear. She was given to saying prayers. As *maîtresse en titre* she lasted about two years, when she was brusquely shoved aside by her younger and more wolfish sister, Madame de Vintimille. This second of the de Nesle sisters was a rough, mannish woman of whom her husband was heard to say, "The bitch stinks like a monkey." She interested herself in politics and troop movements and was just settling down to boss things when death carried her away from the scene of her many hopes.

Shortly after the removal of Madame de Vintimille a third of the de Nesle sisters, one Madame de la Tournelle, stepped boldly onto the stage. Madame de la Tournelle was a cold-blooded, calculating gold digger who boasted neither heart nor scruple. Of the three sisters she was the most beautiful—and by far the cleverest. She was without the slightest affection for the King, or for that matter anybody. The demands on her cold nature, which the maintenance of favor frequently imposed, didn't in the least disturb her. Madame de la Tournelle lacked the Pompadour's fastidious sensibility: there were no headaches here, no hysterics. She knew precisely what she wanted, she knew exactly what the price was: she paid it. First on her list of demands was the exile of her de Mailly sister: second was the elevation of herself to the rank of Duchesse. The King gave her the Duchy of Châteauroux and it is from here that she took the name by which she is known to history.

The Duchesse de Châteauroux had a confidant (and very

probably a lover) in the person of the dissolute and cynical Duc de Richelieu, great-nephew of the Cardinal and First Gentleman of the Bedchamber (apt appointment!) to His Majesty. The surreptitious and shocking correspondence between Madame de Châteauroux and Richelieu reads so much like something out of *Les Liaisons dangereuses* that one seriously might wonder if Laclos had not somehow had access to this shameless record of cold-blooded machination.

"I heard him [the King] scratching at my door," she confides in one of her earlier letters, "but when he saw that I did not get up he went away. He's going to have to get used to this sort of thing."

"As you know," the Duchesse purrs in a later letter, "I carefully conceal any interest or knowledge in public affairs in order to encourage him to instruct me. We must go slow here . . . the less I talk of events the more he likes to tell me of them. Then is the moment to pounce. Unhesitatingly, dear Uncle, I shall follow your advice and will never act without consulting you."

Through the wily Richelieu the Duchesse's hands were soon plunged deep into the ever-turbulent waters of palace intrigue.

"Cardinal Tencin seems to be cultivating me and I wonder what you think of this? His sister is a liability. She's a clever little piece, but she is unable to conceal her ambition. I have had several anonymous letters, doubtless from her, full of complaints about Maurepas. Her views change with her interests."

The Duchesse (and Richelieu) loathed Maurepas, the King's chief Minister: "I hate him and he is the torment of my life. Get me the facts about him and I promise to turn them to good account." Just as twenty years later Richelieu was to achieve the downfall of his enemy Choiseul through Madame du Barry, so now was he scheming through Madame de Châteauroux to effect the ruin of the hated Maurepas.

The history of Eighteenth Century France, and by extension a good part of the history of Europe, is not to be discovered in the record of its wars, its treaties or its fiscal policies. It is to be found in the ceaseless busy intrigues of Versailles, hidden in deep tunnels of a thousand sharp-clawed moles, lost forever in the furtive whispers of the ever-forming, ever-dissolving cliques and petty conspiracies of the most malicious and the cleverest people in Europe. From the day the Court first inhabited it until the day one hundred fifty years later when it was abandoned forever, the history of Versailles is one of never-ending intrigue. It hummed perpetually like some monstrous wasps' nest. Buzzing and burrowing, its energetic little tenants were forever on the move, busying themselves with this or that purpose of spite, lust or greed. At Versailles there was always something afoot; the air was continually electric with pending or freshly past excitement.

Such a spectacle lends small credit to human nature and the serious historian frequently averts his eye from it. But contemptible as the event may appear, the downfall of so important a wasp as a Mailly or Châteauroux was a happening that to history could be a matter instinct with the most far-reaching consequences. On the downfall or the favor of a Mistress frequently depended the downfall or favor of a Minister—and on the Minister and his adherents depended policy. It was not to the King or to any of his Ministers that Maria Theresa first proposed the alliance which was to rock the foundations of European diplomacy. It was, wisely, to Madame de Pompadour. Trivial as these intrigues may have been in purpose, in consequence they were often deadly serious.

In 1744 Madame de Châteauroux was arrogantly riding the crest of fortune's wave. She was detested by the Court and especially by Louis' long-suffering and pious wife, the good Queen Marie Leczinska. But cold silences from the dreary prayer-reading Queen were no more likely to disturb this hardened woman of the world than the false smiles of false friends. "I close my eyes to these intrigues so common against those in my position. The very people who want to injure me most are those who show me the greatest attentions."

Her star, and with it Richelieu's, was just fixing itself in the firmament when there occurred an event that was to set the nest a-humming as it rarely was to hum again. The girl who one day would become the Comtesse du Barry was one year of age at the time; thirty years later the episode of Metz would give her nightmares. The very name of Metz was to send shudders down the spine of Madame de Pompadour.

In May of 1744, egged on by the relentless Duchesse, who in this move saw a means to destroy the influence of Maurepas, the King departed for the front to exhort his troops, then engaged in battle with the Austrians near the Alsatian frontier. The Duchesse restlessly remained in Paris reading with mingled anxiety and pleasure the reports from Richelieu which told her step by step of the success of the King's trip. As the weeks went by hints started reaching her, from this and that source, of a growing collusion between the

Queen and Maurepas. It was whispered that a plot was being hatched and that a fourth de Nesle sister, Madame de Flavacourt, was not unattractive to His Majesty and that Maurepas and the Queen, seizing upon the advantage of the King's prolonged absence, were contriving the Duchesse's downfall through the instrument of Madame de Flavacourt. Absence did not make Louis XV's heart grow fonder. "Out of sight, out of mind" was the maxim that more fitted the apathetic King and none knew this better than the Duchesse, a keen observer of men. In July, unable to contain herself any longer, she set out for the front. Since permission to do so had specifically been denied her, the trip represented something of a gamble on her part. Accompanying her were the Princesse de Conti, the Duchesse de Bourbon, the Duchesse de Modena and the Duchesse d'Orléans, each headed for a husband or lover. As they neared the front, their train of gold-emblazoned carriages tearing angrily through the rustic mire must have presented a singular sight to the local hoydens and bumpkins who gaped from the roadside at this imperious procession. The Duchesse was of course received with open arms. Such as she rarely lose a gamble on human nature. ("I assure you," she once boasted to Richelieu about the King, "I know every twist of his soul.") The lovers stayed briefly at the front where the sight of their King, His Most Christian Majesty, with the brazen Favorite in all her triumph lolling at his side, no doubt edified the stalwart sons of France. Then they journeyed slowly on to Metz.

On August 8, 1744, two days after their arrival, a dinner reception was given to the Prussian Ambassador. The King appeared tired, but his Bourbon appetite was in no way impaired. He ate his usual heavy meal, talked in that majestic yet amiable manner which was uniquely his, and retired at his usual hour. He awoke the next morning with a high fever. For a while a cluster of sycophant women and frightened attendants tried to keep the matter a secret, but the disease moved with swift virulence and within hours it had become alarming. The doctors having done their worst now made way for the priests. The King was not expected to live.

In the face of every evidence to the contrary, Louis XV was an intensely religious man. The form, the rite, the ritual filled him with mingled emotions of awe and terror. Unlike so many of his sophisticated subjects he believed in God. How exactly he managed to reconcile the habits of his private life with the convictions of his religion it would be difficult to guess. Probably his picture of the Almighty was of a King very much like himself, but Omnipotent and Everlasting. Such a One would be inclined to understand and perhaps forgive an occasional trespass. In any case he never tried to reconcile the two at the cost of the Sacraments. To receive Communion meant Confession; to receive Absolution might, therefore, mean the expulsion of the current Favorite. To be *au courant* of the "situation" in the Sovereign's privy chambers, it was the practice at Versailles to observe whether or not he received the Sacraments at Easter. Death filled the King with thoughts of direst terror. In his frequent seizures of melancholy he would brood for hours on graves, skeletons and worms. It was a Mistress's foremost duty to distract him from these gloomy obsessions, and to "sleek o'er his troubled looks." He reminds one in these moods of some Asiatic potentate, some Khan or Khedive or Sultan. There was perhaps a touch of madness in his great and ancient race. Any mention of graves filled his mistresses with despair, for from graves to priests and from priests to Sacraments and renunciation lay a chain of thought too obvious for comfort. For her own safety the first object of every Favorite was to keep the King as far away from the Sacraments as possible or, to put it in terms of Louis' faith, to keep him in a condition of damnation as long as possible.

Such was the predicament at Metz. If he were dying it was unthinkable that a son of Saint-Louis should leave his realm without Grace, headed perhaps for Purgatory or even, conceivably, for Hell. To receive Grace, however—and the priests made this point very clear—he would have to dismiss the Mistress. Should he recover there could be no return of Madame de Châteauroux for by dismissal the Bishop of Soissons meant renunciation. The dilemma was now largely the Duchesse's. With her would fall Richelieu and, with Richelieu, the entire faction. In his extremity there remained little doubt in the King's mind. He had no intention of meeting his Maker without the proper credentials. There was, moreover, an outside chance that if he were to confess and make due sacrifice God might show mercy and permit him to live. The Queen was already speeding to his bedside. And so with a gentleness that spoke too clearly his regret the King dismissed the once-haughty Favorite. "It is best," he murmured, "that we part."

After receiving the Viaticum, the King kept his promise to the Bishop of Soissons and summoned his officials and the officials of Metz to his bedside where he asked pardon for the ungodly example he had shown his people, and announced that the Duchesse de Châteauroux had been dismissed forever from his Court. The Bishop with a firmness that was commendable, but a temerity that was perhaps impolitic, ordered this apology and promise to be read from every pulpit in France. Torn between genuine anxiety over their King's extremity and savage glee at what it had wrought to the bold virago (she was as much detested in the streets as she was in the palaces), the whole country was in an uproar.

Half-crazed with rage and shame, the fallen creature repaired not to Paris where she had been ordered, but to an estate at nearby Sainte-Menehould where she could better keep an eye on developments at Metz. She never doubted that, were he to recover, her charms would seduce the King from his solemn vows. What scores she would have to pay off then! The hooting glee of the *canaille* who danced about her carriage flinging mud and insult troubled her very little. It was the supercilious scorn of the courtiers, the wasps, that stung her almost to madness. "Nothing can make up for the humiliations I have suffered. As I was about to step into my carriage I met [the Comte] d'Argenson who cut me with an air of cold contempt. Everyone avoided me . . . I should love to avenge myself on those people who thinking that I was finished tried to humiliate me." Or again: "If he recovers what a joy it will be! I shall regard it as Heaven's method of opening his eyes and punishing evildoers. If he pulls through you will agree that our star will carry us a very long way, and nothing will then be beyond our grasp."

The King did recover. All hope had been abandoned when from nowhere there appeared a quiet gentleman who promised a cure if the royal physicians would step aside and permit him to try his remedy. It was probably the departure of the doctors more than the mysterious visitor's herb concoction that restored the King to life, for they were a notorious lot and a visit from them with their terrible clysters and their bleedings spelt almost certain death. The King recovered, but only to face the mortification and chagrin of a spectacular and needless repentance, to face the prospect of a dreary lifetime by the side of his boring wife. Health quickly returned and with it a renewed appreciation of the world he had almost left and of its many delights. From Paris the temptress's voice was wafted to his ears. As the weight of boredom and melancholy grew heavier so did the promises of the siren grow sweeter. After a struggle with himself that was neither intense nor long, the King's frail scruples collapsed and the Duchesse was summoned back to Versailles.

It was a turning-point in his life. Apart from what he appeared now in the eyes of his people, Louis was surely disgraced in his own. In the struggle between temptation and resolution, temptation, he now admitted, would always win. It is not for our sins that on this earth we suffer, but for our conscience. The humiliating episode at Metz and its more humiliating outcome had a profound effect on his character because Louis, unhappily for himself, had both conscience and scruple. He knew that he was doing wrong, but he couldn't help himself. And such, according to Dante, is the condition of damnation. It is Hell's special torture that it is always by our own preference that we choose to be there. For Louis the seizures of malaise, of boredom and melancholy, grew more frequent and more intense and the need of a *maîtresse en titre* consequently more exacting.

In Paris, fire blazing from her proud nostrils, the vindictive Duchesse prepared for her return. Her enemies and those false friends who on her dismissal had unwisely thrown off their masks must have shivered at the news. But their fears were quickly allayed for now in the giddy hour of the creature's ultimate triumph she was struck down by the hand that had failed to fell her lover. One evening after a hot bath, sudden and frightful pains, probably those of peritonitis, convulsed her body. She, and later Richelieu, insisted that she had been poisoned by Maurepas and his faction. Nine times did she manage to survive the physicians' bleedings; history does not record the number of clysters. Paris and the Court were in an ecstasy of joy for this time death was not to be cheated of his victim. She died in a spirit of sweet piety that edified the Jesuit who had been summoned to receive her confession. That it be spared the outrages of the Paris mob who howled with joy, her corpse was entombed in the greatest secrecy. Thus, at twenty-seven years of age, did the Duchesse de Châteauroux depart this world.

Among the celebrating Parisians on that day there was one who must surely have held a quiet little holiday in her heart. Clever little Madame Le Normant d'Étioles had no grudge against the vanished Duchesse. She was bourgeoise and the gate to those exalted circles in which the Duchesse by virtue of birth and favor moved was closed to her. The future Madame de Pompadour was scarcely known to the Duchesse, for Paris and Versailles comprised two very distant societies. Some years before when Madame d'Étioles was a girl and her name was Poisson a prophecy had been given her by one of those fortune tellers who seem to have been so active and accurate in the Eighteenth Century. She would one day be Mistress to the King. Just as today a perspicacious gypsy might flatter the aspirations of an ambitious young Vassar freshman by foreseeing for her the career of sales manager, novelist, or personnel efficiency expert, so in those more frivolous days the dream of every normal young French girl could have been shrewdly forecast in the picture of the King's Mistress. And Jeanne Poisson with all the tenacity of impressionable girlhood, believed. Her family, half in jest, and half in doubt in the hope that their little girl might someday really become the King's Mistress, nicknamed her Reinette—Little Queen.

Few who knew Madame d'Étioles, now in her early twenties, would deny the uniqueness of her qualifications for the position to which she aspired. In that sparkling confluence of French waters where in Paris the stream of Society met that of Letters, no one twinkled more brightly than pretty little Madame Le Normant d'Étioles. Every accomplishment seemed to be hers; she sang, she played the harpsichord, she sketched, she acted and she could converse with both animation and intelligence. Not only could she do all these things, she did them consummately well. In her person seemed to be combined all the enameled, slightly hard perfections which were the ideal of the skeptical, urbane, highly sophisticated society which she graced so exquisitely. Indeed she was not entirely unknown to the King, who during the Châteauroux's lifetime had gone so far as to send her a hamper of game and a basket or two of hothouse fruit. But Madame de Châteauroux was a formidable obstacle; it would have taken a tougher *intrigante* than the future Madame de Pompadour to overturn that imperious beauty. Death now did swiftly what the slow poison of malice and the temptation of rival charms had failed to accomplish. For Madame d'Étioles it was now or never if she was to bring her singular qualifications to the King's attention. She did. Within a year of that occasion Monsieur Le Normant d'Étioles' wife had become the Marquise de Pompadour.

Of the "reign" of Madame de Pompadour, which was by no means the scandalous affair that contemporary sensationalists and their descendants have made of it, much that is creditable might be said. To the arts she brought her faultless taste and her seemingly limitless bounty. To the gloomy King she brought distraction; to the Court she brought an elevation not a lowering of tone. Her stamp is on everything that is French and fine and delightful about the culture of her time: Sèvres, Boucher, Fragonard, they are inseparable from the name of Pompadour.

When consternation and shock at the appointment of a

bourgeoise to the King's favor had died away most courtiers found her a good deal easier to take than the late Duchesse. "If he has to have one, better this than the other," sighed the forgotten Queen. Madame de Pompadour was always scrupulously respectful toward the Queen. She was a loyal friend, although a vindictive and dangerous enemy. Her extravagance was appalling. With her begins the tradition in France of financial profligacy by women nearest the Treasury: Madame du Barry, Marie Antoinette, Joséphine, these were her successors.

She introduced the King to the delights of architecture and of landscape gardening, those most dangerous of all diversions which have sucked Kings and Popes and princes of finance into a quagmire of ruin. During her term of favor she owned more than seventeen different estates. The Château de Bellevue alone cost more than twelve million dollars to build and furnish. "Although not very large it is really rather delightful," the former Mademoiselle Poisson was able to write unblushingly of Bellevue, a pleasure palace on the scale of a lesser Versailles, "and with no pretense at magnificence."

Startling as they are, such extravagances neither condemn the Marquise nor herald the Revolution. Even at this level they remain exactly what they were: the personal expenses of a spendthrift woman, and they made that sized dent in the Treasury. They injured but by no means crippled it. Not for her love of baubles and bonnets, nor even for her greed for châteaux can the historian condemn Madame de Pompadour. (Sèvres probably contributed to foreign trade and on her death the estates were bequeathed to the Crown.) Her continual and active meddling in affairs of state was a matter of far graver significance.

"The life, the whole life of Madame de Pompadour belongs to history," write the Goncourts. "It was a life of affairs, of intrigues, of negotiations, the maintenance of a political role, a public exercise of power, a commerce at all hours with Secretaries of State, with men of the sword, with men of money, with men of the robe, a control of the interests of the nation and of the will of the King, an influence on the destinies of France and of Europe." Her heels clicked efficiently over the floors of Versailles as she busied herself with this matter or with that with an intensity of pleasure that suggests she may have been a bit touched by the *folie des grandeurs*. Her plump little fingers gracefully but very firmly held the reins of power. The Abbé Bernis, a worldly and superficial prelate who wrote delightful poetry and was amusing company for the ladies, was her appointment to the Ministry of Foreign Affairs. Choiseul, brilliant but dangerously vain ("a fool with genius," was Pope Benedict's description of him), was her final appointment to this crucial office. For the critical rôle he played in the Diplomatic Revolution Choiseul may be considered one of the most important statesmen of Eighteenth Century Europe. Without the favor of Madame de Pompadour he would certainly never have attained his position and probably not have held it.

Delightful as she was in the rôle of Muse, her posture as Elder Statesman is open to the sharpest criticism. She lacked entirely the cold and dispassionate eye, requisite to the man of State, which sees its goal and moves relentlessly toward it. Trivia by the wayside distracted her. Flattery (and conversely insult) quickly blurred her limited vision. She was shrewd, but in a mean sense of the word. Her practical intelligence was of the sort that reckons accurately but in small figures. She might have run a successful vegetable stall or a small hat shop on the Left Bank. Par excellence she was a woman (or what men believed a woman to be): intuitive, sensitive, capricious and often unable to separate personal feeling from intellect. As it is with many people, she seemed to believe that she was the center of the universe. Such egotists exist in a network of complicated likes and dislikes, almost always personal, and with these as guideposts will live out their lives. Whatever their success in other lines of endeavor: hardware salesmen, stockbrokers or wardheelers, they have always made conspicuously poor statesmen.

The most famous and disastrous of the Marquise's undertakings was the Seven Years War. It is impossible to estimate the extent of her complicity in this affair, but any dispassionate account of it makes sorry reading indeed for those who would like to believe that history is hewn by the giants of this earth. On to an ego sorely wounded by the merciless malice of Frederick of Prussia, the Austrian Ambassador gently poured the imperial balm of Maria Theresa's overtures. Would she, the Marquise de Pompadour, be willing on behalf of the Empress's Ambassador to undertake an assignment of the most delicate and critical nature? She, Maria Theresa, Queen of Hungary and Holy Roman Empress, approached Madame de Pompadour in utmost confidence. . . . On the part of Maria Theresa it was a masterful stroke.

In a vapor of self-importance the giddy Favorite set herself to undoing France's traditional alliances, with all the fervor and energy of a suburban clubwoman supporting a Worthy Cause. Floods of dispatches flowed through her hands: reports from distant embassies, reports from the ubiquitous spies in the chancellories of Europe, reports from her privy council. Night and day the busy creature worked over a mound of secret papers that poured in to her from the corners of Europe; night and day she insinuated her projects in the King's ear.

Since the reign of Francis I, Austria and France had bellowed at each other across the reaches of Europe in an enmity that by the 1750's had grown deeper than reason or expediency. But the hour had now struck—so Maria Theresa and her Minister, Prince Kaunitz, realized, and so in his heart did Louis—for France and Austria to come to terms with their ancient (and now-senseless) rivalry, forget the past and realize that what in the time of the great Cardinal had been a necessary and purposeful policy of state, had become in the time of his descendants a meaningless and empty custom, as perfunctory as the steps in some Court ritual but desperately dangerous. The time had arrived for these two crowns, the most ancient in Europe, to guard together the splendid patrimony of Charlemagne, of which on this earth the King of France and the Daughter of the Caesars were the signal and magnificent heirs. With the Mistress's active support and the King's tacit consent the alliance was finally promulgated. It was done with a dangerous splitting of deep and ancient roots and at the cost of a reluctant and sorely divided France, but done it was. To the consternation of Europe, France and Austria had become allies. A new era—and the Seven Years War—had begun.

In the ensuing horror the Marquise held to her object with all the tenacity of despair. At times it seems that only her consuming hatred, her passionate loathing, of Frederick the Great kept her going. In one of the most disastrous wars in French history, victory for the French would not have gained them much more than the ruin of Prussia, the triumph, so to speak, of the Marquise over its sour, woman-hating King. While there may have been very little to gain there was, on the other hand, a great deal to lose no matter how the wheel of fortune turned. A Treasury bled white, a suffering, starved nation, the colonies in America lost, the bread of bitterness, sorrow and humiliation: this was the price of the Seven Years War. Madame de Pompadour went into it young, she came out an ailing, exhausted woman. She died within a year of its conclusion. It was the war she had in mind when she opened her heart to Madame de la Ferté telling her how grieved she was at the state of the kingdom. It was the war that the Duc de Croy had in mind when on Pompadour's death he said: "France suffered many misfortunes in her time."

No one regretted her passing. Her enemies were delighted: her "faction" headed by Choiseul was now too deeply imbedded in affairs of state to be casually uprooted. On the whole they were probably relieved to have her out of the way. One can only surmise the depth of the King's despair. On such matters he rarely opened his heart. "We have lost the poor Marquise," wrote the Dauphine. "The King is very distressed and controls himself with difficulty in public. Our greatest hope is that he will now concentrate his affections on his children and find his happiness with us and that God will touch his heart."

For the King the sun was now setting fast and the shadow of age lengthened ominously before his path. With the passing of the Marquise had passed laughter and an irreplaceable delight. The vast palace was full of ghosts. There was a great deal of talk about God by his depressing family and many prayers were offered for his return to their bosom. There were, to be sure, plenty of women at Court eager to fill the empty post. But they were dull and in the case of Louis they made the mistake of supposing that his Mistress's sole function was to share his couch. They forgot the table and the fireside, always so important to the King who was able to gratify his senses at his private brothel, the Parc-aux-Cerfs. Companionship he needed, and amusement. Neither the Court nor his family, nor the furtive visits to the Parc-aux-Cerfs could offer him these. Gloom and loneliness hung like a thick miasma over the morbid, aging monarch.

Death grew busy at Versailles: Louis's favorite daughter, the Duchess of Parma; the eldest of his grandsons; Madame de Pompadour; and then his only son quickly followed by his son's wife, the gentle Dauphine, vanished one by one into the night. In 1768 the Queen died, glad no doubt to be done with a life outwardly so splendid, but inwardly so full of sorrow, humiliation and disappointment. She bore her burden with Christian submission and even with wisdom, for in the good, generous heart of Marie Leczinska there was no bitterness. Madame Campan, that energetic chronicler who would live to see far stranger sights, was a girl then and a "reader" to the King's spinster daughters. The sumptuous gloom of Court mourning that followed the Queen's death made an indelible picture on her young mind. She never forgot the sight of "those magnificent apartments heavily hung in richest black; the state chairs raised on steps and overhung with canopies adorned with black plumes; the caparisoned horses, the immense processions, all in deepest mourning; the pages and footmen with enormous shoulder knots embroidered in gold and silver spangles."

Since the Queen had no influence (the King's visits to her had been perfunctory appointments), her little circle of friends was genuine. She had no enemies and even the most hardened courtiers agreed that although she was a bore she was a good woman. The few who mourned her passing were soon glad that she had departed the scene when she had. Scarcely had the poor woman been laid to rest when the air was crackling with rumor. The wasps' nest suddenly began to hum excitedly. For it was reported that the King had fallen in love and that soon there would be a new Favorite the like of whom had never before been seen in the gold and crystal halls of Versailles.

Chapter 2

A YEAR BEFORE the episode at Metz, in the little village of Vaucouleurs located in what is now called the Department of the Meuse (but which in 1743 was more pleasantly known as the Province of Champagne) a woman of the name Anne Bécu gave birth to a daughter. That the mother was unmarried was a matter of no particular interest either to herself or to the community. In France at that time marriage was viewed more as a joining of properties than of people. That someone might consider it as a serious Sacrament would have been a piece of sentimentality that would have invited astonishment from the class into which little Jeanne Bécu was born, and contemptuous amusement from that to which she would one day attain. Life is brief and life is earnest and there is every evidence that the baby's mother supplemented the meagre income which she earned as a sempstress, by an occasional sale on the side of certain riches with which nature had conspicuously provided her. She seemed to have been one of those women who in the words of a contemporary journalist "hold themselves aloof from professional prostitutes, making no special study of the arts of love, but readily accept the little pleasures that come their way. They take pains to please and are conscientious in the performance of their duties. They are honest, decent girls."

Mademoiselle Bécu was, in any case, either unable or unwilling to offer any suggestions as to who exactly the baby's father might have been, leaving this mystery to the unborn biographers of Madame du Barry. Of these the more romantically inclined have suggested some passing soldier to whom the hospitable woman had offered the warmth of her bed; others, more plausibly, have suggested a monk named Gomard, known in religion as Brother Angel. The monk was well acquainted with Mademoiselle Bécu and had been living near Vaucouleurs at a time which would support this theory. He rather mysteriously appears and disappears at moments in the Comtesse du Barry's life and was indeed a witness to her wedding contract.

When Jeanne Bécu was five years old her mother decided to move to Paris where two of her brothers and a sister were in domestic service. With their help Anne Bécu was able soon after her arrival to find a situation as cook in the household of a rich contractor named Dumonceaux, a man, it is recorded, of considerable artistic sensibility and much taste. Dumonceaux, struck by the extraordinary beauty and breeding of the six-year-old child, became a kind of godfather to her and with the encouragement of his mistress, Francesca—a famous courtesan of the day—and perhaps with that too of the mysterious Brother Angel, made arrangements that she should be accepted as a boarder in the Convent of Saint-Aure in Paris.

Saint-Aure was not one of those dim, sumptuous places of retreat for world-weary Princesses of the Blood, neither was it one of those too notorious cloisters, the scandal even of Eighteenth Century Europe, where the night was rent by the drunken screams of reeling, riotous nuns. It was a modest place whose doors were open to young girls of decent background "who may find themselves in circumstances in which they are in danger of ruin." Here, in an air of austere decorum such girls were instructed in reading, writing, embroidery, and housekeeping: accomplishments that would be helpful to them and perhaps lend a little lustre to the modest station in life to which it was hoped that the pupils might aspire. The food was plain, the uniform—a white serge frock and coarse woolen hood—severe. The sisters kept a sharp eye turned for such symptoms of incipient worldliness as affected airs or a taste for frippery.

Jeanne Bécu entered Saint-Aure at the age of seven; she left it at sixteen. Obscurity hangs over those years, but she must have been happy there because the mark of a convent education never left her. To the end of her life she was impeccably observant of the rituals of her Church and always generous to persons of the cloth. During the Revolution one of the charges that was to bring her head to the guillotine was that she had sheltered priests. She did not deny the accusation. Saint-Aure gave her an education quite as respectable as had some of those at Versailles who so loudly laughed at what they supposed to be her ignorance. Foreigners and people not of the Court who saw her during her years of notoriety were to a person astonished at the sweet face devoid of paint and the gentle, unassuming air of the woman whose name was the flaming scandal of Europe. The mark of the convent thus stood her in good stead, though probably not in such a way as the good Sisters of Saint-Aure might have desired.

At sixteen she bade farewell to her girlhood and the little

harbor of tranquility where it had been passed. When the gates of the cloister had clanged behind her, it must have been with a pang of apprehension that she saw ahead the turbulent waters of Paris through which she would now have to ply her frail bark. Many indeed were the monsters that lurked in the rocks and caverns of that pleasure-mad city. No social workers were available to tender succor and apart from certain Sisters of Charity there were few organizations of mercy. The hard, unchangeable laws of life were not softened or disguised. One swam or one sank and the cold truth then, as it is now, was that no one much cared but yourself. The child of Eighteenth Century Paris, rich or poor, may not have known the security of proper psychiatric guidance, or the satisfactions of group activity, but he learned very quickly to read the human heart and to calculate accurately exactly how what he had read would affect him. Young Jeanne Bécu (or Rançon, as she now called herself, since some years earlier her mother had married a man of that name) was ravishingly lovely and so powerfully attractive that from this moment she seemed to have inflamed every man who crossed her path. Trouble was not long in coming.

One day she went with her mother to pay a call on her aunt—Hélène Bécu—who was a maid in the household of a certain Madame Peugevin. One can picture the two sisters chatting belowstairs over a good glass of wine, the lovely daughter quietly sitting in her corner. Above, Madame was having her hair curled in the elaborate style of the day. His task finished, and it was an exacting one, the young hairdresser stopped downstairs on his way home for a little gossip. Here Monsieur Lametz was introduced to the Rançons, *mère et fille*. The problem of Madame's hair was no doubt discussed and then, when the sighs were over, the matter of hairdressing in general. Eager to locate her daughter in some paying profession, Madame Rançon hopefully suggested that Monsieur Lametz give the girl a few free lessons in his art. Lametz, who by now had had a good look at the daughter, accepted this proposal with alacrity. The better part of the next few months he spent closeted with his voluptuous pupil instructing her in "the craft of hairdressing."

Unfortunately much of the time that Lametz so generously gave to this philanthropy was borrowed from that which he ordinarily spent at home with a widowed mother. Suddenly alert to danger, the widowed mother, her every instinct bristling, began cautiously to make investigation. When she had spied out the Rançon land she suddenly appeared one day at the door and accused Madame Rançon's daughter of seducing her son. Madame Rançon naturally flew to her daughter's defense and a scuffle ensued. Vehement accusations and shrill insults were exchanged. The widowed mother flounced indignantly off, threatening to report the seductress to the curé of the parish. This was not a threat to be laughed off, as the curé in those times was fully empowered to have the girl sent to a reformatory.

But Madame Rançon knew her way about Paris, and where her adversary had invoked the aid of the Church, she now lost no time in soliciting that of the Civil Law, two arms of His Majesty's authority that were as much at odds with one another on the level of the parish as they were on that of the Court. She accused Madame Lametz of a disturbance of the peace and the affair might have had serious consequences for all involved in it had not the authorities to whom they applied managed to calm the agitated women. Some private settlement of differences was finally arrived at and Jeanne's apprenticeship in hairdressing, probably along with her first love affair, came to its undistinguished end.

Scarcely was the hairdresser episode over when Jeanne unwittingly found herself in the midst of another storm. Her next position was companion to a Madame de la Garde, a rich and respectable old woman who lived not far from Paris in the Château de Corneuve. Madame de la Garde, who was the widow of a tax collector, entertained the world of finance at her table. Inevitably the lovely, laughing companion was the center of an attention she probably had not asked for.

The most ardent of her admirers were soon Madame de la Garde's two middle-aged sons, both of whom were married, the eldest to a Mademoiselle de Saint-Vrain (whose family château at Saint-Vrain would one day be bought by the Comtesse du Barry), and the younger to one Comtesse de Ligneville whose curious tastes tempted scandal to place her among the most urgent of Jeanne's *soupirants* of the Château de Corneuve. With two of her sons, and probably her daughter-in-law, disputing for the goddess's glance, the old lady's days were soon made miserable. Jealous presumptions darkened the Château de Corneuve and the air crackled with snapping nerves. The tension seems to have concluded in some sort of muffled explosion, but even the Duc de Choiseul's assiduous spies were unable in later years to unearth the details. A veil of reticence was hurriedly drawn over the whole affair, and Jeanne, having had a tantalizing glimpse of the warm world of the rich, was once more out in the cold world in which she seemed fated to live out her days.

Because it promises so much and generally returns so little, personal beauty is the most tragic of the gods' gifts. Unless it has been decently transmuted into a portrait or piece of statuary the world affects to despite it, whereas far from actually despising it, one half of the world is likely to be inflamed by lust at the sight of it and the other half by envy. Unlike virtue—and the virtuous have seen to this—it is rarely its own reward. Unlike intelligence, character, wit or artistic sensibility it rarely can be put to use and returned transmuted to the gods (as all their gifts should be) in some life-enhancing form. Personal beauty, the rarest—and perhaps the first—of nature's blessings is generally the most wasted, and by its very nature the saddest of all responsibilities. For how many farm girls has the Hollywood contract never come? For how many Jeanne Bécus no Louis XV? And time, which destroys everything, destroys beauty first. In the three years that followed her dismissal from the Château de Corneuve Jeanne seems to have fallen low indeed. She was now in full possession of her beauty and it had availed her nothing. Did she wonder as she looked into her glass to what end all this might bring her? Very probably, for what she saw there was the face and body of one of the most attractive women of her time, a veritable *morceau de roi,* wasted, some sound instinct must have hinted, on hairdressers and the like whom she met in her squalid surroundings.

For a time she worked as salesgirl in the Maison Labille, a millinery shop on the rue Neuve-des-Petits-Champs. Once again she smelled the warm scented air of a world just beyond her reach, a world of pretty ribbons and frothy fripperies, accessories to those saucy little nests of lace and ruffles where, in the fashionable language of the day, Venus's acolytes slyly hid their creamy treasures. Maison Labille was as much frequented by men as it was by women: plump abbés, rouged old rakes, young fops and idle macaronis who on the pretext of buying a piece of ribbon or a bit of lace were able to make the acquaintance of one of the pert apprentices or shopgirls. In those days the working girl lived on the premises. When her day's work was finished she was shepherded upstairs to the dormitory and locked in for the night.

But there were ways of escape as well as days off, and Jeanne Bécu, now nineteen, often made her way into the raucous night to who knows what rendezvous. On a holiday she would go with some *ami* to one of the marvelous fêtes or fairs that were so delightful a part of that age. There was an avid *joie de vivre* in those times, an appetite for spectacle and excitement that has since left the earth but whose ghost still wanders distressedly in some of the poorer towns of southern Italy. The Fête of Saint-Cloud, for instance, was not an elaborate amusement given by some Prince of the Blood to his friends, although Fragonard's great painting of it certainly suggests so; rather it was an affair open to all who could make their merry way out to Saint-Cloud to enjoy it. Here on the greensward, under the ancient trees of the estate, there were pierrots and punchinellos, music and dancing and all manner of tricky devices to keep the eyes sparkling and the mouth agape. The Prince was borne in his sedan chair, the wigmaker walked, but in their mutual eagerness to enjoy themselves they were one. When Talleyrand made the statement years after the Revolution that those who had not lived under the Old Regime could never know what the "sweetness of life" really was, it was as much to these fêtes as to Versailles that he referred. And when the Fête of Saint-Cloud was no more it was this same hunger for spectacle, this need for something to keep the eye excited, that seems more than anything else to explain the terrible, surging mobs about the guillotine.

It is not known how long the future Comtesse du Barry remained at Maison Labille. We glimpse her but fleetingly in the next few years. Possibly some "customer" at Labille lured her away from the shop with the promise of a more tempting situation; possibly she left of her own accord. A few years later it would become a matter of utmost interest to certain people at Versailles to uncover evidence that she had been a professional woman of the town. Nothing was found; her name was on no police record at this time nor was it enrolled on the register of the notorious Madame Gourdan where Jeanne was supposed to have put her services on call. But if she was innocent in the legal sense, in the moral sense she clearly was not and what research failed to provide, rumor strongly hinted. One fact is in any case certain: it was no frightened virgin who finally fluttered into the embraces of the King of France.

In the smoky, tawdry world in which she lived, she had the habit of going to a certain gambling house run by one "Marquise" de Duquenoy, and probably it was here toward the close of 1763 that destiny, in the person of the Comte Jean du Barry, finally directed her steps toward the path that was to lead to Versailles and to the guillotine.

This du Barry was an extraordinary man and so perfectly

the Eighteenth Century rake and adventurer that he seems almost a caricature of his type. Brazenly unscrupulous, a cardsharp, a wencher, a fop, this dapper, witty man about town seems to have redeemed some of his many faults by his insouciant tolerance of the same faults in others. He was a liar; never a hypocrite. In the glittering world which he frequented, where the raciest element of the Court met the most dissipated of Paris, he was affectionately known as the Roué and such hardened old libertines as the Ducs de Nivernais and Richelieu, the most notorious men of the century, were awestruck by the excesses of the Comte Jean. Although his family was old and of gentle origin, his title was spurious. The fact that, if anybody, it was his older brother who was the Comte troubled him not in the least. His brother and the rest of the du Barrys were moldering in their shabby château in remote Gascony, too poor and too seedy to make an appearance in the wicked city.

Comte Jean had left them behind him many years before; after he had run through his young wife's provincial fortune, he had struck out for Paris where his sharp wits could serve his fortune better than among the goats and geese of his mother's barnyard. His nimble fingers were soon in and out of many pies: a diplomatic career which had begun with promise under the influence of his relative Rouillé soon faded for want of support from the all-powerful Minister, Choiseul. Next he landed some "contracts," as nebulous an expression then as it is today, but which seem to have been the source of some very concrete returns. The proceeds from the "contracts" he invested in a brisk little side line that he ran as much for pleasure as for profit. Just as an art dealer will buy certain canvases cheap and by cleaning them, framing them, or hoping for a rise in the market aspire to make some money on his investment, so did Jean du Barry invest in women.

He would discover some shabby *grisette* and, having seduced her, would instruct her in the manners and little graces that his fashionable friends, the Nivernais and Richelieus, found irresistible, disposing of her eventually at a tidy profit to himself. His little business had on one occasion taken him as far as the King's antechamber, but his price for the article in question, La Belle Dorothée, was too steep and the alert Pompadour quickly spiked this transaction with her heel.

He was outrageous and he was a scoundrel, but his faults were by no means the human worst. Such as he had, he cheerfully—indeed boastfully—admitted to, while he was notably free from jealousy, resentment, and "the lean and hungry look." Even the police seem to have had a grudging respect for him: "When he begins to weary of a woman he invariably sells her off. But," continues the report, "it must be admitted that he is a connoisseur and his merchandise is eminently salable."

When at the end of the year 1763 his path crossed that of the ravishing Jeanne Bécu (or rather Jeanne Beauvarnier as she was now calling herself), du Barry must have realized that his fortune was made. In the ensuing negotiation no time seems to have been lost by either party. The Roué was lavish of hand, and his mistresses, glittering with diamonds, were driven about in a dashing coach so that all Paris could behold and envy the splendor of their fall. Jeanne Bécu even then had a dangerous weakness for diamonds, those stones whose cold fire were destined one day to play as sinister a part in her life as they were, even more spectacularly, in the life of Marie Antoinette.

Mademoiselle Beauvarnier was soon installed in du Barry's house as hostess. To lend a note of respectability to this arrangement (a bit of cynicism that doubtless fetched an icy smile to the lips of Richelieu and Nivernais), Madame Rançon, the mother, was brought along too. Jeanne had now attained to the highest stratum of the Paris demimonde. She was seen everywhere and was known to many of the princes of the greatest Houses in France: Lauzun, Fitzjames, Ligne, Richelieu. The police were kept busy following her movements, certain sign of "arrival" in the France of 1764: "The Marquis [*sic*] du Barry who was responsible for having brought La Belle Dorothée to Paris and for having given the Demoiselle Beauvoisin her start in life, exhibited his latest mistress in his box at the Comédie Italienne last Monday night, the Demoiselle Beauvarnier. She is a person nineteen years old, tall, well-made and of distinguished appearance with an extremely pretty face. No doubt he intends to dispose of her advantageously."

One evening she appeared at the Opéra Ball, unmasked and dressed entirely in white. "Never," recalled the diarist d'Espinchal, "have I seen anyone more beautiful than this heavenly woman as she was that night: she was Hebe, a Grace. Voltaire's picture of Agnès Sorel fitted her perfectly:

> Love had never wrought such as this,
> She was all, and in her toils she might have taken
> Heroes, wizards, sages and kings. . . ."

The Comte d'Espinchal, who has the distinction of being remembered as the greatest gossip of his century, became a warm friend and admirer of Madame du Barry. Another future friend, the Prince de Ligne, gives us a more concrete description of her as she appeared to him at this time. "She is tall, well-made, ravishingly pale with an open forehead, fine eyes, beautiful lashes, an oval face with little moles upon her cheeks which only serve to enhance her beauty, a laughing mouth and breasts with which most women would be wise to shun comparison."

Of these contemporary descriptions the most curious and amusing is the one that purports to come from the pen of the procuress Madame Gourdan. It is quoted by Pidansat de Mairobert in his scandalous book *Anecdotes About Madame du Barry* which was published in 1775 (the year after Louis XV's death and Madame du Barry's downfall). The scene he pretends to describe is, like almost everything else in the book, a complete invention but it is worth quotation as an example of the kind of piquante writing that titillated the senses of that time.

Upon hearing of the arrival at Maison Labille of a new and wonderfully beautiful shopgirl, Madame Gourdan, like a *bonne bourgeoise* out shopping for a bargain in the meat market, hurried to Labille's to verify the report. When she saw the future Madame du Barry she could scarcely contain her excitement: "What I could see of her made me wildly impatient to see that which I could *not!*" Accordingly Madame Gourdan gave the girl a few louis d'or with the promise of many more if she would one day pay her a visit. As may be expected the girl finally appeared and on a pretext Madame Gourdan persuaded her to undress. "I saw her naked as she was born! I drew closer. I saw a ravishing body, a throat . . . well, my hands have caressed a good many throats in their time, but never one of this elasticity, of this shape, of this irresistible softness. The plunge of her breasts threw me into an ecstasy; her dazzling white thighs, her delicious little buttocks—the Sculptors themselves have never produced anything more perfect. As for the rest, I was connoisseur enough to realize that the *pucelage* was in a very equivocal condition to say the least of it, but with the application of certain astringents it might be sold a few more times!"

At the Roué's establishment Jeanne presided over little supper parties where she entertained such exalted personages as Lord March, the future Duke of Queensbury, and his companion the Comtesse La Rena, whose favors were said to cost him fifty thousand dollars a year. Lauzun came to dine and the Duc de Duras and Radix de Sainte-Foy (of whom the busy police wrote: "Mademoiselle de Beauvarnier, milch-cow of the du Barry, is presently engaged in fleecing Monsieur de Sainte-Foy, Treasurer of the Marine, with the encouragement of Monsieur du Barry"). There was a great deal of champagne, a great deal of laughter of the sort that was too hearty to be genteel, a great deal of high-pitched conviviality. On du Barry's recommendation she again changed her name, calling herself Jeanne de Vaubernier which with its added *de* and exchange of syllable had a more aristocratic ring about it than the more modest Beauvarnier.

For four years, from 1764 until 1768, she "did the honors" of du Barry's house, and if it may be supposed that as that gentleman's *vache-à-lait* she gave him a good return on his money, there is no doubt that for her part Jeanne was rewarded in a coin less tangible. These were years of apprenticeship, years of discipline and of training, years that polished to gleaming perfection the talents and instincts with which nature had so generously endowed her. In Jean du Barry's sparkling salon she had met the flower of the French aristocracy, had observed with every sense the tastes and conventions out of which they built their image of the entirely desirable woman. An accomplished courtesan is but she who can conform as closely as possible to man's image of the perfect woman. Her function is to alleviate boredom, to amuse, beguile and sympathize, as much as it is to arouse and assuage passion. She is what wives are supposed to be but after a few years of marriage are not. She is a pearl beyond price.

By birth, by inclination, and now by training, Jeanne de Vaubernier was a great courtesan. Under du Barry's roof she had been but rehearsing in the wings of the theatre. Now she was ready to step onto the floodlit stage of history and whether it was by accident, by design or whether by a bit of both, in the early summer of 1768 at Versailles she met face to face with Louis XV. Within a month he was prepared to sacrifice for her the last shreds of his tattered reputation, for she was a woman such as he had never before beheld.

Chapter 3

IT WAS AN IRONY probably never apparent to him that the Duc de Choiseul was himself responsible for first bringing Jeanne de Vaubernier to Versailles, becoming therefore the inadvertent agent of his own eventual destruction. Along with diamonds and feathers Jean du Barry had turned over to Mademoiselle de Vaubernier the revenues from a government contract in Corsica. A change of policy by the Ministry had brought the income from this to a standstill and it became necessary for Jeanne to go to Versailles to solicit from Choiseul its continuance.

The palace was always open to any person who was decently dressed and all who chose to do so could wander about and enjoy such spectacles as the King eating, the Princes of the Blood on their way to Mass or, when it happened, the Queen giving birth to child. Crowds of wide-eyed bumpkins and tourists were continually ambling about, gawking and gaping at the intricate ritual of Monarchy. (It is no wonder that when the great palace was stormed twenty years later the mob lost no steps finding its way through that labyrinth of vast corridors, wings and interior courtyards.) By knowing the hour of Mass or the hour when he was to sup, it was possible, by stationing yourself along his route, to see the King pass, and—if you looked like Jeanne de Vaubernier—be seen by him. This unquestionably is what happened. Their eyes met, probably on several occasions, inquiries were made, and the King's valet-pimp, Lebel, was soon in Paris with a discreetly worded invitation which, needless to say, was accepted with alacrity by the girl and greeted with transports of joy by her *ci-devant* lover.

The first "interview" between the King and the future Comtesse du Barry took place in the early part of July, 1768. From that instant he was bewitched and could scarcely bring himself to part with her. The Court was in mourning for Queen Maria Leczinska (who had died on the twenty-third of June) and was too distracted by that excitement to notice the presence of Mademoiselle de Vaubernier who, in any case, was sequestered in the depths of the palace. If she was noticed at all, and no doubt a few sharp eyes had observed her, it would have been supposed that she was only one more of the many pretty Parisiennes who, in a continuing stream, were brought to Versailles for the old satyr's passing pleasure.

More than anything else it is indicative of Madame du Barry's consummate charm (and of Jean du Barry's persistence) that she did not end up in the obscurity of the Parc-aux-Cerfs, that common hostelry of passing caprice where she might have disappeared with the other women who did not even leave a memory with the King. From the first it seems to have been his wish that she should eventually be presented to him publicly at Court and that she should then live openly with him as his declared *maîtresse en titre,* that "magnificent dishonor" which traditionally was reserved for women of noble birth. That a woman who had aunts and uncles in domestic service should become the Favorite and consequently step on the necks of the nobility of the proudest and oldest Monarchy in Europe, was a possibility too extravagant to have occurred to the Court.

The Court, however, was in for a sharp surprise because, unknown to it, events were now moving very rapidly. Louis had met Jeanne de Vaubernier in early July. The Court, after its ceaseless round, was scheduled to remove to Compiègne at the end of that month. For Jeanne to follow the King there it was necessary, such was the custom, for her to be married; and the King made it known to her that he most urgently desired her presence.

Du Barry, whose ship was at last in sight of shore, must have cursed that far-off day when he had married his provincial heiress. The fortune had been quickly spent, but the heiress, alas, remained: "A handsome, honest person who had nothing to say about the shameful conduct of her husband." She lived somewhere in the country. Eager as he might have been to be the husband of the King's Mistress, not even the unscrupulous du Barry was likely to resort to murder and still less to bigamy which in the France of that day was met with the severest penalties. Wasting no time on regret, the quick-witted scoundrel hurriedly calculated what, for his purposes, was the next best move. He then remembered his older brother, the clodhopper Guillaume du Barry, who with his two spinster sisters and an aged mother, moldered unmarried in the rural mire of remote Lévignac, shooting hare and chasing stag.

The simple-minded folk at the Château du Barry in Lévignac had heard little from their disreputable relative since his departure from them some years earlier and no doubt they were astonished when a letter in his hand was suddenly delivered to them. Madame, head of the household, was too old to grasp the meaning of its contents. Her two ugly daughters, whose wits had never been dulled by romance, carefully explained the situation to her and the simple soul, still somewhat puzzled, finally gave her permission. Guillaume du Barry, the chosen sacrifice to his family's new-found fortune was suspicious until he discovered that a considerable sum of money had been sent to defray the expense of the trip to Paris. With nothing to lose he agreed to the arrangement and a procuration was accordingly signed by the old lady at Toulouse. A few days later the bridegroom and his two bright sisters were on their way to Paris. They arrived there on July twenty-second and on the following day the marriage contract was signed.

During these weeks Jean du Barry had been busy forging and embellishing the documents necessary to this ceremony. The future husband was no doubt startled to find himself styled "high and puissant seigneur, messire Guillaume, Comte du Barry"; only a week before in the procuration at Toulouse he had been plain Guillaume du Barry. His disreputable brother suddenly became "Gouverneur de Lévignac," a dignity that might have lost some of its flourish were it known that Lévignac consisted of five or six miserable houses, a goat pen and a few hen roosts. The bride was now "Mademoiselle Jeanne Gomard de Vaubernier, daughter of dame Rançon and *of her first husband* [!], the sieur Jean Jacques Gomard de Vaubernier." This addition to her name is interesting because the monk who had known Anne Bécu back at Vaucouleurs some twenty-three years before had been named Gomard, and this gentleman now suddenly appeared at the wedding, done up in a "frock of maroon *bouroucan* with big gold buttons," under false credentials like everyone else at the ceremony, and styling himself "Almoner to the King." In the forged birth certificates which were produced for the religious ceremony, the Roué had wisely killed off the fictitious father; Gomard appeared in the capacity of uncle of the bride and as witness to this intricate tissue of falsehoods and distortions.

The religious ceremony took place on September first. The bride bade her husband farewell at the church door and never saw him again. For his complaisance Guillaume du Barry was awarded a pension of five thousand livres, and he now quickly proceeded to spend on his own vices that which he had realized from the King's. He tarried in Paris and soon acquired a mistress of his own, one Mademoiselle

Lemoine, "a piquante blonde with a saucy mouth and dazzling white teeth." He took her back to the farm where in the solitude of Lévignac the happy couple raised a family. After the execution of his wife in 1793, du Barry married his mistress of twenty-five years.

Jeanne, now officially the Comtesse du Barry, hastened to join her royal lover at Compiègne where she was lodged in a house apart from the palace. At the end of September, however, the Court moved to Fontainebleau and here she was no longer concealed. She appeared openly, prancing about in an elegant equipage, carried to the King's apartments and to Mass in a richly cushioned chaise, attended by a train of liveried servants. The wasps' nest, which for some weeks had been stirring uneasily now began to hum excitedly as the wasps scurried about taking their position in the coming struggle. The issue over which the battle would be fought was clear to all: would she or would she not be presented? Without a presentation the Comtesse would hang in an uncertain (and probably short) limbo between the Parc-aux-Cerfs and the council chambers of significance. Presented, however, she would become an incalculable power upon whose smile or frown would hang the fate of ministries and mitres; of brevets, commissions and pensions. Overnight the one time shopgirl had become a personage of international significance. To Rome, to Saint Petersburg, to Berlin went the encoded confidential reports.

To Vienna, Maria Theresa's Ambassador, Comte Mercy-Argenteau, wrote a clear-sighted report on the affair as it might affect Austrian interests: "She is lodged in the court called *des fontaines* near the apartment which Madame de Pompadour used to occupy; she has a number of servants with brilliant liveries and on Sunday one sees her at the King's Mass in one of the chapels which is reserved for her. I have ascertained that this woman expects to be presented at Court and that a cabal of some persons of very high rank favors this project. . . . The serious turn this affair has taken finally prompted me to speak of it to the Spanish Ambassador, Señor Fuentes. Señor Fuentes agreed that he ought to give his views on the matter to Monsieur de Choiseul, representing to Monsieur de Choiseul how grievously the person of the King would be degraded by such a scandal. He succeeded in fixing the attention of Monsieur de Choiseul on this matter and together they pondered a means of averting the presentation. Monsieur de Fuentes was to compose a letter which he would write to his Court, which, when it had been intercepted by Monsieur Choiseul's spies, would be brought to the notice of His Most Christian Majesty. Through the medium of the Spanish Ambassador *I am trying to turn this affair to good use,* persuading Monsieur de Choiseul how greatly it would be to the advantage of both the State and the King himself that this prince who clings to the pleasures of the senses should by a fresh marriage liberate himself from all these disorders which are a source of intrigue disturbing to the Ministers and injurious to the proper conduct of affairs."

Maria Theresa, who had one daughter—Marie Antoinette—engaged to the Dauphin, had another, Elizabeth, whom her Ministers were trying to marry off to the widowed King. Such was Mercy's secret iron in the fire. The arrival on the scene of the Comtesse du Barry was an event he quickly put to good use. By frightening Choiseul with the possibility of a presentation, by dangling this fresh mortification before the Royal Family, the agile Mercy promoted the interests of his own Court and maneuvered to gain approval of a marriage heretofore odious in the eyes of the Minister and the Royal Family. A presentation was not to the interest of the Austrian Ambassador, but the threat of it distinctly was, and so he moved about assiduously dropping a hint here, expressing his heartfelt concern there, an imperturbable presence on whose masklike and powdered countenance could be read but one expression: discretion. "As soon as it could be done without exciting suspicion," he reports, "I insinuated my views into every quarter."

The courtiers, experienced in the ways of intrigue, quickly calculated the position most favorable to their own interests and took sides accordingly. The Court was soon divided into the Barryiens and the anti-Barryiens: those who favored and those who opposed the presentation of Madame du Barry. The ranks of the latter were impressive, consisting of the Choiseul party and all who held favor under his Ministry. These viewed a presentation with fear and foreboding which they disguised as Moral Indignation, a scarcely convincing attitude since they themselves had been raised to power by the bejeweled fingers of the late Pompadour. They were joined by most of the women at Court who felt themselves cheated out of a position to which they had a better claim. Moral outrage in this instance barely concealed spite.

The most unhappy recruits to the anti-Barry party were the four spinster daughters of the King, known collectively as Mesdames, who were caught between the Scylla of their hatred of Choiseul and the Charybdis of their horror of Madame du Barry. Mesdames made up in the consequence of their birth for what they had missed in the way of domestic felicity, consoling themselves with the thought that Daughter of France was a rank higher than any that could possibly come to them by any marriage on this earth. They lived in semi-retirement in vast connecting apartments at Versailles and here, dominated by the elder, Madame Adélaïde, they brooded over ineffectual plots which rarely hatched. Madame Adélaïde was a sour, thin-beaked old maid, immensely proud and of a haughty aspect, who was filled with disgust by the unseemly conduct of her father, the King. She never dared confront His Majesty directly with her distaste, but attacked obliquely and in secret. In the privacy of their chambers the sisters continually stirred up a brew of mischief, never realizing that their drops of poison were eating into the foundations of the very edifice which supported them. Adélaïde and Victoire would live to see the consequences of their malice. They would barely escape the guillotine, leaving Paris in 1791 in the dead of night on the pretext of a pious pilgrimage to Rome. In Rome, under the protection of the Holy Father, they lived in exile, praying to God that He spit down flames of vengeance to destroy the monsters of the Revolution, never reflecting that they themselves had been among the first to intrigue against the Monarchy. They loathed Choiseul both as the upstart creature of the Pompadour and as the instrument of the expulsion of the Jesuits in 1762. Nothing could have been sweeter to them than the ruin of this man whom they viewed as a socially questionable Antichrist, but the price—Madame du Barry—they could not bring themselves to pay.

Fully aware of their dilemma Mercy was soon dipping his fine, white hand in these troubled waters. He bribed their lady-in-waiting, Madame de Durfort, to keep him informed of the lay of the land in their apartments, at the same time recommending that she advance to them the advantages which would accrue by a marriage of the King to the Archduchess Elizabeth. Much as they detested the Austrian Alliance and Austria, they quickly realized that here lay a solution to their problem and they were soon ardent supporters of the project. For once in their lives they summoned up courage to broach a matter directly to the King.

His Majesty greeted their proposal with moderate interest and might well have followed the matter to some sort of conclusion had it not been for the short-sighted greed and uncompromising ambition of the rash leader of the anti-Barry party, he about whose person such violent storms, mostly of his own making, were so soon to break. "Certain persons in power here," writes the observant Mercy, "feel that a judicious and amiable queen who succeeded in gaining the affection of her husband, might open his eyes to the irregularities and enormous abuses which exist in all departments here and cause much embarrassment to those who direct them. They are consequently of the opinion that it behooves them to direct the mind of the King from all ideas of marriage. . . ." The Ambassador was speaking of Choiseul: a man who would destroy in a rage that which he could not himself have.

Born of great family but poor estate in the obscurity of Lorraine where scarcely a glimmer of life-giving rays penetrated from far-off Versailles, Étienne François, Comte de Stainville, like the woman he now opposed, had had to make his own way along the long path that led to the foot of the Throne. Compared with the means used by the future Duc de Choiseul, the Comtesse du Barry's seem innocent. He married a great heiress, exchanging name for fortune. Although with his wife's money he was able to cut quite a figure at Court, favor and appointment eluded the Comte de Stainville's grasp. The Pompadour was then at the summit of her glory, but rumors were abroad that her emotional apparatus could no longer keep pace with the King's and that soon she would fall. The future Duc de Choiseul threw in his lot with the anti-Pompadours, loudly proclaiming his scorn of the presumptuous Favorite. In 1752 his chance came. The nest was humming with excitement over the impending crash. Intrigue was everywhere afoot, and destiny now brought Choiseul into the very heart of the most serious plot.

He had a cousin, a Comtesse de Choiseul-Romanet, whom the Pompadour's enemies had succeeded in introducing to the King's bed. The opposition's hopes were suddenly centered on this attractive young woman because it was soon clear that the King had fallen in love with her. Joy knew no bounds when one evening at Fontainebleau the door to the Minister of War's apartment burst open and the young Comtesse, hair askew, flushed in the face, breathlessly announced to her assembled backers: "All is over! I am loved. She will be dismissed. He has given me his word."

In the excitement of this apparent victory the incautious Comtesse turned to her cousin for some very confidential advice. She revealed to him the most secret matters, even showing him certain letters which she had received from the King. When the interview was over Choiseul coolly assured her that the matter would be kept in strictest confidence. And with that he took himself as fast as his pudgy feet could carry him to the sanctum of Madame de Pompadour. There, with professions of eternal loyalty to her person, he revealed every detail that he knew of the plot against her. Armed with this information the clever Marquise was able quickly to crush her adversaries. It was a rash and masterful move on Choiseul's part, entirely typical of his methods on the diplomatic scene. He played a bold and dangerous game, plunging recklessly into that tide which taken at the full leads on to fortune. Thus by a single piece of treachery did Choiseul make the fortune of himself and of his House. Madame de Pompadour, a vindictive enemy but grateful friend, set no bounds on her gratitude and he was awarded the Embassy at Vienna, where with Kaunitz he spun the fabric of the Austrian Alliance, arranging among other things for the eventual marriage of the Archduchess Marie Antoinette with the Dauphin of France. During the Seven Years War he was recalled to France and appointed Minister of Foreign Affairs.

From this moment his star rose to such a zenith as has rarely been paralleled in the records of French history. In his single person he combined the functions of three crucial departments: Foreign Affairs, the Army, and, in effect, the Marine. Every important post in France was filled by some relative or favorite. He became Colonel-General of the Swiss Guard and head of the Postal Service which permitted him to violate the privacy of all correspondence. Wealth, power and glory showered upon him as though from Heaven. To cap his good fortune, the Pompadour, irritating reminder of his origins and of a power greater than his own, finally passed from the scene leaving Choiseul and his clan and clique in absolute command of France, answerable only to the apathetic King who was always content to leave well enough alone.

It is no wonder then that even the idea of the King taking another Mistress filled the Choiseuls with fear. After the death of the Marquise, a good part of their time had been devoted to nipping incipient love affairs in the bud, and until the advent of the Comtesse du Barry their ruthless methods had met with no serious resistance. That the King might remarry filled them with as much alarm as did the possibility that he might take another Mistress; for all their defensive stance before the dignity of the Crown, it was not this that they were protecting, but rather their own long-established interests.

For all his talk about morality, Choiseul had, in fact, for

some time had a candidate of his own for the position that Madame de Pompadour had vacated: his own sister, the Duchesse de Gramont. This terrible woman, blinded by rage and jealousy at seeing the prize for which she and her brother had fruitlessly schemed suddenly seized from her, lost all prudence and reason. The Minister himself was frightened by his sister and in his ensuing battle with Madame du Barry lost whatever coolness of mind he might have had and was led entirely by the convulsive passion of Madame de Gramont.

The Duchesse de Gramont, Béatrix de Choiseul-Stainville, was a masterful, big-boned woman, raw-skinned, red-headed, half Valkyrie, half Borgia, who since childhood had been her brother's closest friend. Together they had shared the sparse pleasures of Lorraine ("Château Ennui" their ancestral home had been dubbed). When his star rose Choiseul called his sister out of the retirement of the cloister of Remiremont, where she was a Canoness, back into the world of dispute and passion for which she was uniquely fitted. He married her to the rich Duc de Gramont whom she left almost immediately in order to be with her brother, the only man—she boldly confessed—for whom she could ever really care. Open incest could scarcely ruffle the waters of that easy-going society. "A more than fraternal intimacy existed between the two," wrote the Goncourts, "both of whom were sufficiently independent of appearances not to be restrained by religion or public decency." Poems and lampoons were circulated about Paris and the Court with sly references to the Ptolemies, and that was about the end of it.

The Duchesse de Gramont laughed brazenly in the face of scandal. She viewed convention as a very necessary restraint on the passions of the little *nouveaux riches* of Paris, but it could hardly have anything to do with one who had been born a Stainville and was above such provincial nonsense as religion or morality. She did not, like the social climbers, follow fashion; she made it. It could be said of her that she did not so much disbelieve in God as, in the manner of certain of the *philosophes,* she despised Him. God seemed to her to be slightly middle class. With the death of the Pompadour a great hope was born in the heart of this Amazon and, with her encouragement, in the heart of her brother too. Nothing could more firmly set a cap on the fortunes of the House of Choiseul than having the sister (and lover) of the King's chief Minister declared the King's Mistress. What one branch of the family could not put over in the Council

Chamber, the other might well succeed in accomplishing in the Bedchamber. So sanguine were the vain Duchesse's hopes, so imperiously did she ride the crest of this wave that her dreams carried her yet further into the ocean of fantasy. She bethought herself of the great Montespan and of Madame de Maintenon: she envisioned morganatic marriage or legitimized bastards. Not even a glimpse in the mirror could discourage her for, as she saw it, it was more important to be Béatrix de Choiseul-Stainville than to be merely young and pretty. After all, was not her brother chief Minister? Had not the King once given his favor to Madame de Vintimille who stank like a monkey and walked like a Hessian?

Nothing, not even the King, daunted the resolute woman, and so full of vanity was she that it seemed to her that the culmination of all her desires had been nearly realized when, like a bolt from the blue, the radiant Comtesse du Barry stepped from the gutters of Paris into the dazzling publicity of the Galerie des Glaces. Her rage and fury could not be concealed, and like her masterful ancestors of yore, like some giantess of the Rhenish Black Forest, the whilom Canoness of Remiremont girded her ample loins for battle. Into her ranks she pressed the majority of the women at Court, many of whom were more apprehensive of the furious Duchesse than outraged by the triumphant hussy, and fought under the banner of Moral Indignation more as nervous draftees than resolute volunteers. She goaded her brother, never distinguished for his discretion in any situation, into violence and follies that more than anything else accomplished the purposes of the opposing party and brought about the eventual destruction of the Choiseul party and of herself.

Such were the anti-Barryiens: formidable opposition indeed to a girl, innocent, in any real sense, of the ways of the world. Without the help of experienced hands, without the aid of astute counsel she would have been torn to bits, as though by sharks, in a matter of weeks. But at Versailles where jealousy and spite reached a nervous pitch such as has rarely been seen on this earth, the instrument of a Minister's possible overthrow could never lack supporters. Choiseul's long Ministry was particularly disliked, as much for the thoroughness of its hold as for the violence of its politics: the Austrian Alliance, the expulsion of the Jesuits, the compromises with the detested Parlements. These were policies that had dangerously offended the sensibilities of certain powerful factions. Choiseul walked roughshod over the proud toes of those he felt could not further his interests and he was insolent to those he knew to be his enemies.

The man about whom the Du Barry party rallied was his most energetic opponent: that perennial old sinner, the Duc de Richelieu, the man who many years before had aspired to power through his "niece," the now-forgotten Duchesse du Châteauroux. Seventy years had no more impaired his ambition than they had his lust. Witty, urbane, utterly cynical, Richelieu was the Versailles courtier par excellence: a man to whom manner and appearance were all, and fact beneath his contempt. During the reign of the Pompadour, whom he detested, he had suffered something of an eclipse, but his company was far too agreeable to the King, a *debauché* like himself, for them to be long parted. He was reappointed to his old post of First Gentleman of the Bedchamber and was thus able to enjoy again his Sovereign's interesting confidences. It would not be difficult to imagine the general trend and tone of these conversations. The King, although he mistrusted the Duc's political judgment, placed a high value on his experience in other matters, and no doubt in listening to the Duc's witty account of Paris and its forbidden pleasures, he found as much amusement as he found satisfaction in the Duc's immoral but probably sane recommendations respecting his love life. Next to Nivernais, who could tell the right from the left wing of a chicken by its taste, Richelieu was the greatest gentleman in Europe. He was, in fact, so thoroughly a gentleman that in the opinion of his contemporaries, "he remained a gentleman even when he tried most to be one." Nothing, not even the behavior of the Duc, could dull the polish on that hard, perfect glaze.

At first he had had his doubts about the firmness of the Comtesse du Barry's hold on the King's fickle affections. When he realized that with a little encouragement the *affaire* could be made serious, all misgivings left him. Perfect courtier as he was, Richelieu was a stickler for the appearances (of which in private he made ironic mockery) and the arrival at Court of the Roué's hostess, whom he had known in other circumstances, gave him momentary pause. But in his eyes, no doubt, the rules had already been broken for Madame de Pompadour, a creature from the same murky obscurity as Madame du Barry. Whatever little distinctions of rank people not born to the Court might invent for use among themselves, they were lost on a Duke and Peer of France. Three hundred years of noble birth was the rule, and it had been broken just as blatantly for Jeanne Poisson as it would be for Jeanne Bécu. In supporting the Comtesse du Barry, Richelieu probably derived a certain satisfaction in deflating the pretensions of her predecessor.

Since he had the King's ear and since the King respected his judgment in matters of the heart, Richelieu's became a powerful influence in the cause of the new Mistress. He was able to neutralize the effects of Choiseul's vile slanders and so bring firmness to the King's wobbling wish that the Comtesse be presented and declared the Favorite. Richelieu was himself supported by his nephew the Duc d'Aiguillon, a man who so passionately loathed Choiseul that he would have backed an ape for Mistress, had such been the King's preference and the potential instrument of Choiseul's downfall. The Richelieu-d'Aiguillon faction was quickly strengthened by, pretty irony, the most conservative religious element of the Court: the ultramontanes, the priests, and all who deplored the expulsion of the Jesuits. "What was incredible," writes the Duc de Croy, "was that in their hatred of Monsieur de Choiseul the most religious party was the quickest to lend its support. It is really an appalling reflection on human nature that jealousy and personal rancor can so blind a person." The Duc de Vauguyon, tutor to the Dauphin, and Madame de Marsan, who was governess to the Princesse Élisabeth, openly admitted that in the Comtesse du Barry they saw God's chosen instrument to bring about the fall of the haughty Minister. In Paris a priest was heard to lift his glass in a toast:

"To the presentation," he proposed.

"Whose presentation?" inquired a curious foreigner.

"To that of the new Esther," replied the sly priest, "who is to supplant Haman and thus deliver the Jewish people from oppression."

Many at Court were not governed by personal feelings concerning the Minister, but by cold expediency concerning themselves. These, such as the Chancellor Maupeou, and the Abbé Terray, while not actually committing themselves, watched the developing crisis with shrewd, appraising eyes. They planned to strike after the presentation when the first risky battle had been won and all positions had been consolidated.

The Comtesse's most active personal support came from Jean du Barry who was wise enough to absent himself from the scene of the struggle, where his presence could only have served as a reminder of his protégée's origins, but who with dexterity managed her interests from behind the scenes, keeping in touch with her by means of disguised couriers between Versailles and Paris. As a kind of agent, du Barry dispatched his sister Chon to Versailles to act as companion to the Comtesse. Between these two women, one lame and ugly and the other radiant and lovely, there grew up a deep and genuine friendship that does credit to them both.

Chon du Barry was an intelligent woman, quick-witted and a keen observer of the human comedy. It is said that she contributed articles to the *Mercure de France* under another name. She was without jealousy of her sister-in-law's manifest blessings, only appreciative of what they vicariously brought her, Chon. In her turn, the Comtesse, the most warmhearted of women, found in Chon the friendship which she craved, but which was not offered to her during the early part of her stay at Versailles. Apart from affection, Mademoiselle du Barry was able to give her friend a good deal of shrewd advice and there is little doubt that Madame du Barry's open overtures of friendship toward d'Aiguillon—an easy conquest—sprang from the advice of Chon who realized that in d'Aiguillon lay a powerful friend as well as a dangerous enemy.

The Roué was a gambler. On the Comtesse he now staked all that he had in the world, going into debt and even mortgaging his future income in order to provide his "investment" with the appurtenances proper to her high station. In this delicate interim he saw very clearly that it would be dangerous for her to solicit any favors from the King, who not untypically of his kind, was a pinch-penny when it came to small sums. His Majesty could spend thousands without a tremor, but was loath to part with the tens and twenties; the thousands were obtained by drafts on the Treasury, but the tens and twenties came out of his little personal hoard in which he took a miser's pride. The fine carriage in which the Comtesse took her morning air, the exquisite clothes, the diamonds, the rubies, the servants, all these were unpaid for and represented du Barry's enormous gamble. He won his bet and his money was returned to him many times over. Several years later the inveterate gambler lost another large bet, this time at cards. He paid willingly, smiling ironically as he said: "Don't feel sorry for me, my friends. It's you taxpayers who are paying."

The most impressive weapon of the du Barry party was the radiant young lady herself. Her person seemed to be the incarnation of man's romantic fantasies. She was a creature born for love: the epitome of what her age dreamed that woman should be. Love was the breath of her life, the primary nourishment of all her being. She could not, and did not, exist without it. Health, sweetness of disposition, a deep generosity of soul entirely lacking in malice or envy, these were the rewards of a nature that remained, for all the assaults made on it, uncorrupted. Her effect on the King, exhausted by so many years of morbid sexuality, was instantaneous. The women of the Parc-aux-Cerfs were dismissed, his whole being seemed to radiate a fresh youth. "At sixty years of age," writes the Duc de Croy who saw him at that time, "the King was more in love than he had ever been. He seemed rejuvenated and I had never seen him in better spirits: in extremely good humor and far more outgoing than he had ever been."

Louis himself described her best and most succinctly. One evening during one of their tête-à-têtes, Richelieu asked the King what it was that he saw in her.

"Only this," answered His Majesty, "that she makes me forget that soon I will be sixty."

Choiseul opened his campaign with a barrage of calumny and libel. The nimble-witted courtiers at Versailles made the poison of slander more palatable (and deadly) by serving it up in a little patty shell of verse, prettily scalloped about the edges. These *chansons*, as they were called, were no mere songs: they were cruelly sharpened barbs dipped in venom. All were meant to wound and some were meant to slay. As the century wore to its close the *chansons* increased in number and malignance, falling thick as autumn leaves over the dying order, and culminated in the bloodthirsty songs of the Revolution. Frivolous as they might appear on the surface, the *chansons* were a deadly weapon, as malignant in intent as a poison-pen letter and as devastating in effect as any well-written propaganda has ever proven itself to be. Marie Antoinette was the hapless victim of the worst of them, but Madame du Barry in her time got a dose such as had not been seen before.

The Minister's agents went to the gutters of Paris to dredge their mud. What they could not find they did not scruple to invent. Paris and the Court were soon inundated by pamphlets and placards of varying degrees of filth and insinuation. Majesty itself was not spared. The King was represented as a drooling, senile old lecher, "*un vieux paillard*." The audacity of these attacks shocked the Austrian Ambassador: "Every day placards of the sort that would make you shiver are hung out in Paris; these, along with the most frightful epithets make one realize that France is still capable of producing another Damiens or Ravaillac." The theatre lent its arm to the campaign and a ribald burlesque called *La Bourbonnaise* enjoyed a brief season. The identity of the protagonists was scarcely disguised, but so outrageously distorted was the sketchy skeleton of truth that the production could boast of being one long libel. Paris was whipped into as much of an uproar as the Court. "In the streets and theatres people talk only of the infamy of these du Barrys and of how deplorable it is to see Royalty in danger of being at the mercy of such people."

Unfortunately much of the mud thrown at her during this period has stuck to Madame du Barry. She is generally dismissed by historians as "a prostitute," a degradation to the dignity of the Throne and a herald of, if not an excuse for, the oncoming Revolution. Choiseul not only managed to stir up the masses against her but, in his hatred, against the Crown itself. In this sense she was indeed the herald of the Revolution. So dextrously did he pursue his goal that he not only succeeded in blackening the Comtesse's name (and with it by implication the King's) but he managed at the same time to polish his own. "People imagined that it was on moral grounds that the Duc de Choiseul was opposed to Madame du Barry, and owing to this belief he became the idol of the magistrates and finally of the entire public." Monsieur de Choiseul purchased his own credit with the public at the expense of the King's.

In overstepping the truth as they did, the anti-Barry party went too far and succeeded merely in casting doubt on such legitimate facts as might by themselves have deterred the King from his intention. Had they contented themselves with picturing the lady as low-born and of a shadowy background they might have spoken to his remaining scruples. Instead they depicted her as a coarse-tongued, gin-soaked slut, and this Louis knew with his own eyes she was not. Far from intimidating or disgusting him as it had been the intention of these lampoons to do, they aroused his sense of chivalry and hastened him to the defense of an innocent and helpless woman.

His intention that she should be presented grew firmer and in December he took the active step of trying to find a woman of quarterings willing to act as the Comtesse's sponsor. Such a woman was hard to find. Greed was appealed to, but the ladies of Versailles put too high a price on their pride, one of them asking for a sum close to a million dollars and the brevet of Duchesse: only with this would she apparently feel herself adequately armed against disgrace. Richelieu finally unearthed a needy aunt, one Comtesse de Béarn whose family had known its best days at the court of the Valois. Poverty and the expense of a lawsuit so ancient that its origins were wrapped in legend had long kept the old woman from a Court she probably in her heart despised. She was delighted to comply with Richelieu's request, her fee being the payment of her debts.

Richelieu now set the date: January 25, 1769. The Court was in a frenzy. "They say that tomorrow is to be the great day," wrote Madame du Deffand to her friend Horace Walpole, "the day when a dress will decide the fate of Europe and the destiny of ministers. Bets are being placed. A few bet on a nightgown, but the majority on full Court dress. No, *no*, I can't believe it! The matter will be stopped by shame, by simple decency. . . ."

In the excitement, the hysterical Choiseul tried to introduce another woman to the King's attention: one Madame Millin described as "young and pretty," but who was unable to touch the King's distracted affections. But Choiseul's party was given an unexpected reprieve. At the last minute word was sent from the Comtesse de Béarn's apartment that she had "sprained her ankle." In reality the old lady had been frozen to the marrow of her bones by the terrifying looks she had received from Madame Adélaïde, and in fear and trembling had crept off to bed, too unnerved for the moment to fulfill her promise.

Fate itself seemed to conspire against the presentation. A few weeks later Louis, while hunting, had a bad fall from his horse and injured his arm seriously enough to give him a scare. Mesdames, it was observed, and not the Comtesse, sat by his bed. The weeks slipped by and nothing happened. The weeks became months and although slander and smut continued to pour from the printing presses of Paris, the Court's fickle attention was gradually distracted by other matters.

The time of the great wedding—that of the Archduchess Marie Antoinette to the Dauphin—was now but a year away. An event of this magnitude, the mingling of Europe's two oldest dynasties, was beset with problems of etiquette and ceremony that occupied everybody's attention many months in advance of the event. The air crackled with envy and triumph at imagined favors or slights as preparations were made for the arrival in France of the fifteen-year-old Marie Antoinette.

On the sixth of April the wedding of the Duc de Chartres (the King's cousin, and the future Duc d'Orléans and Revolutionary, Philippe-Égalité) to Mademoiselle de Penthièvre—heiress to the great Montpensier fortune—took place, a preview of greater things to come and an affair of great magnificence.

Scarcely had people recovered from this when, like a thunderbolt, came the terse announcement that on April twenty-second the King would hold a presentation at which he would receive the Comtesse du Barry. Everyone realized that unless Fate again stepped in, the business was now as good as accomplished. The King's will was done. This time the Comtesse de Béarn steeled her spine, straightening it no doubt with the thought that the Béarns were, after all, descendants of Eudes of Aquitaine and had known honor under the Merovingians.

The scene that took place at Versailles in the evening of that twenty-second of April, 1769, belongs as much to French history as it does to Madame du Barry, It is one of the famous Versailles *vignettes*.

Louis, his arm in a sling, surrounded by all his retinue, paced nervously up and down the floor of his apartment. From beyond the gates leading to the central courtyard below could be heard the hum of the curious crowd which had flocked out from Paris to catch a glimpse of the affair. Within the King's Chamber the murmur gradually grew louder as it was realized that the lady was late. Choiseul had absented himself, but his clique exchanged sly, triumphant glances as it became apparent that the Comtesse was not going to appear. The King could scarcely conceal his gathering irritation. He was not a man to be kept waiting and he was just at the point of ordering Richelieu to dismiss the assembly when the clatter of horses' hooves was heard in the courtyard below, and in great excitement it was whispered that the lady had arrived. The carriage was heard to stop. Within the room there was utter silence as the Comtesse and her sponsor were ushered up the Escalier d'Honneur and through the long rooms of state to the King. After what seemed an eternity a footman flung open the doors and Richelieu, his face flushed with triumph, announced the Comtesse du Barry.

All gloom left the King's person when he saw the beautiful woman who now entered behind the Comtesse de Béarn. The occasion needed no other excuse. All in the room were spellbound as, blazing in a half million dollars' worth of diamonds, she advanced with that peculiar lilting movement which was the stamp of Versailles, and made a deep curtsy before the enamoured Sovereign. Her hair, after the custom of these ceremonies, was powdered to a snowy white that brought forth the fragile rose of her skin and the sapphire of the half-closed, slightly slanting eyes. She received the King's formal recognition and then, with cool composure, kicked back the long train as she made the requisite three reverences, leaving the King's presence backwards.

One of the women present has left an interesting account: "I went to the presentation of my aunt," writes Madame de Genlis, "and was highly amused for it was the same occasion on which Madame du Barry was presented. It was recognized by everyone present that she was tastefully and splendidly dressed. By daylight her face was a little faded and her complexion spoiled by freckles. But it must be admitted that she looked extremely well at night. We reached the card tables in the evening a few minutes before her. When she entered the room all the ladies who were near the door rushed hurriedly forward in the opposite direction in order to avoid sitting near her, so that between her and the last lady in the room there was an interval of four or five empty chairs. She regarded all this with perfect composure; nothing upset her. When the King appeared at the conclusion of the game, she looked up at him and smiled. The indignation at Versailles was unbounded. Never had there happened anything quite so scandalous, not even the triumph of Madame de Pompadour. It was certainly very strange to see at Court a Madame la Marquise de Pompadour whose husband Monsieur Le Normant d'Étioles was nobody but a tax-farmer, but it was still more terrible to see a woman of the streets presented with pomp to the whole Royal Family. This with many other instances of unparalleled indecency cruelly degraded Royalty, and consequently contributed to bring about the Revolution."

Snobbish Madame de Genlis might well have looked to her own questionable quarterings. Since by the time she wrote this description she herself had played the rôle of Madame du Barry to the Duc d'Orléans, the regicide Philippe-Égalité, her views may be taken as a bit of irony as well as description. If any individual contributed to bring about the Revolution it was surely the half-crazy paramour of Madame de Genlis.

Scarcely was the presentation over than the diplomatic pouches left Paris bearing the news to the courts of Europe: to the Bourbon cousins of Naples, Spain and Parma; to Austria; to the Court of Catherine, Semiramis of the North; to Prussia and to the Holy See. All had some interest or other that would be affected by the event.

So did the daughter of Anne Bécu step into the pages of history.

Chapter 4

"SHE WAS KIND," writes the Comte d'Espinchal, "and always generous, gentle in company and an excellent friend who was both charitable and obliging."

Not once during her term of favor did Madame du Barry assert her power to do harm to others. Not an imprisonment, not even an exile is on record to speak against her. More than once she actively interceded to help those who had fallen into serious disfavor—in several cases people who were in disfavor because they had venomously attacked her. She was singularly endowed with the gift of charity and on the very threshold of her "reign" she was given several opportunities to put her new-found powers to work for the benefit of others.

The law at that time condemned to death any woman whose child was still-born and who had not notified the authorities of her pregnancy. Such case was brought to the Comtesse's attention who, shocked at this piece of barbarism, immediately dispatched a note to the Chancellor Maupeou:

> MONSIEUR LE CHANCELIER:
>
> I understand nothing of your laws; but they are barbaric and run counter to all reason and humanity when they condemn to death a poor creature because she gives birth to a still-born child without having given formal notification. Such, according to the documents I am attaching, is the situation of the one who now pleads for mercy; it appears that she is condemned either because she was unaware of the regulation, or because, with a very natural modesty, she did not carry it out. I commend the affair to your attention and to your sense of justice. This poor girl deserves mercy. At the very least I implore a modification of the punishment. Your own feelings will dictate the rest.

The Chancellor, who for many reasons was trying to ingratiate himself with the new Favorite, was only too glad to comply with her request, and a life was thereby saved. It was not a calculated move on the Comtesse's part, but the story soon got about and it spoke in her favor. After twenty years of the Pompadour who never acted to release anyone from any sentence, who on the contrary was more inclined to fill the prisons than empty them, this simple act on the part of the new Favorite caused something of a sensation. Because of it, she was approached a month later on a matter of a still grimmer nature.

In a ruined old château in the province of Orléans, there lived a threadbare, elderly couple, the Comte and Comtesse Pé de Louësme. Despite the popular picture of it, the plight of the aristocracy before the Revolution was frequently deplorable. The greater part of the nobility, people in fact like the du Barrys and the Comtesse de Béarn, eked out a wretched existence crushed between debt and complicated traditions and laws which forbade people of noble birth from earning their living. The aged Pé de Louësmes were at the last extremity, virtually at the point of starvation when their last poor possessions and the old château itself were sequestered by an up-and-coming tradesman, one Dourcy, for debt. The couple refused to give up possession of their property and, in the manner of those who had fought in the Fronde a hundred years before, flooded the moat and pulled up the drawbridge. When Dourcy and the police arrived, the Comte warned them of his intention to hold the castle by arms if necessary. The police breached the walls and in the ensuing scuffle one of them was shot and killed by the Comtesse. The party hurried away to gather reinforcements and the Louësmes with their few loyal retainers prepared to withstand siege. The pitiful but plucky defenders finally surrendered, although not until a two-day battle had been fought and the Comtesse herself wounded.

Reminiscent as it was of the Fronde, this affair caused quite a stir and because of the rank of the defendants the trial was held before the Parlement in Paris. The old Comte and Comtesse were sentenced to have their heads chopped off on the block. Their two married daughters, in despair, rushed from the Chancellor to the Throne, imploring the King's mercy. Both Maupeou and the King were adamant: the sentence, under due law, had to be executed. There was no hope of a reprieve. At this point a relative of the unhappy pair, who knew the Comtesse de Béarn, had the inspiration to suggest that through the Comtesse de Béarn they should approach Madame du Barry and solicit her sympathy. As soon as she had heard the story the Favorite hurried to the King and fell on her knees before him, begging for the mercy he had so stonily refused to give the unhappy daughters. For a while the King remained firm, but the Comtesse threatened never to rise if he didn't grant her this petition. Her tears could not be resisted and after a moment the King raised her from the floor.

"I am delighted, Madame," he declared, "that the first favor you ask of me should be an act of mercy."

When this story became known many people who had disliked the Comtesse on principle or on hearsay took a closer look at her. Her credit rose appreciably both on account of this disinterested act of compassion, and as evidence of a stronger sway over the King's intentions than had heretofore been supposed. She had nothing to gain by saving the lives of two elderly and unimportant people, and exactly for this reason she gained much. Her reputation for kindness soon brought others to her door and a few months later she was able to save the life of a soldier, named Charpentier, who had been sentenced to death for desertion. This wretch, who was fortunate enough to have a commanding officer who took an interest in the circumstances of his case, had run home to the farm in a seizure of homesickness and, being caught, was sentenced to death. His officer wrote to a friend at Court who was attached to the Lightguard and, explaining the situation, asked if he might in some way bring influence to bear for a pardon. Belleval, the guardsman appealed to, went to the Duc d'Aiguillon, Commander of the Lightguard, and asked him what could be done to save the "deserter's" life. D'Aiguillon assured him that the quickest way to secure the King's compassion was through the Comtesse du Barry and arranged to introduce him to that lady.

"At the hour appointed," writes Belleval, "I presented myself at the Duc's residence in full uniform. He was waiting for me and went immediately to the Favorite's apartments.

"I had frequently seen the Comtesse du Barry, but only from a distance so that I had never been able to study her famous beauty in detail. She was reclining carelessly on a large *fauteuil* and wore a dress of some white material with garlands of roses which even as I write this, fifteen years later, I can still see very vividly. She was one of the prettiest women at the Court where there were so many, and assuredly the most fascinating because of the perfections of her whole person. Her hair, which she often left unpowdered, was fair and of a most beautiful color in such a profusion that she seemed at a loss to know what to do with it. Her blue eyes had a kind and open expression and she always fixed them closely upon those to whom she spoke, seeming to follow in their faces the effects of her words. She had a tiny nose, a very small mouth and a skin of dazzling whiteness. She quickly bewitched everyone and in the delight I had in gazing at her I very nearly forgot my petition. I was then about twenty-five years old. She quickly perceived my embarrassment as did the Duc d'Aiguillon who very adroitly turned it off with one of those compliments at which he excelled. I then presented my petition, adding some explanation and stressing the necessity there was for haste if we were to save the life of this unfortunate Charpentier.

" 'I give you my promise to speak to the King, Monsieur,' she answered, 'and I trust that His Majesty will not refuse me this favor. Monsieur le Duc knows well that his friends are always mine, and I thank him for sending you to me,' she added, turning to him with a charming smile. She questioned me about my family, and as to how long I had served and then dismissed us, telling me that I should soon have news from her. She offered her hand to the Duc d'Aiguillon who kissed it with the observation: 'This is for the Commander; is there nothing for the Company?' She laughed as she bestowed upon me the same favor of which I hastened to take advantage.

"The following day, while I was on guard, a lackey in the well-known livery of the Comtesse approached and informed me that she expected me at six o'clock. At that hour I presented myself at the door of her apartment and was admitted. There were several persons there including the King who was standing with his back to the chimney-piece. When she saw me Madame du Barry said to His Majesty: 'Sire, here is my guardsman who has come to offer his thanks to Your Majesty.'

" 'Thank, in the first place, Madame la Comtesse,' said Louis XV, 'and tell your petitioner that if I pardon him he must, by his attention to my service, cause the fault of which he has been guilty to be forgotten.'

"I can't recall what answer I made to the King, but the Duc d'Aiguillon later assured me that I had acted properly and that the King was satisfied with me. The same evening the good news was dispatched to Provins where poor Charpentier was expecting nothing but death. He afterwards made a good soldier and was a credit to his regiment.

"The account which I gave my fellow Lightguardsmen of the kindness of the Comtesse was received with great applause and the Vicomte du Barry [son of the Roué] promised to report our compliments to her. We afterwards believed that he really did, because she always showed a marked preference for the Lightguard above all the other troops in the King's

Household. For my part, I was always afterward treated with kindness and I often met her at the house of the Duchesse d'Aiguillon to whom she was much attached on account of Madame d'Aiguillon's husband. I never again visited her apartments. But a simple Lightguardsman did not belong in the midst of all the courtiers who thronged her apartment to pay court to her or to meet His Majesty. She understood that and had the tact—though she treated me in a very kindly manner whenever we met—never to ask me why I did not visit her, as so many other women would have done. The situation was different at the Duc d'Aiguillon's where we 'redcoats' often gathered. 'Ah! There's my Lightguardsman!' was the phrase with which the Comtesse would always greet me and then she would ask if there were anything she could do for me. I always replied that there was not and she would then turn to the Duc and say: 'He always answers "no" when there are so many who would answer "yes." My dear Duc, are they all like that in your Company?' 'Certainly not!' the Duc would reply, and the laughter and gaiety which followed seemed as though it would never end."

For all her kindness of heart, the Comtesse remained cruelly quarantined by the ladies of the Court. Madame de Gramont, far from conceding the fight, declared by her activities that it had only just begun. She and her clique refused to attend any gathering where the new Favorite was present. When by Royal Command their refusal was made impossible, they appeared with the worst possible grace, shunning the lonely Comtesse and snubbing her overtures of friendship. In the privacy of the Petits Cabinets there were sobs, and a tear-brimmed pair of pretty eyes were often dabbed by a furtive handkerchief.

The King, ever a kind man, took steps to form a little circle for his isolated lady. Mademoiselle Chon and the elderly Comtesse de Béarn, who had too much the air of an aunt on hire, were not enough. He now turned to an old friend, the Maréchale de Mirepoix, a clever, monkey-faced old woman, who had been the most intimate of Madame de Pompadour's friends and by marriage with the brother of the Princesse de Beauvau, as well as by long association, was in the very heart of the Choiseul party. She was as amusing as she was heartless: a hard-bitten realist whose own interests were never obscured by the sentimental fumes of friendship or of loyalty. She lived entirely for pleasure, and the only pleasures that could matter to her were those she found in the hard, bright light of favor and fashion. Conversation (always with that intellectual tincture which bore the stamp of Versailles), gossip, the never-ending buzz of palace intrigue, these were the food and breath of her life. They nourished her well, for the raddled, worldly old woman died at a very advanced age in Brussels during the Revolution, bright-eyed to the last. On the morning of her death, shortly after the Last Rites had been administered, her doctor announced that he found her remarkably improved. "What a bore!" answered the old woman. "Everything has been packed and I was all ready to depart."

Although very rich, the Maréchale had an insatiable appetite for gambling which was reported to keep her in an annual debt of over forty thousand dollars a year. The King was genuinely fond of her—she was one of the few people who could be counted on to amuse him—and often gave her a substantial present to help face this embarrassment. He offered now to increase this sum by a very generous amount if only the old woman would come to the rescue of Madame du Barry. The Maréchale wasted no time thinking over this proposal; her relatives and friends in the Choiseul camp were outraged.

"Madame de Mirepoix is playing a disgraceful rôle," wrote her friend Madame du Deffand to Horace Walpole. "In order to diminish her own shame she is now on the lookout for recruits; thus far without much success."

Where the sun shines warmest there do the lilies of the field turn their face, and it was not long before others who had this or that to gain were sheepishly tiptoeing from the ranks of sterile righteousness into the camp of fruitful vice. The Princesse de Montmorency, whose husband wanted to be appointed to the suite of the Dauphin; the Princesse de Monaco, whose paramour the Prince de Condé hoped for an appointment from the King; the Marquise de l'Hôpital, sent by her lover, the Prince de Soubise, all these and others were soon dining off the Comtesse's plate and laughing at one another's jokes, much to the open joy of the Comtesse and no doubt to the secret and more malicious delight of the renegade Maréchale. "Bit by bit," remarked the Duc de Croy, "people began to visit the Comtesse more often. She was established in the apartment in the Cabinets where the late Dauphine had died. From this she derived the advantage of being generally acknowledged as a lady of the Court; she went to all the fêtes helter-skelter with the rest; people slowly became used to it."

Horace Walpole, who had come over to Paris to gossip with his old friend Madame du Deffand, hurried out to Versailles to see the woman whose name was on every tongue in Europe. He has left an interesting account of the lady as she appeared soon after her presentation: "Thence to the Chapel, where a first row in the balconies was kept for us. Madame du Barri arrived over against us below, without rouge, without powder and indeed *sans avoir fait sa toilette*; an odd appearance, as she was so conspicuous, close to the altar and amidst both Court and people. She is pretty, when you consider her; yet so little striking that I should never have asked who she was. There is nothing bold, assuming or affected in her manner. Her husband's sister [Chon] was along with her. In the Tribune above, surrounded by prelates, was the amorous and still handsome King. One could not help smiling at the mixture of pomp, piety and carnality."

Walpole, like so many after him, had expected to see some flaming Jezebel. Nothing could have been farther from the truth as all who wrote of her, even her enemies, testify. Madame de Genlis sneers at her freckles, but to another age this would speak in her favor. In a Court where even the men were rouged to the eyebrows she would indeed have been "conspicuously inconspicuous." Health, youth and her natural beauty needed no gilding and beyond a minutely fastidious care of her person, a rite that took several hours of every morning, she rarely had recourse to the excesses of *maquillage* which were the custom of the Court.

Drouais painted her likeness at this time in two different portraits and what Walpole could not convey in words the artist very happily conveys in paint. Declaring that he could not handle so much beauty in a single portrait, Drouais solved the problem by painting two pictures: one representing her as Flora with a wreath of roses; the other as a huntress, dressed in masculine attire. The paintings hung on exhibit in the Louvre and created an immense sensation. They were followed by a rash of flowery poems each more complimentary than the other of the Favorite's radiant loveliness. Very possibly the hands that penned these pretty flourishes were the same that an hour later dipped a quill in venom and turned out Monsieur de Choiseul's daily order of poison. Such in the *ancien régime* was the condition of the Muse whose acolytes rarely starved.

In the summer of that year of 1769 Louis made the first significant gift to his Comtesse. The Château of Louveciennes which stood at the edge of the royal park at Marly, not far from Paris, had been unoccupied since the death there, several years before, of the young Prince de Lamballe, dissolute son of the Duc de Penthièvre. His widow, the sensitive Princesse de Lamballe who was destined to meet an atrocious death during the Revolution, had no wish to live in it again and the building reverted to the Crown. Louis now made a present of it to his mistress. Although it was admirably situated in one of those wild and faintly *triste* settings which were coming to be the taste, and while it had a splendid view, the building itself was small and inconvenient. Under the supervision of the great Gabriel a battery of builders were soon at work on it converting it into a property suitable to the Favorite of a King of France.

Almost every life has some particular place where associations with it are strongest. In Madame du Barry's life this place was not Versailles, but Louveciennes. Louveciennes knew the nights of splendor when she gave her magnificent receptions to the King and his Court, when the mirrors blazed with the reflected light of a thousand candles and the walls gave back the laughter of a glittering, sycophant crowd. It was Louveciennes she called "home" when King and crowd had vanished forever and she lived out the long, pleasant days of her "retirement," potting jam, attending the parish poor, receiving a few old friends and now and then making new ones. She was as close with her memories as were the walls and mirrors, but as she grew older an occasional sigh would escape. "It was in this room," she once said to Madame Vigée-Lebrun when showing her through the château, "that some years ago Louis XV did me the honor of dining." At Louveciennes in 1793 she was arrested and taken to Paris to face prison, trial and death. During her period of favor many additions, including an orangerie, a chapel, and the exquisite Pavilion of Louveciennes were made at Louveciennes.

The growing warmth of favor which radiated from the Comtesse now brought two reptiles cautiously slithering toward her person. The Chancellor Maupeou and the Abbé Terray distinguished themselves at Versailles in being the two most dreaded figures of their time. Crafty, cold and perfidious, the spectacle of this sinister twosome acting in collusion was enough to strike terror in the bosoms of the most hardened intriguers.

Because he aspired to more conspicuous rôles and was consequently better known, Maupeou was the more detested of the two. A little black-haired man who vainly tried to conceal a hideously green complexion beneath layers of dirty rouge and caking powder, Maupeou was said to show on his face all the signs of the baseness of his soul. Beneath a pair of bushy eyebrows that flared like Gothic arches into a low, mean forehead were set two keen and piercing eyes that darted about restlessly, as though in search of prey. Like the shadow of a hawk over a henroost, his mere presence was enough to silence a room.

The Abbé Terray, if possible, seems to have been more hideous than even the Chancellor Maupeou: "His exterior was rugged, sinister, even terrifying: a tall, gaunt figure with haggard eyes and a shifty glance which conveyed the impression of falseness and perfidy, uncouth manners, a raspy voice, utterly lacking in openness of soul, judging all men unfavorably because he judged them by himself, a terrible, dry, caustic laugh. Although he was harsh to a degree with those who were unable to injure him, he was revoltingly servile toward those he believed to have credit. Never did there exist a more icy heart nor one more inaccessible to affection save that of lust and for money as a means of gratifying lust."

Common cause now brought these two cold and subtle intelligences together. It is probably true that more damage has been done to humankind by the idealistically inclined who unfortunately happen to be a little stupid than by such men as Maupeou and Terray (or their better known equivalents, Bismarck and Cardinal Richelieu) who view the human heart without illusion and are able to deal with the unpleasant realities of this imperfect world without passion. For such men, of course, the end is all and the means to that end—treachery, baseness, even cruelty—are of no consideration. "If we can gain anything by being honest men," declared Frederick the Great, "why then for heaven's sake let us be honest; but if we can gain something by being knaves, then let us be knaves." Since the end for such people is rarely so simple a thing as private gain, such men by a curious irony often turn out to be the real idealists, willing to sacrifice not only others, but occasionally even themselves to their object, living in austerity, working night and day with tireless energy toward a goal that causes them to be hated by their contemporaries and more often than not despised by their descendants.

In the case of the Chancellor and the Abbé this goal was no less than the crushing of the rebellious Parlements and a restoration to the Crown of its once-unquestioned sovereignty. The Parlements bore little resemblance to the English institution of similar name. Far from being a step forward toward Constitutional Monarchy, the growing power of the Parlements threatened a step backward in the direction of medieval chaos and disunity. Each Parlement in its district represented the most mean-minded of provincial interests, a lingering and dangerous remnant of the divided France which Cardinal Richelieu with hand of steel had welded together. The provincial nobility, the rural politicians, the up-and-coming business class whose money would never buy them a position in the giddy, arrogant Court where their lumpy, fashionably-dressed wives and themselves were rudely laughed at by such dowdy old witches as the Maréchale de Mirepoix whom they could buy and sell ten times over: such as these gave more of the little loyalty that they had to give to their local Parlement rather than to the King. To Louis XV these Parlements were a source of unending trouble. The history of his reign is punctuated by almost continual squabbling between Crown and Parlement, a deep-seated and dangerous ill in the body politic that flared up often, but never quite resolved itself through crisis. Madame de Pompadour and Choiseul had supported the Parlements' claims of jurisdiction and authority. In the years following her death they had been quieter, but they had also grown stronger and more insistent in their claim of the right to veto the King's edicts.

The Chancellor Maupeou with passionless eye saw very clearly that France was approaching a crossroads. Every reform, every measure of innovation which the times called for was overridden or stalemated by the antiquated and cumbersome legal machinery of the Parlements, which considered neither the wishes of the King nor the needs of the people. Maupeou realized that no resolution of difference between these two contending parties was possible; ultimately no compromise could solve the issue. The King or the Parlements must go. Maupeou's goal was the destruction of the power of Parlements and restitution thereafter of central authority to the Crown. Had his eventual successes in this direction been supported, the history of France might have moved in a different course. It took the strong fist of Napoleon finally to smash this broken-down remnant of the Middle Ages which for so long had been as much a burden on the people of France as on their King. But it was not for want of recognizing the evil or for trying to eliminate it that Maupeou failed in his purpose. He was a ruthless and cold-blooded intriguer, totally without principle, but he was also one of the most capable and intelligent men of his time, a power-house of efficiently directed energy. It must be allowed (with the advantage of hindsight) that he acted in the best interests of his country. Choiseul himself had appointed Maupeou to the Chancellorship with the explanation: "I know quite well that the man is dangerous, but he is the most capable in France for the Chancellorship. If he starts to make trouble for me, I shall dismiss him."

Maupeou groveled in false gratitude before the Minister's feet, setting no limits to the oily profusion of his flattery, no bounds to his oaths of eternal loyalty to the Minister's person. In the meanwhile he was briskly working toward his downfall. The ascendancy of Madame du Barry and of the d'Aiguillon-Richelieu party gave him the chance for which he had been waiting. He was soon conspiring openly against his benefactor. No wonder then that he honored the Favorite's whimsical little requests for mercy for those condemned to death.

His first open conflict with Choiseul came over the appointment of the Abbé Terray to the Ministry of Finance. Choiseul had his own candidate for this critical post and it was a severe blow to his position to find that Maupeou's dark purpose had prevailed and Terray, a more implacable enemy than even the Chancellor Maupeou, had been appointed Comptroller-General of France. Like Maupeou, the Abbé Terray hoped to put his clear, icy intelligence to work in effecting drastic and desperately needed changes in the fiscal system. The State revenue was almost entirely made up of duties and indirect taxation. Such an income was not enough to cover State expenditure, and the problem had reached a critical impasse. It was Terray's solution that the propertied classes of France who, thanks to an antiquated system of exemption and privilege managed to escape payment of most taxes, should now be made liable for a share in the support of State revenue.

The Parlements, representing the propertied classes, had no intention of ever approving such legislation as would make them subject to taxation. It was as much a blow to them as to Choiseul that the Abbé should have been appointed to this critical post. As with Maupeou it must be admitted that Terray's objectives were long-sighted and commendable. Like Maupeou too, the Abbé obsequiously indulged the Favorite in her whims and saw to it that the Treasury honored without question the little chits which in gathering volume fluttered down on it first like a snowstorm and then like a blizzard from the Comtesse's boudoir. What, he reasoned, are a paltry ten or fifteen millions, if through their expenditure a system of drastic and beneficial reform might be achieved? By throwing ten or twenty million dollars' worth of diamonds at the Favorite to keep her in good humor, Terray aspired to achieve a renovated system of taxation which would increase State income many fold and place the tottering Treasury back on its feet.

With such motives did Maupeou and Terray cross into the camp of the Comtesse and of the Duc de Aiguillon, an alarming reinforcement to the Barry party and a bad blow to the party of Choiseul. The dark waters of intrigue were suddenly boiling and surging about the person of young Madame du Barry. Vast issues, programs of far-reaching consequences, policies instinct with the weight of history took birth in the hope of her favor. How much, one wonders, could these things have meant to her? "The most important events that took place during her ascendancy passed before her eyes like the figures in a shadowbox," wrote Sénac de Meilhan after a visit at Louveciennes some years later. "She bore no part in them and they lingered only as a vague memory in her mind."

She was no fool—few Frenchwomen of her class are—but her opinions and her preferences (well-intentioned though they generally were) remained entirely personal. Like her predecessor, the Pompadour, she was unable to separate judgment from prejudice; unlike the Marquise, however, she did not aggressively meddle in politics. She liked the Duc d'Aiguillon because in his courtly and insurpassable manner he was unfailingly attentive to her. She disliked Choiseul for the very sufficient, and human, reason that he disliked her. This was quite enough to fix her political attachments. Kindhearted and easygoing as she was, Madame du Barry, apart from a grateful attachment to those who were polite to her, showed little inclination to dip her toes in the swirling political waters. She would have been quite content to sun herself on the comfortable safety of the beach. "She has neither affection nor hatred for anybody," Madame du Deffand reported to Walpole. "She says what they make her say like a parrot, without interest or passion; no one contrives to govern with a character like that."

The good-natured woman asked only peace and quiet to enjoy the good things of life that, suddenly as though by the wave of some powerful wand, had now become hers. She had all the diamonds a simple creature's heart could cry for, she had the finest clothes in France, the most dazzling retinue of any woman at Court. She wanted no more than this. Her ambition did not extend to the launching of armies, the promulgating of treaties or the advising of ministries.

Unfortunately she was but human and while she may not have asked for the actual applause of her adversaries (she would have been well content with a silent neutrality), she could not support the continuing harsh and envenomed attacks on her character, the malicious, spiteful little acts and cautiously calculated insults from the Minister and his dwindling adherents. She had endured Choiseul's hostility with an admirable tolerance that is admitted by even the most sympathetic of that Duc's biographers. But her every overture of reconciliation had been met by sullen indifference or arrogant contempt. Fortified by his harridan of a sister and by his relative the Princesse de Beauvau, Choiseul's hatred soon became a madness that dragged France close to revolution and to the very brink of war.

Nothing can more clearly illustrate the fascinating proximity of the petty to the enormous, of statecraft to personality as it was at Versailles, than the two ensuing struggles into which the Comtesse du Barry was witlessly dragged: the first with Choiseul and the second, more extraordinary still, with Marie Antoinette. Ministries toppled, alliances tottered, parlements were dismissed, armies were mobilized and ultimatums drafted—all because in the first instance the Minister disliked the Mistress and in the second because the Dauphine would not speak to her.

Chapter 5

THE VEHEMENCE of Choiseul's press continued unabated. Wild incredible stories that would have done credit to the Court of Heliogabalus circulated about Paris and the provinces. But a certain spicy malice, the recognizable tang of Gallic seasoning marks most of them as the Eighteenth Century's own. The Romans were not very amusing about their vices.

One such story tells of a certain morning when Madame du Barry imperiously summoned the Archbishop of Paris and the Papal Nuncio to her bedside. When the King and his notary had entered, the trollop suddenly flung aside the covers and stark naked arose from her nest of lace and satin, demanding to receive her slippers from the astonished dignitaries. "The two priests," smirks the chronicler, "considered themselves well repaid for the humiliation they had suffered by the ravishing glimpse they had had of the Beauty's secret charms." Another story, as interesting, no doubt, to the psychologist (with its hints of Rousseau and the Marquis de Sade) as it is to the satirist, tells of the fate of a certain Marquise des Rosses. Outraged by the impertinence of this lovely but saucy peeress toward the King, Madame du Barry commanded her attendants to spank her. Transported by the squeals and struggles of the wriggling Marquise, the Son of Saint-Louis seized his Favorite and then and there the "two mad creatures" poured a libation to Venus.

The Comtesse, child of the Paris streets, was the first to laugh at such anecdotes or verses, the bawdier the better. When the police announced to her the discovery of a fresh pamphlet she would ask to have it read to her. Even cruel and personal attack left her remarkably good humored.

Had Choiseul limited his assaults to mere slander his term of power would probably have lasted out the reign. Unfortunately he waged his campaign against her with the vigor and energy he might better have applied to establishing a more favorable balance of trade or a reformed fiscal system. Closer and closer, in circles ever more daring and defiant he skated toward thin ice. The Austrian Ambassador and the Court of Vienna who saw in him the cornerstone of their alliance with France watched, appalled. No one but Choiseul himself, it almost appeared, really wished his downfall.

The King, always loath to lose a Minister and particularly one so familiar to him as Monsieur de Choiseul, did everything in his power to bring about peace between the contending parties. He gave a supper party at Bellevue, hoping that if the Comtesse and the Minister had a chance to meet one another and talk they might find some common ground of interest or friendship. In vain. The Duc behaved as rudely as he dared in the presence of Majesty. The King spoke to him privately, an extraordinary step for a Sovereign who was not called upon to explain his private life to a minister. In vain. Not long after, the King was writing to him: "You promised me that I should hear no more from you about her. I speak to you again in confidence and friendship. . . ." There had been a scene after maneuvers at Compiègne. A battalion in a spontaneous gesture of friendship for the generous Comtesse who had entertained them at a sumptuous banquet the evening before, had saluted her presence. Choiseul outraged by this unprecedented honor, had threatened, as Minister of War, to break the commanding officer. Once more the King implored his Minister to behave with prudence.

So strained were matters becoming that the Roué now discreetly stepped into the picture. The Comtesse, genuinely disturbed by the disagreeable turn of affairs, implored her brother-in-law to do something to heal the fast-widening breach. Du Barry immediately addressed himself to a nephew of the Minister whom he arranged to meet secretly in the park at Compiègne. He begged the intermediary to tell the Duc that Madame du Barry, having nothing but respect for the Minister's great abilities, wished from the bottom of her heart to be at peace with him. It would not be easy for him to force her to be his enemy, but should he succeed it would be most unfortunate because she had far more power with the King than Madame de Pompadour ever had. If this was a warning, it was also a genuine plea for peace.

When the message was conveyed to him, Madame de Gramont happened to be in the Duc's apartment. The old toad spat venom not only on the name of du Barry but on that of the King too. The Comtesse's olive branch was thrown to the floor with contempt and scorn. Goaded on by his sister, the Duc pursued his campaign of meanness and malice with a yet more reckless intensity, angered rather than sobered by the danger signs that were becoming apparent to the whole Court. "The winds are blowing in all directions," writes Madame du Deffand. "I wonder if they will uproot any trees?" Horace Walpole passed on the gossip to his friend Sir Horace Mann: "A fortnight ago the Mistress sent for Choiseul to ask a favor for a dependent. He replied that she might come to him. She insisted and he went and stayed above an hour, and yet did not grant what she asked. It's a thousand to one but some éclat happens during the approaching visit to Fontainebleau when the Choiseul women will have returned from abroad."

D'Aiguillon, who was not a Choiseul candidate, had been appointed Commander of the Lightguard. The Abbé Terray, not Choiseul's candidate, had been made Comptroller-General. Maupeou, Choiseul's own appointment, had openly defected to the d'Aiguillon party. At public gatherings and the *petits soupers* of the King it was observed that the crowd was thickest and the laughter loudest about the persons of d'Aiguillon and the Comtesse. No one troubled any more to laugh at the little witticisms of Choiseul which not many months before would have seemed so amusing to so many. He talked to a dwindling audience.

Too late the Minister finally conceded the power of the lady's hold on the King. He sought an interview in which he made it clear that he was willing to grant a few concessions. They talked for over three hours, but to no avail. Choiseul had already destroyed himself in the lady's eyes. She could consider him only as an implacable and dangerous enemy. He had made it too clear to her that they could not live together in peace, and she now looked forward to the day when finally she should be rid of him and of his mischief-making sister.

"The lady now no longer conceals her hatred of him," reports the indefatigable Madame du Deffand in November, 1769, shortly after this interview. "The conversation he had with her was a false move on his part because it was utterly useless. Every day he is subject to such little annoyances as not being invited to the *petits soupers*. When he happens to be her partner at whist there are grimaces, mockeries, shruggings of the shoulders, all the little schoolgirl tricks. . . ."

To flaunt her open support of d'Aiguillon, the Comtesse gave a magnificent reception for him at Louveciennes. Louis attended. In alarm Choiseul wrote to the King.

"How could you believe," answered Louis, "that d'Aiguillon could replace you? . . . You manage my affairs well and I am satisfied with you; but you must be wary of those who surround you and who give you advice. I have always hated such people and I now hate them more than ever. You know Madame du Barry. She is pretty and I am pleased with her.

I advise her every day to beware of those who surround her and who try to give advice. You can well believe that these are plenty. She bears no grudge against you. The attack on her has been appalling and for the most part without any justification. People would be on their knees to her if only . . . well, such is the world. She is very pretty; she makes me happy. That is all that need be said. Would you like me to take a lady of quality? If the Archduchess pleased me I would marry her. The fair sex will always trouble me, but you will never find me with a Dame de Maintenon. This is enough for the present. . . ."

As d'Aiguillon's star began to rise and that of Choiseul to sink, there occurred an event of the gravest significance to the fortunes of France and one which brought to a crisis the relationship between these two antagonists. In the years previous to the arrival at Court of Madame du Barry, d'Aiguillon had been Governor-General of Brittany. Of all the fair provinces of France, Brittany had always been the most difficult for Paris (or rather Versailles) to govern. Proud traditions and ancient continuities had kept that sullen, stubborn, rock-bound people loyal to the recollection of independence. Bitterly did its provincial nobility and its hard-bitten magistrates resent subservience to the far-off cage of gold and crystal where the chattering birds-of-paradise minced and simpered, flaunting their plumage. Bitterly did they resent the high-handed and arrogant emissaries of the Crown who came among them to superintend what they fondly imagined to be their own affairs. The Breton Parlement and the King's Governor were at constant odds. D'Aiguillon with his foppish airs and his cold, contemptuous arrogance soon made himself heartily disliked. Mutual simmering resentment finally reached a boiling point when the Parlement refused to register or collect a tax which the Governor had levied, and declared it to be illegal. D'Aiguillon summarily ordered the arrest of several of the magistrates and the dissolution of the Parlement, forming another of his own. The sullen Bretons refused to recognize the authority of the new Parlement and remained in a condition of revolt against the Government. After four years of this impasse the Crown finally permitted the old Parlement to reassemble and in 1768 d'Aiguillon was recalled to Court.

He returned there vowing vengeance on his enemy Choiseul in whose dark intrigues with the Parlements he sensed the source of all his troubles. Destiny, with the arrival at Versailles of Madame du Barry, unexpectedly smiled on his hopes, and hurriedly he hitched his wagon to that star. The friendless and warmhearted Comtesse gratefully responded to this consummate courtier's overtures of friendship and when her own power had been safely consolidated she saw to it that he was rewarded with the important post of Commander of the Lightguard: a position she was able to obtain for him over Choiseul's candidate. His never-failing courtesy, his exquisite and always courtly attention to her well-being soon gained for him the almost passionate attachment and admiration of the Comtesse du Barry. He took pains never to abuse his power. "He manages her not so much by an open ascendancy," reported Mercy, "as by suppleness, consideration and tact."

In 1770 the day dawned when d'Aiguillon had good reason to be very glad for his pains in gaining the attachment of the loyal and kindly Comtesse. Once more the troublesome Parlement of Brittany rose to dog his steps. Not content with merely the restoration of their authority, the magistrates, encouraged by certain masked but powerful interests at Versailles, determined to carry their battle right into the enemy's camp. On general charges of malfeasance of duty, they demanded the trial of the Duc d'Aiguillon and d'Aiguillon, convinced of his innocence, persuaded the reluctant King to accept the Parlement's challenge and permit a former representative of the Crown to go on trial. So began one of the sensational political events of Louis's reign. Scarcely had the trial got under way than the Duc began bitterly to regret the impetuous step he had taken in persuading the King to allow it to start in the first place. "Prejudice, perjury and intrigue" soon made themselves disagreeably apparent. Very possibly, too, a certain element of truth may have added to the Duc's embarrassment, although this is not suggested.

Intense as was the magistrates' thirst for the blood of the Duc d'Aiguillon, it became clear that they were pressing charges not only against him personally, but against him with equal rancor as the representative of the King. They could not hope to send the King to prison or strip him of his rank, but they could do so vicariously. So having got their quarry into the dock, they attacked him with vengeful fury. There is no doubt that matters would have gone ill indeed for the Duc d'Aiguillon had not his friend Madame du Barry been present to inspirit the King. The King needed no one to direct his sympathies in the trial. He detested the Parlements. But he had never been a man given to action. It had always been his inclination to let moving things take their course, never to stop them. It was on this well-known weakness that the magistrates and the Duc de Choiseul (whose hand was everywhere in this affair) had banked. But they had not reckoned with Madame du Barry who, upset at the danger in which her friend suddenly found himself, began to shed copious tears, imploring and beseeching the King to put a stop to this disgraceful trial. To the Favorite's heart-melting pleas was soon added the firm counsel of the wily Chancellor Maupeou, who now stepped from behind the curtain of silence which usually cloaked him. The Duc d'Aiguillon might have burned at the stake for all Maupeou cared, but in this altercation he saw at last his chance to crush the quarrelsome Parlements. With the weeping Comtesse on one hand and the firm-willed, terrifying Chancellor on the other, the King now took an extraordinary step. With no warning at all he suddenly held a *lit de justice*, that *ultima ratio* of the royal prerogative, and exonerating both Duc and Parlement, declared that the trial was to proceed no further.

The consternation of the magistrates knew no bounds. They could scarcely credit their senses and in a transport of rage they now proceeded to defy the King's veto—the very cornerstone of the Monarchy—and declared the Duc d'Aiguillon guilty. As one the provincial Parlements leaped to the support of their fellow magistrates in Paris. D'Aiguillon was declared stripped of his privileges as Duke and Peer of France. At Rennes he was burnt in effigy. The King, now really angry, retaliated with arrests and prison sentences. Maupeou, in a paroxysm, flung fuel on the fast-growing flames. On the evening of September 2, 1770, the King suddenly announced his intention of entering Paris and holding yet another *lit de justice* in the Palais de Justice, the very stronghold of the rebellious magistrates. This was a very serious step indeed and, short of outright revolution, it meant that an end had now come to this affair.

He entered his capital on the following day and there, in the sumptuous and antique ritual of the *lit de justice*, the King pronounced his will: the records, documents and minutes of the trial were to be confiscated and placed under seal and the proceedings were never again to be spoken of. Madame du Barry was present at this somber ceremony. Choiseul, who had excused himself from it on the pretext of an appointment with the Court banker, was not. It represented a serious check to his intrigues, and indeed it marked the end of his favor with the King. There was not the slightest doubt that he had been secretly conspiring with the Parlements in order to destroy the Duc d'Aiguillon. Traveling through the provinces that summer, the Duchesse de Gramont had actually incited the local Parlements to uphold the decision against the King's veto. Louis could no longer trust or care for this man who attempted to retain power by such dangerous methods. The Duc's days were numbered, and the Duc knew it.

Accordingly the desperate Minister decided to take one last gamble, fling out onto the table a final hidden card and attempt to recoup the enormous stakes which he had already squandered. He decided to embroil France in a war. He knew that the King would never dare dismiss a man of his experience during wartime and that his services therefore would become indispensable. The cost of a war, moreover, is staggering and the rambunctious Parlements would never decree the necessary increased taxation for Maupeou or for d'Aiguillon whom they hated. Only Choiseul, who had ingratiated himself with the magistrates, would be able to raise the necessary funds; only Choiseul, who had many friends abroad and a long experience in the Foreign Office, could cope with the allies at Madrid and Vienna.

Fate conspired with the Duc, for in the summer of 1770, in the very middle of the row with the Parlements, a wretched cluster of gorse and rock off the coast of Argentina known as the Falklands was invaded by the Spanish and after a brief scuffle was wrested from the British settlers who, under the impression that it belonged to them, had been living there for some years, raising sheep. A stern ultimatum was immediately presented to Spain by the English Government. Spain, at that time in the full downward rush of her magnificent decline, was in no condition to go to war. Without support of an ally she would have been obliged to submit to the English demand. But between the descendants of Louis XIV there existed a *Pacte de Famille* (one of Choiseul's creations) wherein the Bourbon rulers of Europe contracted to support one another in time of war. The King of Spain, counting on France to fight for him the war with England which he himself could not afford, sent a sharp reply to England. The belligerent parties and all of Europe, now held their breaths to see which way France would turn, for on France's move depended war or peace.

Playing a dark and dangerous game of his own, Choiseul was furiously writing secret assurances to the Spanish Minister, Grimaldi, with one hand, and open threats to the English with the other. Louis, whose memory of the Seven Years War and its horrors was still vivid, informed his Minister that he wanted no war. Because of his relations with the Parlements the thought of war at this moment was particularly frightening to the King. It would probably mean the dismissal of Maupeou, the agent he now counted on to smash the magistrates, and of Terray and d'Aiguillon: exactly, in fact, what the Duc de Choiseul intended that it should mean. The Minister, coolly ignoring his Sovereign's express wishes, continued under the cloak of official secrecy to pursue his goal.

Maupeou and d'Aiguillon, perfectly aware of the Minister's reckless game and of the danger in which they themselves were consequently put, urgently began to impress on the King the advantages of the Minister's immediate dismissal. Their logic was fortified by the sobs and pleas of the lovely Mistress who, moreover, fancied that Choiseul was stirring up the recently arrived Marie Antoinette against her.

The King, who disliked decision even more than dispute, was caught between the now-continual nagging of the Maupeou party and his awareness of the popularity which his difficult Minister commanded throughout the kingdom. To dismiss him would be to invite another of those howls which his ears dreaded to hear. In the eyes of the French masses Choiseul represented moral rectitude, a guardian of the decencies at a dissolute court. In the eyes of certain of the nobility he was the torchbearer of Liberalism, in all ages a rôle certain to be applaudad by the rich and the leisured who, in supporting what they believed to be New Ideas, are able to show themselves as more intelligent and open-minded than their parents or their friends. Abroad, his stock was so high that he was called *"le Cocher de l'Europe."* Such was the agility of Choiseul's legerdemain, moreover, that Louis, despite the clear evidence of his senses, still held his Minister's capacities in a certain awe; such was the King's long experience with intrigue that he could not bring himself to succumb to the imprecations of Maupeou and d'Aiguillon whom he suspected, with good reason, to be acting only in self-interest.

In the meantime the drums of war were beating louder and with an ominous persistence. Matters were fast rushing toward a crisis and Maupeou, realizing that there was not a moment to spare, now sought allies who, because they appeared disinterested, might lend the color of respectability to his purposes. He approached the Princesse de Monaco. Madame de Monaco was mistress of the Prince de Condé, the King's cousin, and, having her own axe to grind, was only too glad to intercede with her lover in favor of the Maupeou cabal. The Prince's price was that upon Choiseul's dismissal he should control the appointment to the Ministry of War and that he himself should be appointed Grand Master of the

Artillery. When the bargain had been settled to the satisfaction of both parties, Condé, a man of immense prestige who lived in retirement at his great Château de Chantilly, ordered his carriage and arrived at Versailles, soliciting an audience of his cousin, the King. They remained closeted for three hours while Condé, in no uncertain terms, recommended the immediate dismissal of the troublesome Minister. That night, December 19, 1770, the King wrote a *lettre de cachet* addressed to the Duc de Choiseul. "I command my cousin to deliver the resignation of his offices of Minister of State and of the Postal Service into the hands of the Duc de la Vrillière and to retire to Chanteloup [Choiseul's nearby estate] until further orders from me."

Still he could not bring himself to take the fatal step and the *lettre de cachet* lay concealed in his pocket. In despair, for war could now break out at any minute, the Maupeou-d'Aiguillon clique had recourse to a final ruse. Choiseul's communications to the Spanish Minister, Grimaldi, were personal and consequently their content was unknown to all but the two Ministers. The King was as uninformed as everyone else. On the suggestion of an envious clerk in the Foreign Office a trap was set. It was proposed that the King confront Choiseul and order him to draft a letter to the King of Spain saying that Louis XV could not come to the aid of his ally and that nothing could induce France to become embroiled in a war with England. Should Choiseul balk or make excuses it would be clear that he could not draft such a letter because it would be in flagrant contradiction to his own private negotiations with Grimaldi.

With the *lettre de cachet* that he had written four days earlier still in his pocket the King, on the twenty-third of December, met with Choiseul. When the Minister, as was expected, balked at the King's request, Louis angrily demanded an explanation. With incredible rashness the Minister blandly made the statement that war was now inevitable, troops in England, Spain and even France were mobilized, and nothing could now be done to stop "the march of events." Trembling with rage, the King turned on him.

"But I told you," he cried, "that under *no* circumstances did I wish war!"

Horrified, he ordered Choiseul to inform the French Embassy at Madrid that there would be no French support of a war against England and that every effort should be made to persuade Spain to submit to the English demands. The King himself now dispatched a personal letter to his cousin the King of Spain, explaining to him in terms that a fellow monarch could warmly appreciate, the reasons why he could not come to his assistance. According to Talleyrand, generally reliable when he is not speaking of himself, Madame du Barry made the first draft of this letter which Louis later revised to suit his own kingly style:

"Your Majesty, my brother and cousin, is no doubt aware of the degree to which the spirit of fanaticism and revolt has spread through my kingdom. Until now I have been patient and gentle, but my Parlements forgetting themselves to the point of actually questioning the Sovereign Power which I receive from God alone, are forcing me to command obedience by every possible means. War, in this condition, would be an appalling misfortune both for me and for my people. My ministers are but my mouthpiece. Although I may be obliged to change them, nothing can possibly alter my relationship with Your Majesty and we will be united in affection as long as I live. If Your Majesty could possibly make some sacrifice for peace without losing honor, he will render a great service to mankind in general and myself in particular in the circumstances in which I presently find myself."

The King of Spain responded in kind: "The disobedience of the French Parlements," he wrote sternly, "has always been grievous to me. I have nothing but praise for Your Majesty's determination to assert your Sovereign Power and compel obedience. If help should be needed my power stands at your disposal for I am ever happy to fulfill the duties owing to my family. I shall do all that is possible to prevent war."

On the following day the Duc de la Vrillière was ordered to present to the Minister the *lettre de cachet* which contained his dismissal and the order for his exile. "Were it not for Madame de Choiseul," the King explained in his instructions to Vrillière, "I would have exiled him elsewhere as Chanteloup is in Touraine; but he is to conduct himself as though he were not residing there and will see no one except his family and those to whom I may give permission to visit him."

Paris exploded with the news. The Minister's disgrace was, in fact, his greatest triumph. Thousands gathered to do him honor. Despite the King's explicit orders a steady stream of the high and mighty defiantly poured through the Hôtel de Choiseul to offer sympathy and bid the Minister farewell. When on the morrow he departed for the Château de Chanteloup to begin his term of exile, a great parade of sympathizers followed his carriage to the very gates of the city.

The roofs of the houses were lined with waving spectators and busts of the statesman-hero Sully were placed beside those of Choiseul in every shop window.

France has always had an excess of that class of person who is ever on the lookout for some outrage by authority so that it can then organize protest rallies, carry placards about the streets and generally indulge in the delights of mass hysteria concealed as righteous indignation. The occasion of the Duc de Choiseul's dismissal brought such people out in droves, while others, like the Duc d'Orléans who wished to insult the Sovereign with impunity, now could do so by flaunting an excess of regard for the fallen Minister. Such flagrant adulation of a disgraced public figure had never before been witnessed in France. Under Louis XIV a fallen favorite crept away under the contemptuous gaze of his former friends and peers, only too grateful for the obscurity of exile in which he could hide his shame. The times had changed. The winds were rising, and in the public support which the nobility of France gave to a disgraced Minister, many sniffed the coming storm which in twenty years would sweep away all: King, nobility, and—a point that is often overlooked—the reformers themselves.

"Exile," which suggests some barren rock off the coast of Africa or farmhouse in the obscurity of the provinces, lends a pathos to the Duc's situation of which it was hardly deserving. The Château de Chanteloup was, in fact, one of the most princely private residences in Europe. No less than sixty liveried footmen attended to the Duc's wishes; four and five hundred people (including two troupes of comedians) dwelt beneath its roof. The vastness of the grounds, the luxury and extent of the great palace which at night blazed with the light of thousands of candles, the complexity of office and appointment required to keep this huge establishment functioning, suggested more the Court of some independent duchy or principality than the residence of a private subject.

For all the huge benefices and emoluments attaching to the many rich offices which the Duc had held during his years of favor, for all the size of his wife's private fortune, Choiseul, like France, was continually in debt. At the time of his disgrace his friends were able to raise four or five million to tide him over the immediate crisis. The uncompromising scale of life at Chanteloup ("the reckless magnificence," as Talleyrand describes it), combined with the drastic cut in income which followed his loss of office soon carried the extravagant Duc beyond the embarrassment of mere debt to the verge of actual bankruptcy.

A year after his downfall a severe blow was dealt him. The King summarily demanded his resignation as Colonel-General of the Swiss Guard, a post that carried with it a handsome revenue. Traditionally this was a lifetime appointment and Choiseul had supposed that this income, at least, was safe from the ravages of ruin. Shocked by this loss, the Duc immediately dispatched a request to the King for the outright payment of a sum close to a million dollars, and the establishment of a pension in his favor for another one hundred thousand dollars a year in compensation. The King, who had demanded only the Duc's resignation from the Swiss Guard, was outraged by this arrogant answer to his order and, scarcely troubling to dismiss it, once again demanded the Duc's resignation. But Choiseul was not without friends and the friend who had undertaken this delicate mission for him, Comte du Châtelet, had the foresight to turn to the one person he felt could now help him: Madame du Barry.

She heard du Châtelet's story of Choiseul's difficulties with sympathy and his request for her help without astonishment, merely reflecting that she welcomed such an opportunity of showing the Duc her continuing regard for him. "The fault," she declared, "was his, not mine. I would have welcomed his friendship. In the end it was the King, not myself, whom he most offended." Thus began an incredible affair which suddenly found the Comtesse du Barry pleading in Choiseul's favor.

It was no easy task: not only because the King, now completely broken with Choiseul and quite aware of the rancor and even hatred which the Duc entertained toward him, was reluctant to concede him a single favor, but because at this moment the Treasury was almost literally empty. Braving the King's real anger (and that of d'Aiguillon, too, who wanted no quarter shown this vanquished enemy), the Comtesse finally managed to wring a pension of sixty thousand livres and the outright payment of another three hundred thousand for the man who—had their situations been reversed—would almost surely have had her driven naked from the kingdom. It was an act of extraordinary magnanimity even for one naturally generous. Not a line, not even a word ever reached her from Chanteloup. "Neither I nor Madame de Choiseul said a word of thanks to her," explains the Minister in his bitter memoirs. "The injustice and above all the harshness with which we were treated exempted us from any gratitude."

A few years later when Madame du Barry, too, had been exiled, Choiseul met a mutual acquaintance.

"And how go things with Madame du Barry?" he inquired hopefully.

"Very well," was the answer.

"Has she kept all her servants?" demanded the Duc.

"She has."

"Why then she must have a great deal of money!" cried the disgruntled man. He could not bear it that she who had gone to such trouble to help him in time of need, should herself have retained something out of disgrace.

Bankrupt and forgotten, he died in 1786, escaping by a few years the fate which was reserved for his sister, the Duchesse de Gramont. Hailed before the Revolutionary Tribunal and asked if she was in correspondence with the *émigrés,* the indomitable woman paused for a moment and then, no doubt seeing her fate already written in the eyes of her examiners, turned toward them and, in utter contempt, said:

"I was going to lie. It isn't worth the trouble." She was guillotined in July of 1794.

Chapter 6

DURING THE SUMMER of 1770, in the midst of Choiseul's desperate struggle to maintain office, fresh trouble had started to smolder in another quarter of the palace.

On May 7, 1770, after months of frenzied preparation, the Archduchess Marie Antoinette had arrived in France. In the vivacious little porcelain doll who finally alighted from her carriage in the Forest of Compiègne, flinging herself supplely at the feet of Louis XV, none could have remotely imagined the careworn face of the "Widow Capet" twenty-three years later, white-haired at thirty-eight and half-blind, bereft of crown, husband, children and friends, dragged to the scaffold in the back of a manure cart. Impetuous, proud, utterly lacking in any comprehension of malice ("But what have I done that they should hate me so?" she would one day ask), the Dauphine was scarcely on French soil before she was enmeshed in a web of intrigue: first of the many that finally would bind her until she was helpless. The antagonist, herself as much a victim of intrigue as the Dauphine, was Madame du Barry.

Like everyone else at Court, the Comtesse was intensely excited over the coming nuptials and the many elaborate festivities which were to attend them. In anticipation of a "show" that was likely to surpass anything seen in many a year at Versailles, she had had made for her the most sumptuous clothes, had selected with tender, trembling hand each ruby, emerald and diamond which in blazing loops and clusters she would hang on her wrists, her fingers, her throat, her ears, her stomach. But, according to the Duc de Croy who was watching all these preparations, "it was very much of a question whether she would be allowed to go to the wedding at all. She loved dressing up and would have been heartbroken to miss it." The wedding festivities in honor of the fifteen-year-old daughter of Maria Theresa were hardly fit setting for Madame du Barry to make her first official appearance, *en grande tenue*. The Comtesse herself was aware of this and proposed, none too eagerly, to absent herself from Court for a week or two.

D'Aiguillon, instantly alert to the dangers which would

be hatched by her absence and the implications which would be invited by her presence, urgently persuaded her to wheedle an invitation from the King. Because it would be an almost unthinkable audacity on the part of the King to flaunt her, so to speak, before the eyes of the Empress of Austria, precisely was it to the advantage of Richelieu, d'Aiguillon and Maupeou that she be present. It would show the Choiseul faction once and for all the unparalleled zenith of power to which this woman had risen.

The splendid party which had met the Dauphine in the Forest of Compiègne in all the panoply of royalty, attended by clarions and drums, now made a slow, stately return to Versailles. On the evening before its entry, at the small Château de la Muette in the outskirts of the forest, the King gave a supper to the Royal Family, the Dauphin and Dauphine, the Princes and Princesses of the Blood, and a very few people of the highest rank. At the table, ranking high on the list of those who had been invited, sat Madame du Barry.

A thrill of horror went through the Austrian Ambassador. "It seems inconceivable that the King should have chosen such a moment to accord the woman an honor heretofore refused her," he reported to Vienna. "Her presence there," reflected the Duc de Croy, "announced to all that she would succeed in crushing her opponents." The scene, which is a familiar one in the biographies of Marie Antoinette, usually portrays the Favorite in scarlet, flamboyant colors, a macaw boldly flaunting itself among hummingbirds. On the contrary, according to the account of several of those present, her appearance, apart from the fact that as usual she was the most beautiful woman in the room, was remarkably reserved and unassertive. She sat between the Maréchale de Mirepoix and the Duchesse de Chevreuse, not far from the King who "ogled her continually with long, infatuated glances." This, not the lady's appearance, was what attracted the notice of the little Dauphine.

"Who is that woman?" she is reputed to have asked a courtier.

"That is the Comtesse du Barry, Ma'am."

"And what is her function at Court?"

"To amuse the King," came the evasive reply.

"Then I shall be her rival," laughed the Dauphine, coquettishly.

Such a post as that which Madame du Barry occupied in France was unknown at the Court of Vienna. The purest cheek never blushed in the well-regulated Hofburg. The licentious priests, incontinent Ministers and extravagant nobles who flourished at Versailles as though in a hothouse met short shrift from the firm German hand of Maria Theresa. The truth is that the blunt-minded Empress of Austria ("The Queen of Hungary," as Frederick the Great always called her) had a deep-rooted dislike of frenchified tastes and foppish manners. This instinctive antipathy was unfortunately bequeathed to her daughter. Although Marie Antoinette soon lost command of the German tongue, although her friends and associations, her tastes and manner became entirely, indeed perfectly, French, she was never able to lose a certain forthrightness of outlook, a naïveté and frankness of thought that was basic to her Austrian nature and bluntly alien to the nimble, capricious and infinitely sophisticated French character. Her frivolity, which was to provoke so much comment, sprang from the giddiness of youth, not the abandon of corruption. To the end of her life she remained stoutly open of character, puzzled now and then by hints of matters that she did not understand, and recklessly, dangerously heedless of their significance.

On May 17, 1770, in a scene of unparalleled pomp the marriage service was celebrated in the Chapel of Versailles. A week of festivity followed. At one of these celebrations there occurred a slight incident that might have sounded a sharp warning to the Dauphine had she cared to listen. It would have shown her the pettily nasty limits to which rancor and envy could extend themselves at Versailles.

This episode, which in the index of history enjoys a modest place under the heading of The Affair of the Minuet, took place at a ball given in the new Salle de l'Opéra. In a courtly gesture to Maria Theresa, Louis, some days before the ball, had announced that the Princess of Lorraine was to dance the minuet immediately after the Princesses of the Blood Royal. The Dauphine's father, Maria Theresa's late beloved consort, had been Francis of Lorraine and the significance of such a nicety would certainly not be lost on Maria Theresa. It represented a certain amount of thought on the part of Louis and was, in fact, a very pretty flourish and bow in the direction of Vienna. It cost the French Treasury nothing, but the Empress would appreciate it more than all the jewels in France. It discreetly indicated that all went well with her cherished Franco-Austrian Alliance. The gist of the compliment lay in the fact that for one magic evening in her life this foreign Princess, like Cinderella, would take precedence over all the non-royal Princesses and Duchesses of France. Here began the trouble. A compliment in one direction at

Versailles could only be purchased at the expense of an insult in another.

Immeasurably more important than affairs of State in the wasps' nest were the intricacies of etiquette. Every small privilege: the right to sit where others stood, the right to enter where others couldn't, the right to keep on a hat where others must remove it, was a deliciously public affirmation of one's superiority over someone else. Such petty distinctions were guarded by their proud possessors with a ferocious jealousy. The life, the whole life, of the Duc de Saint-Simon was devoted to the re-establishment of ducal precedence over the legitimized Princes, Louis XIV's sons by Madame de Montespan. The War of the Spanish Succession, the Revocation of the Edict of Nantes, the tumultuous storm of events that broke over the reign of Louis XIV meant relatively nothing to Saint-Simon. The culmination of his entire life, the triumph of all his aspirations came on the occasion of the Regent's announcement that the senior Dukes and Peers of France would henceforth be permitted to wear their hats in Council.

The indignation, then the horror, that followed Louis's announcement that Mademoiselle de Lorraine was to do a minuet before the Duchesses of France can scarcely be conceived. In the eyes of many, such an invitation indicated a tendency to establish for the House of Lorraine an intermediate rank between the Princes of the Blood and the first nobles of France. A solemn midnight conclave was convoked. At the Paris residence of the Bishop of Noyon the Dukes and Peers of France met in grave session. After considerable discussion it was decided to send the King a petition: "Sire, the ranking lords of your realm lay at the foot of the Throne the just alarms that have been awakened in them by the widespread rumor that you have ordered that at the ball of Monsieur le Dauphin's marriage Mademoiselle de Lorraine shall dance a minuet preceding the other ladies of the Court. Your lords believe, Sire, that it would be lacking in what was due to their birth if they did not manifest . . ."

The greatest names in France were accordingly affixed to this ridiculous document and it was duly presented to the King. In the *petits cabinets* more midnight oil was burned over this affair as the King discussed it with his Ministers. "There have been bickerings without end," reported Madame du Deffand. "The minuet it to be danced this evening by Mademoiselle de Lorraine and it is vexing a great many people." The King's first wish prevailed. On May 19, 1770, the Princess of Lorraine, by now probably well weary of her little triumph, minced onto the ballroom floor and there on the arm of Monsieur de Lambesc executed a minuet. The rancorous and jealous courtiers, compelled to attend the ball, showed by their every attitude the spite and rage with which such a triumph filled them. Some turned away, others smiled disdainfully. All the Grandees of Spain refused to dance and a good many people simply left the room, causing the King consternation and embarrassment.

Despicably petty, but dangerously significant is The Affair of the Minuet. The time was approaching when the disaffected and spiteful nobles would have it in their power to destroy more than a party.

Directly after the ball the Court removed to the Galerie des Glaces and the palace gardens to enjoy one of the most marvelous and astonishing sights in all the history of Europe: the last of the great Versailles receptions. Three hundred thousand guests filled the vast gardens which were illuminated by every ingenious device that imagination and taste could conspire to invent. Fireworks of an unbelievable intricacy, some of them requiring forty thousand fuses were set off on the Parterre of Latona. By the Grand Canal blazed the Temple of the Sun, an architectural creation of fire; up and down the canal itself drifted a flotilla of illuminated gondolas. In the woods there was dancing and dining beneath chestnut trees festooned with arcades of lanterns. In some parts of the forest crystal chandeliers were hung; in others one came on artificial rivulets and illuminated grottoes, garlanded with ivy and myrtle. Three theatres were established in various parts of the park. Troupes of costumed entertainers, jugglers and magicians wandered at random among the crowd. Riding his chariot through the ceaseless cascade that stirred the waters of his marble basin, Apollo, heralded by the conch-blowing sea gods rode, more through fire than water. Everywhere the magnificent fountains illuminated by unsteady firelight, as it was intended that they should be, splashed and gushed in the intricate pattern of their baroque design. It was a scene such as Watteau or Fragonard might have dreamed of, a fantasy of perfected artificiality.

Above, in the balcony of the central window of the Galerie des Glaces, stood the old King and the young Dauphine, looking down the long slope of the Tapis Vert, lined with its ghostly statuary and colossal marble vases, toward the Grand Canal. Below, strolling on the Parterre, the rising luminaries of the Court-to-come touched elbows with the powers of the old order. From the balcony where she stood the Dauphine might have distinguished many whose destinies were to be woven in such a fatal pattern about her own; the young Princesse de Lamballe and Yolande de Polignac; the Ducs de Lauzun and Chartres and Fitzjames. Between them walked Monsieur de Choiseul and his sister the Duchesse de Gramont; Madame du Barry was there on the arm of the ever-gallant d'Aiguillon. The Court itself seemed to be on parade and on such a night, in such a setting, it no doubt justified Taine's famous description of the most sophisticated race of people ever bred: "They were all accomplished people of the world, gifted with every grace that birth, education, wealth and tradition could bring. Of their kind they were perfect. There was not a gown, not a turn of the head, not a voice or turn of phrase which was not a masterpiece of worldly culture and the distilled quintessence of everything exquisite which the social art has ever elaborated."

Malice, spite, deceit and envy crept off into the shadows and only the artifice, this incomparably fine creation of pruned and disciplined symmetry remained for an instant in the light. The sharp French mind skated over the hard surface of the Eighteenth Century culture with a precision and a daring so dazzling that the eye remains riveted entirely on the performer and very readily overlooks the condition of the rink or the cost of the ice.

To the fifteen-year-old Marie Antoinette, raised on schnitzel and strudl at the stodgy and humdrum Court of Vienna (where the dreary budget took precedence over fantasy), it must have seemed as though it were fairyland or Paradise over which she was one day destined to preside. Her unsuspecting nature saw only the surface; she was unaware of the intrigue that with probing, delicate tentacles was already beginning to surround her.

Some weeks after the wedding the Dauphine had a curious and unexpected conversation with her husband. This awkward young man, already encumbered by the fat that was to distinguish him as Louis XVI, was surely one of the most pathetic victims of the system for which his head would one day fall in sacrifice. Shy and friendless, he stood apart in the shadows of his grandfather's Court, occasionally the target of his envious younger brothers' cautious contempt, but generally ignored. Owing to a slight physical infirmity it was nearly eight years before he was able to be a husband to his high-spirited wife, a matter that (apart from its shattering psychological effect on husband and wife) was instinct with considerable political implication, both domestic and foreign. Frederick the Great and Maria Theresa were but two of the many agencies who employed spies to report on the condition of the royal bed linen. Stammering in embarrassment the Dauphin now entered into various unexpected confidences with his wife, promising among other things *"de lui temoigner la vivacité de son affection"* at Compiègne where the Court was to repair in a few weeks' time. Marie Antoinette, no less isolated than her lonely husband and quite as inexperienced, seized with impetuous gratitude on this opportunity for an exchange of confidence.

"Since we must be together so closely we should feel free to talk to one another in confidence," she replied.

The young couple, scarcely more than children, then entered into a conversation which soon veered toward the topic of Madame du Barry. Not long before, the Dauphin had been well instructed on this matter by Mesdames, his aunts, who in the telling of it had spared nothing. The Dauphin now repeated all this to his wife, stressing particularly the shady origins of the woman. Marie Antoinette, who until now had only mildly disliked the lady whom she saw as her rival in the King's eyes, was shocked and disgusted. In the next letter to her mother she wrote: "The King shows me a thousand kindnesses and I love him tenderly, but the weakness he has for Madame du Barry is pitiful. She is the most foolish and impertinent creature imaginable. She gambled with us every evening at Marly and twice she stood beside me, but she didn't speak and I certainly didn't enter into a conversation with her, although when obliged to, I have spoken to her."

Along with the revulsion which the Dauphin's story had inspired in her, Marie Antoinette was given more immediate cause to dislike the Favorite. The Choiseul party, the party which had promulgated and supported the Austrian Alliance (the agency therefore of the Dauphine's presence at Versailles) hastened to put their new ally *au courant* of the state of things at Court. Choiseul, at the breaking point in his struggle with d'Aiguillon, stood in desperate need of recruits. The Dauphine had arrived just in time and might conceivably save him by destroying either Madame du Barry or d'Aiguillon. When (through the Choiseuls) she was made familiar with the intrigues which were afoot against the Duc and consequently against the alliance, against her mother's interests in France and against herself, the Dauphine's contempt for "the creature" quickly deepened into an intense dislike. Unable to mask hatred with a smile, unable to dissimulate, as it is vitally necessary for those who play a political rôle to do, Marie Antoinette's every contemptuous gesture showed to the Court the repugnance she had suddenly conceived for

Madame du Barry and the party of the Duc d'Aiguillon. The wasps began to stir uneasily and the nest to hum. It was clear to all that a battle was shaping up.

Deep in the center of the palace, in the seclusion of their three adjoining apartments, Mesdames were busy adding trouble to the fast-thickening brew. With a child's instinctive and generally misplaced trust in the sagacity of its elders, the young Dauphine had taken to paying afternoon calls on the maiden aunts. Maria Theresa (who in attempting to mix the oil of virtue with the water of expediency often made trouble for herself) had recommended the society of the aunts to her daughter. "These princesses are full of virtue," she smugly wrote. "And this is a piece of good fortune for you. I hope that you will prove yourself worthy of their friendship." The Empress would soon enough swallow these words.

For their part Mesdames were overjoyed to find their little niece voluntarily making her way to their doorstep. Although in their hearts they detested her, because she was Austrian and because she had displaced them as the ranking women of Court, they were willing to make certain compromises with these natural feelings if able thereby to gain that position of authority and power for which their withering souls had all these years so vainly thirsted. In the Dauphine they saw a rising power and one which, properly handled, might prove malleable.

They gushed and cackled extravagantly when the Dauphine appeared to pay them a call. They racked their brains to think up little diversions and follies to amuse the frivolous girl. She was given her own key to their apartments and an invitation to visit whenever she wished. In the course of these visits it was only natural that the Dauphine, ignorant of much that was happening at Versailles, should turn to the three sisters who had passed their lives there and ask them for helpful information. Exchanging significant glances with one another, the aunts would then proceed to discuss the character and background of the important figures at Court, skillfully molding the Dauphine's amorphous views into a shape to fit their own. Bigotry, spite and envy were the judges that passed sentence on every personality discussed.

Despite her own good sense the Dauphine's opinions began to warp in the direction toward which the aunts' teatime chatter disposed them. Their most consuming enmity was reserved for Madame du Barry. Not once had they spoken a word to the "creature" or even deigned to recognize her presence at Court. Not once, by so much as a word, had they indicated to the King, and certainly not to the lady, that they were aware of her existence. Unfortunately, Madame du Barry for her part, appeared to be scarcely aware of their existence. It infuriated Madame Adélaïde to madness to find that her cold and haughty attitude passed unnoticed by the giddy hussy. Quickly sensing the Dauphine's growing dislike of the Favorite, the aunts wasted no time in twisting it in such a way as might serve their own purpose. A cut from the Dauphine, first lady of the Court and the center of every eye, would wound the du Barry where the aunts had failed to touch her. Up until now the Dauphine, on the prudent advice of Mercy, her mother's Ambassador to Versailles, had remained coolly neutral in her attitude toward the Favorite, nodding distantly and even now and again volunteering a word or two. Egged on by the aunts, however, and encouraged in her antipathy, Marie Antoinette lost sight of her mother's interests at Versailles, forgot that, unlike the aunts, she was a pawn in the grim game of politics, and suddenly began to show a pronounced hostility toward Madame du Barry.

Matters were not helped by a small incident that occurred a few months after the Dauphine's arrival in France. One evening while the Court was at Choisy some theatricals were performed in the little theatre there. The Comtesse du Barry and her inseparable friends the Maréchale de Mirepoix and Madame de Valentinois arrived late to find that the seats reserved for them in the front row were already occupied by several women of the Dauphine's entourage. When asked to move, one of them, the Comtesse de Gramont (sister-in-law of the Duchesse of that name) responded with a barrage of harsh invective and some very disagreeable insults, much to the delight of the assembled audience who found themselves witnessing a scene far more interesting than that on the stage.

Distracted by the fact that the lady was one of the Choiseuls, Madame du Barry probably overlooked the other fact that she was one of the Dauphine's household and rather indiscreetly complained to the King about the episode. The Comtesse de Gramont was instantly exiled fifteen leagues from the Court and there was, in consequence, a great to-do about the matter. The Dauphine was indignant, the Choiseul party outraged. The King remained deaf to the Dauphine's entreaties on behalf of her lady, hinting that perhaps an apology to Madame du Barry was in order. Eventually, through the intercession of Madame du Barry, the Comtesse de Gramont won a reprieve, but not before irreparable damage had been done to the rapidly disintegrating relationship between the Favorite and the Dauphine.

In Vienna Maria Theresa was kept closely informed on each step taken by her daughter during the day. Mercy, assiduous and meticulous, missed nothing. The Dauphine's first successes at Versailles might have pleased her mother, had not certain envenomed whispers reached her ears soon after: "One hears things here that are not favorable to my daughter; they say the King has become reserved and embarrassed with her, that she cuts the Favorite, that the Dauphin is worse than ever, and less than indifferent to my daugther." In her almost daily letters of advice she avoided the delicate subject of the Comtesse du Barry, merely commanding her daughter to defer to the King's wishes and to respect his "friends."

Marie Antoinette, in the meanwhile, was respecting the King's "friend" by the simple but devastating device of not speaking to her. Etiquette at Versailles forbade those of lower rank to open conversation with their betters. A Duke waited for a Royal Prince to address him first; a Marquis waited for a Duke to start the conversation; a Baron waited for a Marquis, and so on up and down the complicated line. Although she held the actuality of power in her hands, Madame du Barry could not initiate a conversation with the Dauphine. She had to wait until spoken to.

And wait she did. Weeks and weeks went by. It became embarrassing. The whole Court was now aware of the Dauphine's little vengeance and was watching its development with delight. The Comtesse would approach with a hopeful, deferent air, while the little Archduchess with the blue, chilling Hapsburg eyes gazed through her as though she were a windowpane. The delighted titter of the fascinated bystanders was more than the humiliated Comtesse could support. Months went by, and still no word, nor even a sign of recognition. In this little maneuver both d'Aiguillon and the Comtesse professed to the King that they detected the hand of Choiseul who was poisoning the Dauphine's mind against the Mistress. The tears flowed. Cruel sobs stabbed at the doting heart of the infatuated King.

It was another argument for the dismissal of the Minister and it is possible that when, in December of that year, Louis finally rid himself of Choiseul, he supposed that incidentally he was bringing harmony back into his household. The effect of his move was exactly the contrary. In Choiseul's disgrace the Dauphine quite correctly saw the triumph of her enemy, Madame du Barry, and became more firmly determined than ever publicly to humiliate the common jade.

At the moment of Choiseul's dismissal, however, this petty battle between two women ceased to be a mere palace squabble and became a matter of serious international significance.

In Vienna the news struck like a torpedo. Choiseul had been the cornerstone in France of the precious alliance. His overthrow presented an ominous check to the Empress's confident hopes. All that now remained in France to bolster the alliance and keep a harmonious relationship between the two countries was young Marie Antoinette. Mercy, quite aware of this, did not wait for orders from Vienna upon the news of Choiseul's dismissal. Without losing an instant he sent a message to the Dauphine warning her to betray by no word or gesture the slightest evidence of anger or disappointment, and to refrain from any allusion to the faction which had destroyed the Minister. Marie Antoinette was entirely sensitive to the implications of the situation and behaved with admirable coolness. There were many courtiers hoping for some indiscreet word that could be reported to the King, many more who eagerly scanned the young Princess's countenance for some sign of inner rage or perhaps even fear. Her face betrayed nothing and such despicable intriguers watched and listened in vain.

Goaded on by Mesdames, however, the Dauphine's attitude toward the Comtesse remained implacable. In the spring and summer that followed Choiseul's dismissal, the situation rapidly grew acute. D'Aiguillon, "creature of the creature," was appointed Foreign Minister to succeed Choiseul. To d'Aiguillon's hands was therefore committed the fate of the crucial alliance. Maria Theresa grew alarmed. And with reason.

Embarrassed as he always was to confront his family with private matters, the King suddenly had had recourse to a delicate expedient to warn the Dauphine to mend her ways. The elderly Comtesse de Noailles, lady-in-waiting and mentor on matters of etiquette to the Dauphine, was summoned in private audience. The King beat around the bush for a few minutes and then came out with the matter which was on his mind. For some time, he said, he had been meaning to speak to her on the subject of the Dauphine. Her many charms and talents made her worthy of every eulogy. Only on three points might one perhaps wish a slight change: while holding Court there was a trifle too vivacious a manner; at the hunt when she distributed largesse there was a certain familiarity which one might regret; and (the Comtesse de Noailles perfectly understood that this was what the King had been leading up to), and—"Madame la Dauphine permits herself to speak too freely of what she sees or believes that she sees. Her remarks might produce certain bad effects within the family circle." The Comtesse, courtier to the tips of her elegant fingers, defended her mistress with her own involuted subjunctives and elaborate circumlocutions, suggesting that these were perhaps the faults of her age and her inexperience and that with His Majesty's advice they might be easily corrected.

"She is unfortunate in her advice," responded the King gravely. "I am quite aware of this. I am also aware of the source of such advice and it most strongly displeases me."

When this remark was reported to Mesdames they were inflamed not by terror but rather by a sense of their success. At last their arrows were striking home. Their answer to Madame de Noailles' frightening report was to incite the Dauphine to further indiscretions.

Observing with growing irritation that the intercession of the lady-in-waiting had had no effect on the impudent girl, the King next had recourse to diplomatic channels. The new Minister d'Aiguillon, whom the Dauphine had snubbed on the occasion of his presentation to her, summoned Mercy to an interview in which he informed him that the King was far from pleased with the Dauphine's deportment toward "certain persons who composed his intimate circle." The King's affection for the young Princess was being destroyed in consequence of her behavior. It was essential that she take measure of the situation. It was essential, in other words, that she address Madame du Barry. When a King of France uttered such blunt words as these, even through the mouth of his Minister, the unquestioned result was the promptest obedience. From the mouth of Louis XIV they would have quaked the earth and rent the veils of temples.

Mercy, the most supple of courtiers, was aghast. He dispatched an immediate report to Vienna in which he flatly stated that the alliance was endangered by the Dauphine's rash conduct. The effect in Vienna was instantaneous. "To refrain from showing respect toward persons in the King's circle is derogratory to that circle," read the letter to the Dauphine. "It is sufficient that the King distinguishes certain people with his favor. It is not for you to examine their merits." Maria Theresa spoke on the subject of Mesdames: "They have never made themselves loved or respected either by their father or by the public. In the end you will be left alone to bear the blame for their intrigues." Shrewd indeed was Mercy's observant eye!

As a result of this reprimand it was observed at their next meeting that the Dauphine's attitude toward d'Aiguillon was remarkably warmer. There was even a faint flicker of recognition for Madame du Barry, but still no word, no longed-for, precious word. The Court was now in a furor over the matter. Each day brought new pressures to bear in the struggle between the two embattled women.

For Madame du Barry it had ceased to be merely a fight for a word, it had become the fight for a principle: and it meant no less than the official recognition of her situation at Court. Her partisans and the anti-Austrian faction at Court spurred her on. Defeat now, before the whole Court, would be a mortal blow to her pride. For the Dauphine, too, the issue had become one of pride. The daughter of Maria Theresa, heiress to a thousand years of imperial blood, was being forced publicly to submit to the haughty demands of a common streetwalker. Each incited by the various factions at Court, both agitated by the idle courtiers avid for fresh spectacles, the two women suddenly found themselves beyond the reach of common sense.

Neither Madame de Noailles' efforts nor those of the Duc d'Aiguillon having borne fruit, the King now had recourse to a final pressure. As usual, the point, although it was sharp, was long in appearing and lay well hidden beneath an elaborate dressing of ruses. Mercy was invited to dine one evening at the residence of Madame de Valentinois, the most intimate of Madame du Barry's friends. He arrived there to find a little party gathered, including the Papal Nuncio (a fervent courtier of Madame du Barry whose sable shadow falls everywhere across this network of intrigue), the Sardinian Ambassador, the Duc and Duchesse d'Aiguillon and the Comtesse du Barry. "It was the first time I had met the woman face to face," reported Mercy to Vienna. "The Sardinian Ambassador greeted her as one whom he has known for a long time; the Nuncio showed considerable eagerness to join in their conversation. I felt it behooved me to observe more reserve and it was not until after the Favorite spoke to me that I fell into a pleasant conversation with her. She showed me considerable more distinction than she did the others."

Mercy, who had dropped Choiseul like a hot potato on the very instant of his downfall ("When the orange has been squeezed," said Frederick the Great, "one throws away the rind"), could not, on the other hand, be too unctuously assiduous in his attentions to the newly risen power. A few months before he had been the most implacable of her adversaries but events had proven the extent of her influence. Therefore Mercy, whose only real loyalty was to his beloved Empress and to his country, hastened to pay court to this lady who might be helpful to his purposes. "I am in high favor with Madame du Barry," he afterward reported to Vienna with satisfaction. "She is beginning to listen to me and has acted favorably on the subject of certain minor political proposals which I ventured to put forth to see how the land lay. I intend to make good use of this woman." The wise ones of this world do not try to change events, but contrive instead to make the best of them and put them to good use.

The urbane Ambassador was perfectly aware of the purpose behind this little supper party and therefore was not surprised when the Duc d'Aiguillon took him aside for a moment and said that the King would very much like to see him privately on the morrow, immediately after the hunt. It was suggested that Mercy appear at the apartments of Madame du Barry at that hour. On the following day the Dauphine, while holding audience with the ambassadors, slipped over to Mercy and whispered: "My compliments on the company you were seen with last night!"

"Madame," answered Mercy, "today there will occur a far more remarkable event on which I shall give you a report later."

The Ambassador reported to the palace at seven in the evening and was conducted by the Duc d'Aiguillon to the apartments of the Comtesse du Barry. The Duc informed him that the King had just returned from the hunt and was dressing. Madame du Barry greeted her guest with great friendliness, asking him to come and sit beside her while they talked. On the pretext of showing them a painting, the Duc led the other guests out of the room, leaving Mercy alone with the Favorite. "She seized this moment to say she was most happy that this idea of the King speaking to me in her apartments was giving her the opportunity to make my acquaintance. She was going to bring up a matter that was the source of much grief to her. She was not unaware of the fact that for some time now there had been people working to ruin her in the eyes of the Dauphine and that to do so these people had had recourse to the most atrocious slanders and were crediting her with disrespectful intentions toward Her Royal Highness. Such was far from the truth. In spite of much, she had nothing but praise to sing on the matter of the Archduchess. It was not against the Archduchess, but against those who had incited her to her attitude that the Comtesse complained."

Mercy here hurriedly interrupted to explain that he was unaware of such sentiments, so uncharacteristic of her, on the part of the Dauphine. The Ambassador, a perfect specimen of his class and era, now lowered his voice a bit, and moved a shade closer to the lady. How could it be possible, he queried, for anyone to harbor such sentiments against so lovely an object? Delicately he shifted the conversation into a tone of gallantry, readily appreciated by the experienced Comtesse, so much more at her ease in the key of coquetry than that of international politics. She because expansive, telling the Ambassador how she came to be installed at Versailles, speaking to him of the King's character, of the difficulties she had in keeping him amused, telling him what she thought of various people at Court. Never able to sustain a rôle that was not natural to her, she gladly abandoned the stiff, "talking-to-an-ambassador" attitude she had earlier assumed and with relief began to speak to him as a man, in the half-flirtatious, the bantering and limpidly sympathetic tone which was native and normal to her. Mercy, who saw considerable future advantage to be harvested from all this, was by no means displeased at the friendly turn the conversation had taken. Cool and entirely dispassionate in his judgments, he had this to report on the character of Madame du Barry as he saw her in this first interview: "She has a fine enough appearance, but her conversation smacks of her former condition. She is utterly without spite, malice or other such disagreeable qualities of character. Knowing how to do so, it is very easy to converse with her. All she wishes is that the Dauphine speak to her just once."

Their conversation had just returned to the matter of the Dauphine when suddenly a curtain parted and the King, entering by a secret door, came into the room. Mercy was considerably taken aback to hear the Mistress address the King of France simply as Monsieur.

"Must I leave, Monsieur?" she asked. The King indicated that he wished to be alone with the Ambassador and the Comtesse accordingly withdrew. The King turned to Mercy.

"Until now, sir," he said, "you have been the Ambassador of the Empress. I now ask you to be mine for a short time. I know that the Empress gives you her confidence; this therefore determines me to give you mine and to approach you on a matter that closely affects my happiness and that of the Royal Family." With some embarrassment the King now spoke of the Dauphine. "I love her with all my heart and I find her charming. But she is young and vivacious. Her husband is in no condition to control her. She has been unable to avoid the many traps which intrigue has laid for her and has become the victim of prejudice and unfortunate counsel, in consequence treating rudely certain people who are admitted to my private circle."

The conversation lasted for some time, but not once in the course of it were the names of either Madame du Barry or Mesdames mentioned. Each respected the other's discretion and each knew what the other meant. The King asked the Ambassador to speak to the Dauphine, even authorizing Mercy to speak on his behalf. "You see what confidence I have in you," he said. "I am telling you of what is on my mind in respect to the private life of my family." For exactly that reason such a commission was an embarrassing one to the Ambassador and he protested mellifluously that as a foreign ambassador he was scarcely in a position to interfere in the private life of the Royal Family. The King, however, remained adamant. He could not face the embarrassment of an interview with the Dauphine himself, consequently (as was always his way) he delegated the embarrassment.

Mercy, who in turn wished to dodge the assignment, immediately had an interview with the Dauphine during which he strongly urged that she should see the King in private and talk to him on the matter. Marie Antoinette shuddered at this suggestion, as did Mesdames who saw all their schemes brought to ruin by such a conversation. Rather than face the King, Marie Antoinette at last succumbed to the pressures on her which were becoming too powerful to resist any longer, and promised that she would speak to Madame du Barry.

Mercy immediately conveyed this good news to the Comtesse and, with the Ambassador acting as intermediary, negotiations between the two hostile parties were soon under way. It was arranged that after the card party at the Dauphine's Sunday evening reception, Mercy would engage the Comtesse du Barry in conversation. The Dauphine as she passed about the room bidding her guests "good night," would affect suddenly to notice Mercy, walk up to him and thus come face to face with Madame du Barry. Pretending to take advantage of this "opportunity" she would then say a few polite words to the Mistress.

The Court, teeming as it was with spies, sensation-seekers and mischief-makers soon had wind of this arrangement and the Dauphine's Sunday evening reception was crowded as it had never been before. All were eagerly waiting to see the outcome of the contest. Bets were placed; sides were taken.

Marie Antoinette's apartments took on the air of a theatre or stadium as step by step she slowly moved down the line of guests, greeting each and not betraying by a gesture the wild beating of her heart as she approached Mercy and her adversary. Four couples away, then three, then two . . . she had just reached them when suddenly Madame Adélaïde who, if she hadn't known before what was afoot had realized it now, came dashing up to the Dauphine and seizing her attention with a loud, commanding voice cried: "Come! It is late. We must leave at once for my sister Victoire's and await the King there." Stretched to the snapping-point, the Dauphine's nerves gave way and with a sudden blush she turned her back on Madame du Barry's eagerly waiting face and rushed away.

This episode created the greatest consternation, and matters were now far worse than they had been before. The word, that long-awaited word on which so much depended, had not yet been spoken. To all appearances indeed it had been bluntly refused. Many of the Comtesse's most ardent partisans: the Papal Nuncio, the Sardinian Ambassador, Madame de Valentinois and the Maréchale de Mirepoix, had been present to witness what was to have been her triumph. A little supper party had even been planned to celebrate the great event. They were witnesses instead to her shame and mortification. At the supper party the King made a brief, sullen appearance. He had already heard the news, and taking Mercy into a corner he said: "Monsieur de Mercy, I see that your advice bears little fruit. I see that I shall have to come to your help." Without giving the unhappy diplomat time to reply, the King turned on his heel and walked away.

In Vienna the matter, which had long ceased to be considered a mere palace intrigue, had now become instinct with the gravest implications. Not only was the Austro-French Alliance in danger of ruin, but the very peace of Europe itself was at stake.

At the Hofburg the ailing Empress had just come to one of the most difficult decisions of her reign. Worn down, inch by inch, by the unceasing persuasion of her son, the Emperor Joseph, and her trusted Minister Prince Kaunitz, she had finally committed Austria to the Partition of Poland. "By what right can we plunder an innocent people whom we have always plumed ourselves on protecting?" cried the sorely tried Empress. "In this thing where not only moral law cries to Heaven against us, but also justice and reason, I must confess I have never in my life been in such trouble. I am ashamed to show my face." Every part of the affair was odious to the honorable Maria Theresa, but probably most odious of all was the company she was forced to keep. Her fellow-plunderers were the Mephistophelean Frederick the Great and the ruthless Catherine of Russia. "The Empress Catherine and I are a pair of brigands," smirked Frederick. "But for this pious Maria Theresa the matter is different. I wonder how she is going to arrange it with her confessor?" It was the last of the Empress's many sacrifices to her country and it was a hard one indeed. But once the deed was decided on, it was necessary to see that it was done properly and that there were no complications. A most important consideration was the attitude that France would assume toward this cold-blooded division of a country that Louis XV for a good part of his life had considered to be a kind of appanage of the French throne. Should the King of France take it upon himself to protest, or even conceivably to intervene in the matter, a contrary alliance might well be put forward and Europe would be brought to the brink of another Seven Years War.

It was, then, vitally necessary that France remain neutral. At this highly delicate juncture in the progress of her diplomacy the news reached the distraught Empress of the Dauphine's latest snub to Madame du Barry, and of the King's extreme displeasure. It was more than she could bear. That she, who had sacrified pride, honor, and ease of mind to the welfare of her country (she who had indeed not hesitated to negotiate with the Pompadour when the occasion had demanded), should see all her work and sacrifice brought to nothing by the whim of her young daughter was more than she could support. Her capable German hand reached for a pen as though it were a hairbrush, and in the bluntest possible terms she set herself to bring this rebellious, featherbrained child to task: "I can no longer keep silent," she wrote. "After your conversation with Mercy, after he told you what the King desired and what your duty demanded you have *dared* to fail him! What excuse can you offer? None. You ought not know or see the Barry except as a lady admitted to the society of the King. You are the King's first subject and you owe him obedience and submission. Only a word . . . and yet you fail him on the first occasion you could oblige!" The Empress now moved on to the subject of Mesdames: "They have reduced you to dependence by treating you as a child, fetching you pony-back rides and thinking up trivial amusements for you with children and puppies. This is why you prefer them to the King. They will make you unloved and unesteemed. I was so overwhelmed by this news which the courier brought me that I have needed time to recover. If you do not play your part . . . I foresee great trouble for you, nothing but mischief-making and petty intrigues. I implore you to take the advice of a mother who knows the world well and who adores her children, who wants only to pass her last sad days in being of use to them."

In addition to her mother's interests yet another filament had been woven into this net of trouble. The Dauphin's brother, the Comte de Provence (that ambitious and enigmatic prince who, forty-five blood-drenched years later and by God knows what dark and devious paths, waddled onto the throne of France as Louis XVIII) had recently married, and the ever-busy intriguers were already at work setting the Comte de Provence's interests against those of Marie Antoinette and the Dauphin. It was soon observed that the Comtesse de Provence was on friendly terms with Madame du Barry. Since the Dauphin was childless, Provence was after him in line to the Throne, and Mercy was not above intimating that in the present condition of things at Court it would be to the obvious interest of certain factions if the Dauphine, whose ascendancy over her husband had become so obvious, were to disappear. The word "poison" was not actually mentioned, but the hint of it (the French Bourbons had the blood of the Medici in their veins) disagreeably hovered about what might have been taken as Mercy's warning.

Once again "arrangements" were made. Once again the stage was carefully set and the cues memorized. This time Mercy took pains to see that the aunts remained ignorant of what was planned.

It was a New Year's Day tradition at Versailles for the Court to pay their respects to the members of the Royal Family. On the first morning of the year 1772, Madame du Barry, accompanied by her friends the Maréchale de Mirepoix and the Duchesse d'Aiguillon, was noticed among the crowd that thronged the Dauphine's chambers. All eyes were fixed on them as they moved slowly down the line toward the Dauphine. Marie Antoinette spoke a few words to the Maréchale and then turned coolly to Madame du Barry and looking her straight in the eye, said: *"Il y a beaucoup de monde à Versailles aujourd'hui."* "There are a great many people at Versailles today!"

The deed was done! The Court boiled out of the room in a turmoil of excitement. The party of the Duc d'Aiguillon could not find words enough properly to extoll the kindness and dignity of the Dauphine. Madame du Barry was in an ecstasy, and the King embraced Marie Antoinette with an excess of affection. Among the aunts, however, all was consternation and indignation. The Dauphine's name became the target for spite and contempt. Reverberations of the Dauphine's simple statement, "There are many people at Versailles today," soon were felt throughout the reach of Europe. At Potsdam, where Frederick hoped to see a rupture in the alliance against him, there was chagrin. At Vienna there was delight and relief. Poland's fate was sealed with its utterance and the Polish Ambassador to France was curtly informed by d'Aiguillon, "There is nothing that we can do for you. This is the result of the vile intrigues of my predecessor and of your own disunity." Maria Theresa's armies swept into Poland. "She wept," acidly commented Frederick, "but while she wept she took. Suddenly she started to take more than her share. She kept right on weeping and taking and the Empress Catherine and I had the greatest difficulty in persuading her to be satisfied with her fair share of the cake. Thus is she."

The price of French silence had been Marie Antoinette's words to the Comtesse du Barry. "We must not speak of Poland in front of you," Louis smilingly said to the Dauphine one day. "Your relatives and I do not share the same opinion." It was his only comment on the Polish Partition. A tacit bargain had been made and tacitly it was fulfilled.

An end was not brought to the matter by the Dauphine's surrender. To Mercy she flatly stated: "That woman will never hear the sound of my voice again." So the exhortations and orders from Vienna continued. To the Ambassador Maria Theresa wrote: "There is only my daughter, aided by your advice, who can render to her family and country the service of keeping the alliance intact. She should do nothing to offend the King. I do not ask anything that is degrading of her, still less do I ask intimacy, but she must treat the Favorite well. It may be that the alliance depends on it."

Every New Year's Day brought with it a fresh crisis. The distracted Dauphine took to God. "I have been praying earnestly," she reports. "I prayed, 'Oh God! if Thou willest me to speak, then make me speak, I will act as Thou deignest to inspire me.'" The Ambassador's dry reply to this bit of piety was that only the voice of her mother was capable of interpreting to her the will of God on matters of etiquette and conduct. An uneasy truce that was to the satisfaction of neither woman was reluctantly respected by both.

In this preposterous affair which does small credit to either side, the du Barry faction at best could be but short-term winners. Scarcely had the laurels been won than the victors began to have uneasy qualms about this prize which they held only on time. A stroke of apoplexy, an undue stress put on a heart that was lucky still to be beating, and the tables would be quickly turned. The Comtesse who had acted rashly and on the instigation of others had paid a high price for the "face" which at Versailles was more valuable than all the rubies and pearls of Cathay. Through intermediaries various proposals of friendship were discreetly made. One of these included the offer of a pair of peerless diamond earrings which heretofore had been beyond the pocketbook of even the King of France. If Madame la Dauphine would like to have them . . . her humble servant the Comtesse du Barry could easily arrange the matter. But such offers were coolly declined. What need had Marie Antoinette of diamonds from the hands of Madame du Barry when in a short time she would be wearing the crown jewels of France? It must have been with a certain uneasiness that the du Barry party furtively scrutinized the face of the future Queen of France, trying to read there some hint of the fate that in the not-distant future awaited them.

Chapter 7

CHOISEUL ROUTED, and the Marie Antoinette problem uneasily resolved, the Comtesse was free to enjoy that which Providence and her own talents had given her. She was now approaching her thirtieth year and was at the apogee of her power. This is the Madame du Barry of history, the "rose and ivy crowned Bacchante" of legend and scandal whose purse was the Treasury.

The King's last passion had become a madness and in the remaining few years of his life he could deny nothing to this woman whose ascendancy over him was unparalleled by all who had preceded her. Because her "reign" was relatively short, and because she was without political ambition, evidences of her hold on the King's heart are not so obvious as they are with the Pompadour who became a very considerable political power and who, moreover, ruled the Court for nearly twenty years. The testimony of all who saw the King at this time leaves no doubt of the extremity of his affection. This was his last, his greatest *affaire;* perhaps, too, his happiest. The twilight of his life was relatively serene; the nightmare of the Seven Years War was long behind him, the kingdom was at peace; thanks to Maupeou the quarrelsome Parlements had been squashed; all three of his grandchildren were married and the succession was presumably secure. The radiant woman who was his Mistress seemed to have lent him some of her own abundant health and vitality; not enough it is true for him to lift himself from the mire of intrigue which had so long engulfed him, but enough for him to take a new lease on life. Such leases are often the most pleasant, and in his declining years the King showed himself to be far more outgoing and far less gloomy than he had been of yore.

Secure in her position, the Comtesse now abandoned herself entirely to temptations which prudence had heretofore held under some restraint and began to pluck the fruit of her folly. The Treasury itself was put at her private disposal, not by the King but by the wily Comptroller-General Terray who in this move saw a sure means (as indeed it was) of securing the alliance of the Mistress. Madame du Barry's drafts were accepted by the Treasury as though they were orders from the King. Her apartments in the *petits cabinets* at Versailles (which once had been occupied by the Dauphin's late mother, Marie Josèphe de Saxe) were in a continual turmoil of redecoration. By the time Gabriel and Marigny had finished with them they were the most exquisite and luxurious in the whole palace and even the blasé courtiers, accustomed to every luxury that wealth and French taste could possibly provide, gasped when they beheld the series of sumptuous boudoirs and salons which the Comtesse had created as a setting to her charms. The talents of the greatest artists and craftsmen in the world were assembled in their various expressions in the salon of Madame du Barry. From the ceiling of the central room blazed a lustre of rock crystal which had cost sixteen thousand livres. Two commodes faced each other, one in old lacquer of a kind no longer to be found on the face of the earth, from which two baboons rose in gilded relief; the other ornamented with five placques of Sèvres porcelain which nowhere had their peer. Marbles, bronzes, porcelains, crystals and lacquers were gathered together in this "asylum of voluptuous pleasure" in a profusion and selection such as had never before been seen. In one corner of the room stood a piece of furniture which held the gambling equipment so necessary in the salons of that time: an ivory backgammon set placed in a table of rosewood marquetry, four quadrille boxes in carved ivory, the counters, pegs and markers being encrusted with solid gold. In another corner stood a piano, a gleaming box of polished rosewood inlaid with blue and white mosaics and adorned with figures and fixtures of gold and bronze; a creation from the manufactory of Clicot.

The bedroom, the sanctuary, so to speak, of this shrine consecrated to pleasure, was a marvel to behold. The altar itself—the bed—was set apart in a kind of alcove and was an incredible construction of precious woods carved and modeled by the greatest sculptors in France, gilded by the hand of the great Clagny himself. Four columns supported a baldachin and these were richly entwined by garlands of carved myrtle and ivy, surmounted by a cascade of roses. A rug of white silk covered the flight of steps by which one approached the voluptuous edifice. About the sides of it were hung curtains of rich silk embroidered in a design of rose clusters which was repeated in the hangings which covered the windows and in the thirteen chairs which, as though set apart for a congregation, were clustered about the foot of the bed. More marvels of the craftsman's art were strewn about this boudoir: a commode of white satinwood inlaid with porcelains; a clock, which was supported by the Three Graces, on the face of which Eros indicated the hour with an arrow of gold. Doves and cupids disported themselves everywhere. Gold, crystal and marble gleamed and glistened in a dazzling excess.

How did the Mistress of France spend an ordinary day at Versailles? The day began at nine o'clock when an attendant entered and quietly pulled apart the curtains, letting the light of a fresh day fall on the lovely creature who slept in her warm nest of pillows, laces and ribbons. After she had awakened her women entered, swathed her in a peignoir, and conducted her to the bath which they had prepared for her. While she lolled in the warm fragrant water, milky with rare perfumes, her morning mail was read to her: invitations, bills, little personal notes of friendship, begging letters, letters from those who had some favor to ask, letters from those who had some dedication to make, all the important frippery inseparable from her position at Court. After the bath she returned to the bedroom where dressed *en négligé* she drank the coffee which her little Bengalese page, Zamore, brought her. Immediately after, she addressed herself to the most important rite of the day. Her portable dressing table was wheeled toward the window to the exact point where it received the harshest light of day. Before her was now set an array of crystal bottles, porcelain jars, lacquered boxes and silver trays, each containing some essence, some secretion, some cream or unguent necessary to the perfecting of her allure. Attached to the table was a large mirror set in a frame of solid gold and cut in a design by the hand of Roettiers de la Tour, and topped by her countal coronet, also in solid gold. As she worked, the merchants were one by one brought in for their morning interview.

These bloodsuckers who for some hours had been waiting in the Comtesse's lilac and yellow antechamber, stirring uneasily among themselves like horses about to be fed, were generally richer by many thousands of livres after their morning session with Madame du Barry. First to enter were the jewelers, Boehmer and Rouen. Boehmer would one day be implicated in the scandal of the Queen's Diamond Necklace that would bring the Crown crashing into the dust. Rouen would one day be one of the witnesses involved in the jewel robbery that would bring Madame du Barry's head under the knife. But the future is mercifully hidden from us, and the Comtesse's love of jewelry in the hour of her triumph scarcely knew caution. Her eyes sparkled like zircons as Boehmer and Rouen opened their cases to display tray upon velvet tray of treasure: ropes of emeralds and pearls, ruby earrings, diamonds set in every conceivable design, rings and tiaras, necklaces, pins and clips; shoes studded with pearls, precious stones cut in intaglio, precious stones cut in cameo. She was never able to resist. The list of her jewelry reads like an inventory of the treasure of Golconda. In this department, at least, she surpassed even the Pompadour, even Marie Antoinette, possibly even the Empress Joséphine. The money spent by these women on jewels alone would have been enough to pay for a war.

When the jewelers departed, the dressmakers, the couturiers, and milliners were ushered in to the Comtesse's sanctuary. Her clothes were the inspiration and despair of every woman in Europe. Each month a doll, dressed in her latest "creation," was sent out of France to the waiting fashion centers in the capitals of Europe. Then, far more than now, Paris was the beacon of taste and fashion toward which the moths and butterflies were helplessly drawn. And of Paris fashions Madame du Barry was admitted queen. Whole ateliers were kept employed cutting and sewing her clothes: *jupes, manteaux, linge de mousseline et de linon:* the articles sound more like themselves in French than in English. Cost had no meaning. Thousands upon thousands upon hundreds of thousands of dollars were squandered without thought on these "creations" that strained the talents and resources of even Paris's ingenious couturiers. At the wedding of the Dauphin's youngest brother, the Comte d'Artois, she appeared in a frock reported to have cost $10,000, a creation of white satin (*"chiné en argent, brodé en papillons verts et roses; les pompoms, la palatine et la tour de cou brodé de petits roses"*) which was designed for her by Pagelle on the rue Saint-Honoré. She thought nothing of paying two or three thousand dollars for a dress. This, in fact, was what she generally did pay, and such little afterthoughts were casually ordered by the dozen. It has been said that French fashion never again reached such a height as during the "reign" of the Comtesse du Barry and the statement is no doubt true. Few woman since have dared to spend so much money on their clothes.

Berline, the hairdresser, next minueted into the room, accompanied by the Comtesse's perfumer, one Viguier. The morning was growing late. During the ministrations of the hairdresser, the doors were opened to the Comtesse's friends and courtiers, flocking to pay their morning respects, to gossip or make plans for some amusement during the day. Offering her hand about, laughing and talking as Berline arranged the ashen-blond locks, she exchanged compliments and chatter with her intimate circle. When the hairdresser had finished his critical task, she returned to the crystal *flacons,* the porcelain jars, the delicate pots of Sèvres and Pâte de Rose with their diamond and ruby clips. When her face was powdered she took a tiny golden knife and carefully scraped away the excess. A bit of carmine was added to her lips, a trace of rose to her nails. She was now ready to begin the day.

When, a few minutes later, the King entered, the room was still fragant with mingled delicious essences, so full for him of heady associations and exciting memories. He remained closeted with her for an hour or so, and then it was time for lunch.

After lunch there was a walk, or rather a "promenade," for this measured and stately affair took place on the parterres of the park and bore little resemblance to that exercise as it was meant by Wordsworth or the Lake Poets. Great attention was first of all paid to the clothing each day appropriate to it. The Comtesse was then borne in a sedan chair, the liveried bearers wearing uniforms of scarlet and silver, out of the palace and down into the gardens. A small regiment of servants followed in attendance: outrunners, footmen, valets, and her little Bengalese page, Zamore, who when she stepped from her chair would hold a painted, silken parasol over her head while she made her little turn. Zamore had been given to her by the King, and she loved this child *"à l'adoration,"* overwhelming him with gifts and trinkets, dressing him in turbans and sashes and all manner of extravagant inventions, stuffing him with chocolates. She lavished on him all the affection a girl gives its doll or a dowager her Pekingese. The King created him "Governor of the Château and Pavilion of Louveciennes" and had Maupeou draw up a toy brevet for the appointment. The promenade finished, the Comtesse was carried back to the palace to prepare for her afternoon reception. For this important event in the day another change of clothing was affected. Music was played, generally on the harpsichord, but occasionally on the Clicot pianoforte, and *thé à l'anglaise* was served to the guests who wandered in and out during the next hours. Madame de Mirepoix, who had a beautiful voice, would sometimes read selections from the plays of Racine.

The final triumph of luxury in the France of that luxury-loving century was not its creamy porcelains, not its matchlessly beautiful furniture (skilled forgeries of which fetch large prices in the art market of today), nor its strong, fragile architecture and its idyllic, lovely painting, but rather its conversation. Never have so few talked so well. This sophisticated, witty and idle race offered their entire lives on the altar of social intercourse—without scruple and certainly without regret. As a consequence the art of entertainment reached a degree of refinement rarely seen before and never since. "It was the most free, the most animated, the most brilliant conversation that it was ever possible to hear," recalled the Abbé Morellet. Literature, love and philosophy walked hand in hand. The dull, the factual, the German, were pitilessly excluded. What was said was not important, for no one was interested in facts. How it was said was all. God, tradition, the sanctities of nature and of human psychology all were sacrificed to the sudden thought, the quick, precise and deadly epigram. The mind was exercised, trained and respected by these people as is the body by the athlete. Even in so relatively disreputable a salon as that of Madame du Barry, the conversation bore this stamp which only that time and that place could impose. Much of what remains agreeable in France today owes its existence to the civilizing idleness of the *ancien régime* where pleasure was considered an art. Literature, love, cooking and philosophy walked hand in hand. Pedantry and Puritanism had not yet separated the pleasures of the mind from those of the flesh. In certain "cultures" learning has come to be regarded as something useful rather than pleasant, and the love of music and of painting are looked upon as worthy accomplishments, as such, to be pursued diligently in the classroom; love has become sex and in consequence a study of the psychiatrist, while food has long since been reduced to nutrition. The earnest German mind has triumphed where its armies have not; and the day of the epicure and dilettante is over.

After tea the King would join his Mistress's party, staying until it was time for him to sit in Council. Then Madame du Barry would give audience to her many petitioners and all those who wished for this or that reason to meet her. Soon after, she retired to prepare for the evening. The ensuing change of clothing and of jewelry was the most critical of the day and the Comtesse's closest attention was given to it. Several hours later she was ready for *souper* and the gambling or entertainment that followed. The King generally joined her circle for an evening of cards or dice (the gambling of those days was ferocious and the sums casually lost or won were staggering: whole estates and patrimonies were recklessly tossed away on the turn of a card or the roll of the dice). The guests were usually the same: Madame de Mirepoix, Madame de Valentinois, Madame d'Aiguillon, the Duc de

Cossé (destined in later years, as the Duc de Brissac, to play an important rôle in Madame du Barry's life), the Duc de Duras and the Prince de Soubise, and others of the inner circle. The Comtesse's main task at Versailles was to keep the King amused. All the distractions and ceremonies of the day were adjusted to that single purpose. The slightest sign of boredom from the King was a warning sign to his Mistress that some new distraction had to be hurriedly thought of lest boredom lead to melancholy and melancholy to remorse, repentance and Communion.

In the day's busy round the Comtesse found time to read. Her library, full of richly bound volumes many of which carried the device of the du Barry, provides an interesting insight into her taste which inclined to history. Among the many books of history were scattered the *Iliad,* Ovid's *Metamorphoses,* Shakespeare (of whom she was an admirer), Voltaire, of course; Villon, Pascal and Montaigne, with a liberal addition of those minor poets who flourished so profusely in the Eighteenth Century. Pornographic literature, into the illustration of which so many of France's greatest artists (among them Fragonard) put their finest efforts, was also generously represented on her shelves.

One of Madame du Barry's responsibilities as Mistress of the King was to literature and to aspiring poets, historians and philosophers. Among her early protégés was the man Morlière who was later to distinguish himself by writing *Les Campagnes de l'Abbé de T . . .*, generally conceded to be the most licentious book ever penned by the hand of man, certain passages of which were so fiery that they were said to have caused notorious libertines to fall senseless to the floor in a state of shock.

In 1773 the Comtesse was the recipient of a precious treasure. The Court banker, Laborde, before leaving on a trip to Switzerland, was asked by Madame du Barry to visit Voltaire on his Olympus at Ferney. She instructed Laborde to carry with him two kisses from her, "one on each cheek," to be delivered to the old man who was the god incarnate of his century, one of the very few mortals whose pen really was mightier than the sword.

Voltaire answered with a letter and two different poems: "*Quoi!*" he cries:

Quoi! deux baisers sur la fin de ma vie!
Quelle passeport vous daignez m'envoyer!
Dieux! C'en est trop adorable Egerie!
Je serais mort de plaisir au premier.

He goes on to say that in exchange he has taken the liberty of kissing her picture:

Vous ne pouvez empêcher cet hommage
Faible tribut de quiconque à des yeux
C'est aux mortels d'adorer votre image
L'original était fait pour les Dieux.

"Deign, Madame," he concludes, "deign to accept the homage of an old hermit (*"un vieux solitaire"*) whose heart hardly knows any other sentiment than that of gratitude." About the edge of Voltaire's profuse flattery there always seems to dance, too nimbly to be caught, the imp of mockery. Unctuous, malicious, spiteful, vindictive, the Sage of Ferney was but the courtier of Versailles magnified in all his faults and compensating merits into the size of genius. His two little bouquets to Madame du Barry, slight as they are, convey a perfect picture of this Voltaire who was ever quick to fawn before the great ones of the world. The verses themselves, so daintily, so perfectly turned, have about them the speed of a serpent's fangs, the deadly precision of a rapier's thrust. Dipped in venom, they would annihilate—as so many who dared cross swords with the "old hermit" had bitter occasion to learn. The Comtesse du Barry was well aware of the value of the little compliment paid to her. The verses enjoyed a certain celebrity and have since become part of Voltaire's collected works. The Choiseuls, who considered Voltaire one of their own, had their noses put out of joint and were indignant at the disloyal philosopher. But Voltaire was loyal to one institution only: himself, and never wasted much time on those who had fallen from their former exalted stations.

Splendid as were the Comtesse's apartments at Versailles they could never be considered in the nature of a permanent or homely residence. In the vast palace under whose roof lived more than four thousand people, the flux and flow of tenantry was as quick as that in a New York apartment house. Death, disfavor, a change of reign, all kept things in a continual condition of impermanence. At best such rooms as even the most powerful had there were small and limited. To house her large staff of servants, her sixteen valets and footman, her coachman, grooms, postilions, runners, secretaries and clerks, Madame du Barry had purchased a house in the town of Versailles. It was the custom of noblemen who could afford it to keep a suite in the palace and a separate residence in the town (in addition to a residence in Paris and two or three châteaux in the country). Madame du Barry therefore purchased a plot of land on the avenue de Paris and ordered her architects to build a *hôtel* there. This was completed in 1773, the year before her downfall; she had little time to enjoy it.

It was toward Louveciennes that her heart most frequently turned. Many improvements and enlargements were made here directly after the King had given it to her, but it was still not adequate for the lavish entertaining which her situation demanded. Accordingly she commissioned Ledoux to build her a pavilion near the main château. This building was started in January of 1771 and reached completion a year later. It was a gem of design, and with the Petit Trianon takes its place as a landmark in French architecture. It was the first important construction in France in the new style, that style that is called "neo-classic" and which owes its origin in France, not to Italy but rather to England where the Palladian seed had come into such successful flower.

Built in the gardens, overlooking the Seine with a view beyond that encompassed Saint-Denis, Saint-Germain and the distant spires of Paris, this white pavilion with its pure, fragile line and its perfectly harmonious proportions resembled some Roman temple of antiquity. Like the Petit Trianon it was almost a perfect square or cube, five windows long in front, three on the side. Four slender columns in the Ionic form supported a peristyle on the pediment of which was worked a bas-relief which represented clusters of children in a Bacchanalian abandon. Inside, the pavilion had three salons in addition to a very large vestibule which served as a dining room when the Comtesse entertained the King or some important personage at dinner. The vestibule was constructed in light gray marble and was a masterpiece of decoration. The bronze and gold ornamentation which was done by Gouthière and Roettiers de la Tour had no equal in Europe. From the door handles to the four marble women who in each corner of the room upheld brackets of candelabra, every detail was worked in a matchless perfection. This room was two or three stories high and at either end of it on the second-story level were tribunes in which musicians would play during dinner. A great dinner here was a magnificent sight. Moreau le Jeune did a water color, now in the Louvre, of one such event and this little painting, almost a photograph, depicts in fascinating detail the splendor and brilliance which would attend a reception given by his Mistress to the King of France.

Directly behind the vestibule was the main salon whose

windows looked out toward the misty view. Here Louis would come after a day's hunt at Marly to rest and gaze out at the dying afternoon and listen to the last echoes of the horn in the forest. Two smaller salons, one at the right and one at the left were on either side of this large room. That on the right was magnificently decorated by Drouais and Vien with the overdoors by Fragonard.

Fragonard was also commissioned to do four wall panels for this room and executed a series known as "A Story of Love and Youth." Not only did the artist surpass himself, but in these four superb panels he has caught forever the breathing spirit of the age. In a garden set in some eternal summerland, almost too sweetly beautiful (but not quite, for Fragonard was the descendant of Watteau, not the forbear of the romantics), the idyll of love moves in its familiar course. With its roses, its myrtle, its cascading waters presided over by Eros, above all with its sultry, summer air, one is transported into a world from which age, illness, anxiety and grief are forever banned. It is said that the shepherd and shepherdess (so exquisitely remote from the vulgarity of sheep) who disport themselves in this Elysian Paradise too explicitly suggested the King of France and Madame du Barry. In any case, Fragonard's masterpieces were declined by the Comtesse. Fragonard removed them to Grasse where in the house of a friend they lay forgotten for many years. In the last century they were brought to light by the art dealer Duveen and sold to the senior Pierpont Morgan. On Morgan's death they were sold for a million dollars to Henry Clay Frick who installed them in his house on Fifth Avenue in a setting appropriate to their style. Apart from their curious history they are one of the great treasures of European art in the United States.

The small salon to the left was all of mirrors with a ceiling decoration by Briard, called "Country Amusements," an allegory of love. This room was dominated by a chimneypiece of carved lapis lazuli.

Such follies as the little Pavilion of Louveciennes soon became the vogue, culminating in the Comte d'Artois's audacious Bagatelle which was constructed in eight weeks as a surprise for his mistress, Louise de Polastron. As the English influence was more felt every château came to have its English garden with a sweep of lawn, a wood, and an informal flower border that so strangely contrasted with the sharp geometric patterns of French tradition. The final flight from reality, the ultimate simplicity, occurred when Marie Antoinette caused her Hameau, the little farm at the Petit Trianon, to be built. With its placid mill-pond, its pigeon cote, its rose-covered cluster of country cottages, the wheel of fashion was brought its farthest turn from the baroque formality of Versailles. Rousseau, at what cost, had triumphed!

The Château of Louveciennes was no less richly appointed than its pavilion. Among its art treasures were to be found the famous Van Dyke portrait of Charles I, now in the Louvre; a seascape by Vernet; romantic ruins from the hand of Hubert Robert; many works of Fragonard and Boucher; and quantities of Dutch and Flemish canvases. In addition there were many portraits of the lady herself, four or five by Drouais, an interesting one by Gauthier-Dagoty, painted at that hour in the morning when Madame du Barry, *en negligé,* was drinking her coffee just before turning to the mirror for her morning "make-up." Later, after her disgrace, there were added the portraits by Madame Vigée-Lebrun.

In addition to the paintings, sculpture was well represented at Louveciennes. The beautiful Pajou bust, a head done by Lemoyne and one attributed to Houdon were among the many tributes to the owner's beauty. Caffieri, Falconet and others carved and chiseled various groups with such fanciful names as "Love and Friendship Surprised." Everywhere in the gardens were to be found those marble vases, those scalloped niches and pedestaled nymphs so much loved by the century.

The Château de Louveciennes was the Comtesse's only home. After the death of the King, she returned there, as soon as she was permitted to do so, to live out the remaining twenty years of her life. The sumptuous furnishings of her apartment at Versailles were moved to Louveciennes, adding such a quantity of treasure to this already-rich hoard as caused visitors to wonder if she had not been the Mistress of ten kings instead of one.

Such were the rewards of the "glorious dishonor" so coveted by the high and mighty of His Christian Majesty's kingdom. Small wonder that those fortunate enough to fill this enviable post should be a target for the malice of an envious Court and the abuse of an outraged nation. It was an appointment that brought with it many unseen pains and anxieties, but history does not show us any woman who ever voluntarily resigned it. The temperament of a Mistress of France was not that of a philosopher. They were all of them women who would rather be rich than happy.

Chapter 8

LIKE THE POPES of the Renaissance, a Mistress of France while serving her term of office often laid the foundation of a dynasty or of an illustrious posterity. While Madame du Barry could not hope to elevate her clan to positions of such eminence and power as the families of Gabrielle d'Estrées and Madame de Montespan had occupied—the day of such ambitions was long past—she did, nevertheless, take good care of those close to her. Shortly after Madame du Barry's elevation, Madame Rançon, her mother, the whilom Anne Bécu, blossomed forth as the Dame de Montrabé. She drove about in a fine carriage and divided the happy years remaining to her between an apartment in Paris and a little farm in the country which Madame du Barry bought for her in 1775. It is not recorded that the Madame de Montrabé ever came to Versailles, but it is probable that Madame du Barry arranged for her mother to visit the palace surreptitiously. The daughter would no doubt have been as eager to show her mother the glittering stage on which she walked as the proud mother would have been curious to see it. Hélène Bécu, Madame du Barry's aunt, was granted a pension as were each of Hélène's four children. The two sisters, Hélène and Anne Bécu, were thus able to spend their declining years in an enjoyment of the good things of life: visiting one another, traveling to the farm, returning with baskets of fruit and hampers filled with poultry, cheese and eggs. Madame du Barry's mother died in 1778. To recompense her widower, Monsieur Rançon, for his "good conduct towards his spouse," Madame du Barry settled a generous pension on him.

But rather than her own family, it was the du Barrys who most conspicuously profited from their relative's position. No estimate could be made of the return which the Roué realized on his "investment." He led a life of the most abandoned profligacy, maintaining a private Parc-aux-Cerfs, dispensing pensions and gratuities as though he were himself a king. His gambling debts were staggering and his demands of his relative the Comtesse (*"ma chère soeur,"* as he called her) were insatiable and continual. Impudently he referred to the King as his "brother-in-law." His ambitions knew no limit. In the first dizzy moments of his triumph he aspired to run the very Government, advancing as his candidate to head the Treasury a close friend, one Guenée de Brochan.

Madame du Barry grew embarrassed by his wild demands and finally was obliged to refuse to advance his interests. A sharp altercation ensued and Jean du Barry received an official letter advising him to take a rest at one of his country establishments: he had become, among other things, seigneur of the County of l'Isle-Jourdain. He spent his time at l'Isle-Jourdain writing anonymous letters and malicious poems which were soon circulating about Paris. Unlike Choiseul or Marie Antoinette the Roué was a cross she had to bear long after she had fallen from favor. He was in almost continual trouble, usually financial, and it was to his sister-in-law, to his Galatea, that he always applied for help. Refused he became waspishly, even dangerously angry; helped, he immediately spent whatever she was able to give him and was soon back again for more. For the rest of her life the Comte Jean was a real problem to her.

Jean du Barry's son, a young man who called himself the "Vicomte" Adolphe du Barry, was, along with Chon, the Comtesse's favorite of the du Barry clan. She conceived an immense, an almost pathetic affection for this rather worthless but good-tempered individual whose years of early training as page in the King's service had given him the foppish, stylish air of a courtier. Adolphe, who was the only du Barry established at Court previous to the Comtesse's arrival there —he held a commission in the King's Regiment—soon found himself the object of his new aunt's bountiful favor. She had him transferred to the Lightguard, a more snobbish troop than the King's Regiment and immediately put herself to finding a wife for him. Since he had little, materially, to offer this was no easy task. The calculating French nobility approached the business of marriage with its sleeves rolled up, bargaining its children away with all the shrewdness of a trader in diamonds. The hook that lay beneath any bait that Madame du Barry could offer them was clearly visible. A daughter exchanged for a share in the temporary good fortune of the du Barrys would in a few years' time be left with the name and not the fortune. No one of the first consequence could be tempted to consider such a risky investment. It was necessary therefore to shop around for less exalted capital. The Comtesse eyed Mademoiselle de Saint-André, Louis XV's natural daugther by the famous Miss

Murphy of Parc-aux-Cerf notoriety. This lovely girl was immured in a convent and Adolphe was sent there to meet her. She seemed to have fallen in love with him at first sight and herself to have hoped for the marriage, but neither her wishes nor those of the Roué (who in an alliance of his son with a bastard Bourbon saw a possible shelter from the blasts of disfavor which would follow the death of Louis XV) were destined to bear fruit. The guardian of the prospective bride persuaded the King that his illegitimate daughter could enter the world with better credentials than those a mere Vicomte du Barry might offer her.

The search for a bride began again and at last a candidate, Hélène de Tournon, was discovered. Hélène de Tournon was a poor relative of the Prince de Rohan-Soubise, a girl of great beauty who had been brought up in the provinces. She arrived at Court largely ignorant of the situation into which she was to be married. Madame du Barry settled the sum of two hundred thousand livres on the couple. Louis XV died in the following year and she was never able to pay the principal, but through all her own troubles she faithfully continued to pay the interest, paid it indeed long after the marriage had ended in tragedy. The marriage contract was witnessed by the entire Royal Family, a hollow promise of future grandeur for the Vicomtesse Hélène du Barry who soon, to her pain, was made to realize the nature of her position at Court. Mischief-making tongues had whispered a lie to the Dauphine which assured the Vicomtesse an even colder reception than that which at best she might have counted on. Marie Antoinette was told that Madame du Barry had selected this niece as Madame de Pompadour had been wont to pick *grisettes* from the streets of Paris in order to populate the Parc-aux-Cerfs. No longer herself able to satisfy the demanding voluptuary, who was the source of all her power, the Mistress was rumored to be proffering the beautiful Hélène de Tournon to the King, trying in this way to keep the du Barrys' source of fortune in the family. Credulous Marie Antoinette was capable of believing any wild story about the Favorite and was shocked to hear of such despicable machinations.

A few days after her marriage the new Vicomtesse was presented at Court. The malicious and inquisitive among the courtiers turned out in droves to witness what promised to be a humiliating reception. Madame du Barry presented her niece first to the King and then, followed by a vast, chattering crowd, conducted her to the apartments of the Dauphine. Taking a shorter route, certain mischief-makers reached there before Madame du Barry and whispered in the Dauphine's ear that the Vicomtesse had just received a cold nod from the King, thus encouraging the Dauphine to give her the same reception. Icily Marie Antoinette acknowledged their reverences, but uttered not a word. The Dauphin was standing in the embrasure of a window talking to one of his suite when the ladies were announced to him. He barely turned around. Pretending not to see them he calmly returned to the window, impatiently tapping his finger nail against the pane. The Vicomtesse's mortification did not end with her presentation. The Dauphine gave instructions to the Comtesse de Noailles that the young Madame du Barry was not to be invited to her balls, nor was she ever to be permitted to accompany her at the hunt. She was entirely excluded from the circle of young people which surrounded the Dauphine. Marie Antoinette never once recognized her presence. To the aunt the Dauphine had been obliged for reasons of State to submit: toward the niece she remained unbendingly aloof. Day in, day out, wherever she went, the Vicomtesse had to suffer the supercilious smirks, the disdainful and pitying smiles of the courtiers who eagerly scanned her face in search of that shame and mortification which was always a gratifying assurance to them of their own superiority.

Jean du Barry's youngest brother, the "Marquis" Elie du Barry, was also provided with a wife, one Mademoiselle de Fumel. She received the same reception as had the Vicomtesse, but since it had never been rumored that she was being trained for the King's bed, Marie Antoinette was able to take pity on her and one day even went so far as to indicate that she saw her.

The rumor that the Vicomtesse Adolphe was the Comtesse's apprentice and successor was itself without any foundation. It rested, however, on another rumor that had about it the ring of truth. At the time of Adolphe du Barry's marriage a whisper was circulating that Madame du Barry's days of favor were numbered. The rumor was sufficiently insistent to find its way into the dispatches of the diplomatic corps stationed in Paris. Since no one at the Court of Louis XV had the audacity of the swashbuckling Duc de Lauzun who once hid himself beneath the couch of Louis XV and Madame de Montespan in order to verify certain rumors, such gossip could only be based on conjecture.

Two circumstances supported this conjecture. The first of these was the recent ascendancy over the King's views by Madame Louise, the youngest of his daughters. This Princess, weary of the continual intrigues at Court and distressed by the godless life led by her father, had taken the veil. Shortly after the presentation of Madame du Barry, this haughty Daughter of France had entered the Carmelite Convent of Saint-Denis where she scrubbed floors and washed laundry, offering her pride as a sacrifice to God. Many years earlier the first love of Louis XIV, Louise de la Vallière, had offered the same expiation to God. When old friends who wished to visit her petitioned Louis XIV for permission to do so they were sternly reminded that while Madame de la Vallière may have become a Bride of Christ, she nonetheless remained a Duchess of France and consequently received the right of *tabouret,* remaining seated while her visitors (unless they were of the Blood) stood.

Such trappings no doubt surrounded the former Madame Louise and her humiliations were more symbolic than actual (when dying in 1787 she was heard to say in a commanding whisper, as though speaking to some coachman sent by God to fetch her: *"à Paradis! à Paradis! au grand gallop."* "To Paradise! To Paradise! Don't spare the horses.") Her decision made a great impression on the King. This plain, rather commonplace daughter, once known to him familiarly as Chiffe, whom he had always looked down on with paternal benevolence modified by kingly condescension, now approached him in the somber vestments of her high calling, vestments that filled the unworthy descendant of Saint-Louis with awe and even, perhaps, fear. In a sudden reversal of established relationships the daughter from whom he had always expected unquestioning obedience had removed herself from the aura of his authority and become, in a sense, his superior. Louis found himself ill at ease in his daughter's presence. When they met it was a Carmelite nun, not the former Madame Louise, that he saw. When they talked he listened to his daughter's words with the close attention that a weak and sinful but pious and frightened Catholic of advancing years might give to one who wore the mantle of sanctity.

"From time to time," reported Mercy in August of 1773, "the King makes remarks concerning his age, health and the frightful account that one day he must render to the Supreme Being for our employment of the life He has accorded us in this world. These reflections, accompanied by the death of some persons of his own age who died almost before his eyes, have greatly alarmed those who retain the frightened monarch in his present errors." Tactfully but tenaciously his daughter, the Carmelite nun, urged her father to forsake the condition of damnation in which the lusts of the flesh held him enthralled. She begged him to dismiss the Favorite so that once more he might know the consolation of the Mass and the inimitable joy of Grace. She urged him to marry and proposed that the young Princesse de Lamballe should be his bride.

Madame du Barry, well aware of the ascendancy which this daughter had attained over her father's conscience, was much alarmed. The King's frequent departures for the Convent of Saint-Denis made her particularly nervous and on one such occasion, it is said, she threw herself upon his mercy, imploring an immediate dismissal so that at least she would have the consolation of receiving it from her lover's lips and not from some intriguing courtier.

All this was known at Court and by itself would have been enough to start a rash of speculation and furnish material for the reports that were daily dispatched to St. Peterburg, Potsdam, London, Naples and the Holy See. Taken in conjunction with a second circumstance, also known to everyone at Court, the rumor quickly gathered substance. Those of Madame du Barry's enemies who questioned whether the King's conscience was strong enough ever to rout her could take heart in the hope that what conscience could probably never accomplish, a renewal of lust might.

At about the time when Madame Louise was most insistently pressing her purpose a rival to Madame du Barry appeared at Versailles. In the position which the Comtesse occupied, rivals were, of course, an occupational hazard. While they had distracted the Pompadour to a point of frenzy and helped to bring about her early death, Madame du Barry with the advantage of youth and energy had cheerfully ignored them. There had been many: an Englishwoman, one Miss Smith, whose name and nationality suggesting as they do the position of governess, strike a peculiar note in the *danse macabre* of the King's illicit love affairs; whatever her recommendation, Miss Smith was the talk of Versailles for but a day, heard of briefly and then no more. The Princesse de Monaco, Condé's mistress, aspired to improve her station in life and was the candidate of several cabals, but the King was too much in love with his du Barry to give more than a passing glance to the Princesse. So it had been with the Abbé Terray's daughter, Madame d'Amerval, with Madame Bêche and all the others.

In 1773, however, there had arrived in Paris a certain Baronne de Nieukirke. This lady had come to France with the declared purpose of winning the King's affections. Ten years earlier Baroness Nieukirke had nearly succeeded in establishing herself in the position she now returned to Paris to solicit. At the time of her first introduction to the King's attention in 1763, she had been accompanied by a husband, a Belgian merchant named Pater. By all accounts Madame Pater appears to have been not only the most beautiful woman of her time, but must indeed have been one of the most beautiful since Helen of Troy. No superlative seems to have been too excessive for those who attempted to describe the beauty of this Juno. Her beauty was, in fact, almost fabulous and when a description of her was given to the King who had lost his Pompadour, he could scarcely contain himself so impatient was he to behold her with own eyes. Through the offices of a mutual friend an invitation to dine at Versailles was extended her, and Madame Pater, elated by this opportunity, was only too willing to meet the destiny which beckoned. Unfortunately Monsieur Pater was a small-minded, jealous husband whose stay in Paris had already been made miserable for him by the cloud of gnats which buzzed around his wife. When he learned that she had been invited to Versailles to meet Louis XV, he lost no time packing his own and his wife's belongings and fled Paris that very night, dragging his disgruntled wife behind him. When this was reported to him, the King was astonished, but he soon found consolation elsewhere.

It must have been with chagrin that Madame Pater learned, a few years after her disappointment, that the glory which might have been hers had been bestowed upon one Madame du Barry. Shedding her husband and disembarrassing herself of his "ridiculous, bourgeois name," Madame Pater, now styling herself the Baronne de Nieukirke, aspired to a situation higher than that occupied by Madame du Barry. She was determined to marry the King. And such a dream could not be dismissed as the hallucination of a madwoman. If Louis XIV, the only really royal personage who has ever been born, was able, without loss of that dignity which caused all who saw him pass to tremble, to marry a woman whose name had been Scarron, there was nothing to discourage a Baronne de Nieukirke from supposing that she might morganatically marry his descendant. In this scheme she was encouraged by the representatives of the fallen Choiseul clique who even in exile never ceased to design the ruin of their enemy Madame du Barry and her supporters. The pleas of the Carmelite nun Madame Louise fitted her own plan perfectly. They would serve to rid the scene of Madame du Barry. Madame de Nieukirke could then step on to it, not as the Mistress, but rather as the wife of Louis XV—to which position, on moral grounds at least, none could offer the slightest objection. Preliminary to her purposes she abjured the Protestant faith into which she had been born and embraced the Communion of Rome. Delighted by her return, the King gave her a large apartment at the Château de Meudon and a sizable pension. Surrounded by courtiers and followed by a crowd of parasites, Madame de Nieukirke thus lived at Meudon in great state, biding her time.

The situation was one that caused Madame du Barry alarm. But her familiarity with the King's nature must have told her that his almost pathological fear of change, his profound and clutching lassitude was her strongest ally. If he found it difficult to dismiss disloyal and dishonest Ministers it was improbable that he would dismiss a woman with whom he was in love. In order to deny the rumors of Madame du Barry's impending downfall which he knew were circulating about the Court, Louis "staged" something of a scene for her at the wedding of the Dauphin's younger brother, the Comte d'Artois. This was an affair only slightly less magnificent than the wedding of the Dauphin himself. The table of the Royal Family was decorated by a device which contained a miniature river that babbled and flowed before them, and was filled with boats and crossed by bridges. It was not the river, however, at which people stared. It was at Madame du Barry, who was wearing "five millions' worth of diamonds" and a dress that cost twenty thousand livres. Blazing like the sun, she sat beside the King. All through the dinner the King (in the words of an observer) "kept ogling her and making the most extraordinary faces." The sight caused a great sensation and, as it was intended that it should, immediately became the topic of all tongues. The rumors quickly subsided.

Madame Pater was not fated to keep her rendezvous with destiny. When, in the following year, the report reached her that Louis XV had fallen seriously ill she hastened from Meudon to Versailles, hoping, as thirty years before at Metz the Duchesse de Châteauroux had hoped, that the King would survive the ministrations of the doctors and the absolution of the priests. With Madame du Barry dismissed, she was given the opportunity for which she so long had been waiting. But the King died and the "sublime" Madame de Nieukirke had finally to content herself with marrying the Marquis de Chamcenetz, as whose wife she played a part of some importance during the Empire.

In the early part of 1774, Madame du Barry's last year at Versailles, a final disagreeable tempest arose in the teapot.

Safe (as he supposed) from the long arm of the French police, there lived in England a professional blackmailer of French origin named Théveneau de Morande. For some time this Morande had been publishing a sheet called *The Journalist in Armour*, subtitled: *Scandalous Stories of the French Court.* Printed in England, these libelous anecdotes were surreptitiously introduced into France, where, human nature being what it is, they enjoyed a brisk sale. The sheet fetched a good price, but it was not from this that Morande earned his living. So atrocious were these libels that the frightened victim of one of them, upon receiving notice of its impending publication, generally hurried to buy the article off at almost any price. Some of the most illustrious personages in France had flung themselves upon the mercy of this scoundrel who could not even be dignified with the name of blackmailer since the greater part of his material lacked the merit of evidence. Having made a pretty killing on the fringes of the Court, Morande now boldly determined to do some hunting in the very sanctuary of the royal preserves.

In January of 1774 Madame du Barry was informed of the impending publication (in four volumes) of a work called *The Secret Memoirs of a Prostitute or the Adventures of the Comtesse Dub*** from her Cradle to the Bed of Honour.* Included for her perusal were some of the spicier extracts. Easygoing as she always had been about such calumnies, Madame du Barry, like every other victim of Morande's lively pen, was shocked by this one. The King, no less a victim than his Mistress, was appalled. The French Ambassador in London hastened to Lord Rochford, English Minister of Foreign Affairs, and applied for extradition of the culprit. But under English law the request had to be denied. Rochford, who had nothing but contempt for Morande, unofficially informed the French Ambassador that his Government might be willing to overlook the kidnaping of this "pest to society and plague to mankind," provided that the "crime" was committed by the French police with discretion.

Following the pattern of all such melodramas of the cloak-and-dagger tradition, a woman was used to bait the trap into which the French police planned to lure Morande. But the woman tipped off the intended victim and Morande, who knew better than to ask protection from the English police, now raised a loud cry in which he appealed to the English public for protection against foreign agents come to abduct him on the sacred soil of liberty. The English looked on their island as a bastion against the heathen activities of the Jesuits, Spanish spies and French secret police who peopled the dark lands beyond the Channel. The stray foreigner who had somehow got "into trouble" in his own country was a familiar figure to the solid Englishman of the Eighteenth Century. Such a one never sought asylum on English soil in vain.

When Morande announced that he was being pursued on English soil by the secret police of the Comtesse du Barry and was in danger of being kidnaped, there was a great outcry of indignation. A squadron of volunteers was formed to protect him, so that when the French police arrived in London and sought to seize their victim they were met by the triumphant Morande at the head of an angry mob. They fled just in time to escape being thrown into the Thames. The outcome of this episode was that Morande, now filled with loud and righteous indignation, refused to have any further traffic with Versailles and, much to the consternation of Louis and Madame du Barry, announced that he would proceed with the publication of his opus, three thousand copies of which had already, in fact, been printed.

In despair, the King now turned to a method of negotiation that he had sometimes found successful in the past. Unknown to his Government, Louis XV had for some years employed a staff of highly confidential agents responsible to himself only. No one—not Pompadour, not du Barry, not even his Ministers—was aware of this hidden network of espionage by means of which the King furtively informed himself of what he believed to be the true nature of affairs and expedited certain matters close to his heart. The most famous of these private agents was that enigmatic personality, the Chevalier d'Éon.

D'Éon, a Captain of Dragoons, had been decorated for bravery during the Seven Years War and was known as the most deadly duelist of his time. None who crossed swords with him lived to tell of it. When he wore a hoopskirt, as often it was his taste to do, the Chevalier d'Éon introduced himself as Mademoiselle Geneviève d'Éon, "a ravishing creature," whose suggestive contours provided Versailles (and Europe) with one of the most piquant mysteries of the day: Was this a man dressed as a woman or a woman dressed as a man? Both as Chevalier and Mademoiselle the creature led a chaste and blameless life. The seductions of both sexes failed to inflame this enigma into ever revealing the truth. Stealthy, cold and nimble, d'Éon was as deadly an opponent in intrigue as he was with the sword. Although he was living in London at this time, d'Éon was under a cloud of disfavor. To handle the Morande problem the King had recourse to another individual, quite as colorful as the Chevalier d'Éon: the playwright-adventurer Beaumarchais.

Beaumarchais, who was himself an occasional blackmailer, had just finished a sensational lawsuit against the venal magistrate Goetzmann in the course of which Beaumarchais had offended the King's delicate sensibilities on the matter of the Maupeou Parlements. His overtures of good will to the palace—a friendship which was vitally necessary to him at this moment, for his enemies in the Parlement had thrown off their masks and were now openly conspiring to ruin him—were met by a proposition which his friend Sartines, head of the French secret police, now laid before him. Explaining the impasse to which negotiations with Morande had come, Sartines asked Beaumarchais if he would be willing to go to London and there, with the utmost discretion, attempt to purchase (and destroy) the terrible publication which was about to be launched throughout France. Success in his mission, he was assured, would almost surely win him the King's gratitude and consequent protection against his enemies.

Beaumarchais, who had a genius for shady negotiation, accepted the mission and in March of 1774 he sailed for England, disguised as the "Chevalier de Ronac." He had no difficulty in coming to an understanding with the man who had eluded the secret police. The two met and instantly recognized one another for what they were. Indeed, they understood each other so well that between them in later years they hatched out a profitable bit of mischief on their own. Not only did Beaumarchais succeed in obtaining favorable terms from Morande, he also obtained from him an agreement to act as informer against his various shady colleagues in London, who, less successfully than himself, were rowing the same boat. "He was a brazen poacher," Beaumarchais reported to Sartines, "but I have converted him into an excellent gamekeeper."

Beaumarchais hastened back to Versailles to report Morande's terms. The King was both amazed and delighted by the speed with which his confidential agent had acted and he accepted Morande's terms with alacrity. When d'Aiguillon met Beaumarchais after his conference with the King, he suggested that once the offending material had been burned, they double-cross Morande. But among thieves there was, in this instance, honor, and Beaumarchais refused to lend himself to such treachery. The King unreservedly supported his agent. So, carrying more than twenty thousand livres in cash and a deed of annuity for four thousand livres, Beaumarchais set sail for England to conclude the business. At Calais he became aware of certain suspicious characters who were furtively following his steps: they were the private agents of d'Aiguillon and to dodge them Beaumarchais was forced into one of those games of hide-and-seek at which he excelled, crossing the Channel at midnight in a small, unscheduled boat. He arrived in London to find Morande in receipt of several anonymous letters warning him against Beaumarchais' treachery. These had apparently been written by d'Aiguillon, but it was impossible to persuade Morande of this fact, and once again Beaumarchais returned to Versailles to obtain the King's evidence of his good word. When Beaumarchais returned to London, Morande was at last persuaded of his sincerity, and on the night of April twenty-fourth the squalid business was concluded in a limekiln some miles outside London where the two men burned the three thousand volumes.

Eager to cap this success, Beaumarchais remained a few weeks longer in London and, on behalf of the King, concluded an agreement with Lord Rochford wherein France and England guaranteed one another sterner treatment in the future of such blackmailing wretches as Morande. Elated by the thought of the King's future favor and anxious to claim his reward as well as his expenses, Beaumarchais set sail for France on May six. He landed at Boulogne on the following day and there he learned the news that put an end to all his hopes: at Versailles Louis XV was dying.

Chapter 9

ON NEW YEAR's Day of 1774 the Comtesse du Barry had held her usual reception. Her crowded antechamber buzzed with the hum of sycophants come to pay her homage. Moving so gracefully, so confidently among her many guests, none might have supposed that four months later the radiant Comtesse would cease to exist for them.

"The King is growing old," Mercy reported to Vienna in the autumn of 1773, "and seems to have regrets. He finds himself isolated, without aid or consolation from his children, without zeal, attachment or fidelity from the bizarre assembly composing his society." In the last months of that year Louis seemed often to be absorbed in some deep, inner thought from which the frightened Mistress would try in vain to rouse him. For some time his doctors had been worried by certain symptoms which spoke to them of a diminution of strength. He was growing fat. It was difficult nowadays to mount him on a horse, and that beauty of countenance which had made him the handsomest man of his time had now given way to an awesome mask of melancholy and boredom, dominated by the mighty Bourbon nose.

"I see that I am no longer young and must begin to rein in the horses," he was heard one day to say to his doctor.

"Sire," came the answer, "you would do better to unharness them."

Thoughts of death filled him with great terror. It was Louis XV's misfortune that he was not the conscienceless debauchee he has too often been pictured as being. On the contrary, he had conscience in such excess that it weighed upon him heavily in even the brightest hours of his youth. Now, in age, as he saw the darkness closing in and glimpsed in the gathering shadows the beckoning spectre, he trembled. In November there had occurred a terrible event. At one of the Comtesse's little after-dinner gatherings where all was usually light, laughter and life, the Marquis de Chauvelin, an affable, worldly gentleman who was the delight of Madame du Barry's intimate circle, leaned over the chair of the Maréchale de Mirepoix. Never had Chauvelin seemed in finer fettle. Now, as he opened his mouth to say something witty to the expectant Maréchale, he suddenly turned dark purple, gasped and fell dead on the floor at the very feet of the horrified King.

"A priest!" cried the King, leaping up. "A priest! Absolution!"—thus betraying the nature of his secret preoccupation.

When a priest finally arrived the Marquis had already been dead for some time, but to calm the King's extreme agitation Absolution was administered on the pretext that "there still seemed to be a little pulse beating." The Marquis was fifty-seven; Louis was sixty-four—a comparison that no doubt held the King's attention in the weeks of morbid brooding that followed this episode. Shortly after this the Abbé de la Ville, while having an audience with the King, fell dead in a stroke of apoplexy. The Genoese Ambassador, too, died without warning; too suddenly to receive Absolution. These were events to make the King tremble.

The approach of Holy Week and the opportunity it offered the King to put himself aright with his Faith and partake of that Sacrament which alone can wash away the sins of this world, caused the Mistress and her circle the greatest anxiety. In Holy Week of the year before the Abbé de Beauvais had preached a sermon at Versailles that had set the congregation aghast: "Solomon, satiated with voluptuousness, exhausted by his efforts to revive his withered senses by every pleasure that surrounded the Throne found a new one in the vilest dregs of public corruption!" So the daring Abbé had thundered in a sermon that not even the sanctity of the pulpit could authorize. It was characteristic of Louis' better traits that he did not take advantage of his position to avenge himself on the audacious Abbé. "He spoke what he believed," commented the King. "It was his duty to say it." The Abbé's sermon this year was yet more terrible. In prophetic tones he lifted his hand and pronounced the awful words: "Yet forty days more and Nineveh shall be destroyed!"

Madame du Barry had been given an equally troubling prophecy. The *Almanac de Liège* of that year announced among its annual predictions that "one of the great ladies at a certain Court will play her last rôle in the coming April." Like one of those characters in Greek drama the frightened Comtesse sought to alter the prophecy by destroying it. She bought up as many copies of the publication as she could and had them burned. To dispel the gloomy thoughts that weighed upon the King and upon herself, she organized many little trips to the country places where for so many years Louis had tried to fill the emptiness of his life: Bellevue, Marly, Saint-Hubert. At Choisy she gave a great party. She imported troupes of comedians and jugglers to amuse the King. Easter passed and the King did not approach the Sacraments. Spring was in the air and the dreaded month of April was drawing to its close. The Comtesse breathed a sigh of relief and on the twenty-sixth of April, 1774, she and the King left Versailles to spend a few days in the warm and scented air of the Petit Trianon.

The King spent April twenty-sixth at the Trianon in the strictest privacy, accompanied only by Madame du Barry, his First Gentleman of the Bedchamber, the Duc d'Aumont, and a few attendants. In the morning of the twenty-seventh he rose feeling unwell, complaining of a headache and dizziness. Despite this, he set out for the hunt. He had always been prone to sudden indispositions and for many years his doctors' standing remedy had been exercise. He returned to Trianon at five-thirty in a state of exhaustion and with a bad headache. During the evening he closeted himself with Madame du Barry who administered medicines and calmed his fears. He retired early, hoping to sleep away his fatigue, but during the night his condition took such a turn for the worse that he sent for Lemonnier, the First Physician, and asked that the Comtesse be awakened to be at his side. Lemonnier found him with a fever, but believing that the indisposition was passing, agreed with the Comtesse and the Duc d'Aumont that it was wisest to keep the matter secret. The King would thus be able to fight his illness in the quiet, peaceful atmosphere of Trianon, away from the turbulent considerations of etiquette that at Versailles surrounded an event so important as the illness of a King. Their instinct was certainly a correct one, and if Louis had had any chance at all of surviving the virulent case of smallpox to which (still unsuspected) he had fallen victim, it would have been at Trianon and not at Versailles, where every interest but that of curing the victim would make itself immediately apparent. Unfortunately such a piece of news as the King's indisposition could not be kept from Versailles, and at three o'clock in the afternoon the King's First Surgeon, La Martinière, made his appearance at Trianon. La Martinière was a thoroughgoing doctor of the *ancien régime,* an advocate of the clyster, the emetic and copious bleedings, and a stickler, moreover, in matters of etiquette, both medical and social. He had no sympathy with the Comtesse's plan to keep the King at Trianon, was shocked to find the sick King left to the ministrations of his Mistress and *valet de chambre.*

"It is at Versailles, Sire, where one must be ill," he pronounced. It was unthinkable that a King of France should be ill anywhere but at his principal residence, surrounded by the entire Faculty of Medicine, the whole battery of "croakers," angrily whispering and wrangling among themselves as to the nature of the ailment and the proper cure for it.

Alarmed, the King was but putty in the hands of his firm First Surgeon and he quickly yielded to his persuasions. The carriages were accordingly ordered and Louis, wrapped in a dressing gown, quit Trianon forever. When he reached Versailles he was taken to the apartment of Madame Adélaïde where he waited while his bed was made up. Soon after he had been put to bed the Dauphine and Mesdames presented themselves in his antechamber. They were informed that the King wished to be alone, which was probably his way of saying that he preferred other care, for no sooner had these ladies departed than the Comtesse du Barry quietly entered the room through an inner door and took her place by the King's side.

It was still assumed that the King's illness was an *indisposition* rather than a *maladie,* a significant distinction in the vocabulary of the day. *"Le roi est indisposé"* was the expression that quickly passed through the palace. It was an exciting piece of gossip, but did not carry with it the explosive implications that the announcement of a *maladie* would carry. During the following night, however, the King's condition took a turn for the worse and it was decided to bleed him. In the meantime Madame du Barry and the Duc d'Aiguillon had summoned their own doctors, Bordeu and Lorry, from Paris. In addition the Dauphin's physician, Lasonne, was called in on consultation. The first bleeding was taken in the morning, but by the time Bordeu and Lorry arrived from Paris it was clear that it had not been successful and the two doctors immediately recommended a second bleeding.

On the camp bed to which, for reasons of comfort and convenience, he had been moved, the King was in a state of extreme agitation, groaning and demanding in a hoarse voice to know the name and nature of his illness. Fourteen members of the Faculty (six doctors, five surgeons and three apothecaries) gravely fluttered about his bed. Far from complaining about their fussy attentions, the desperate King eagerly offered each one his pulse and stuck out his tongue with an alacrity that suggested he childishly imagined that this might somehow cure him. The decision about a second bleeding had meanwhile circulated about the Court and the room was thronged with those courtiers who had the right of the *entrée*—some of whom, had they known the nature of the King's illness, might have been less eager to avail themselves of their privilege. One of them, a Monsieur de Labatière, later died from only having poked his nose into the King's bedroom. The Faculty had not only decided on a second bleeding, but come to the decision that if this proved to be unsuccessful a third should be taken on the following morning. This announcement filled everyone with the greatest excitement.

"Then I am seriously ill!" cried the King. *"C'est donc une maladie!* A third bleeding will dangerously weaken me. Can't it somehow be avoided?"

The King's words rushed through the palace like wildfire. A third bleeding meant the Sacrament. The Sacrament meant Confession and dismissal of the Favorite! Dismissal of the Favorite would mean the downfall of the d'Aiguillon ministry. Memories of the episode at Metz, which with its intrigues so curiously prefigured the King's actual death, were now foremost in everyone's mind. But it was certain that if the King dismissed his Mistress this time, she would never again be recalled. It is one thing for a lustful but pious man to defy the threat of damnation at thirty-four, but quite another to do so at sixty-four. All this was instantly perceived by the various interests at Court who now rushed to their posts and sought to advance their own private purposes.

Intimidated by the King's First Valet, Laborde (a loyal adherent of the d'Aiguillon faction), and emboldened by the pressure of the Mistress's physician among them, the doctors agreed to abandon the project of a third bleeding, thus disappointing the Minister's enemies. The doctors satisfied their professional convictions by making the second bleeding so profuse that it amounted to two separate bleedings, drawing practically all the blood from the King's prostrate body. When this drastic operation was finished, Bordeu, Madame du Barry's representative among the Faculty, went upstairs to the Favorite's apartment where she had retired soon after the arrival of the physicians from Paris. Bordeu informed her that the King's illness could no longer be considered an *indisposition*, but was a *maladie* and that he was in for a long and serious siege of illness.

At about ten that evening, after dinner, the Dauphin, the Dauphine and the Royal Family paid a visit to the King. They were preparing to spend the night in an adjoining room, when someone with a light in his hand happened to approach the King and noticed that his forehead and cheeks were covered with red eruptions. The doctors exchanged swift, significant glances. All had the same thought. Until now a diagnosis of smallpox had not occurred to them for it was supposed that the King had had this disease many years before. It is probable that if Louis had actually had smallpox in 1727 he had long since lost his immunity.

The Duc de Croy was visiting that evening in the apartment of Madame de Marsan and the Dauphin's sister, the Princesse Clothilde. Shortly after eleven a note was delivered to the Princesse who hurriedly opened it. "Good Lord!" she cried. "The King has smallpox!" A moment later the Prince de Soubise arrived and in a state of agitation confirmed the news, adding such details as he was able to give. The dread disease was a menace to the entire Royal Family. Of the royal houses in Europe the Bourbons alone stood aloof from the vogue for inoculation. The Dauphin, heir to the throne, along with his brothers, the Comte d'Artois and the Comte de Provence, and their wives were hurriedly removed from the sickroom. Mesdames alone refused to depart, declaring that their place was by their father—an act of considerable courage since none of them had had smallpox (and all of them, in fact, later came down with it as a consequence of their devotion to the King).

When the first shock was over the Faculty who heretofore had feared a "malignant fever," took comfort in their diagnosis. It is always assuring to know the exact nature of the disease that is likely to kill your patient. Taking comfort from the doctors, Mesdames and the others who hoped for the King's survival went about assuring one another that it was only a matter of nine or ten days and a little patience, recalling the many instances they knew of people who had survived smallpox.

"Listen to all these people who are happy because the King only has smallpox," acidly commented the Duc de Liancourt to the doctor, Bordeu.

"If they are happy," answered the doctor, "it must be because they expect to inherit something from him. At sixty-four with the King's weakened constitution, smallpox is a terrible disease."

The question now was whether or not to tell the King what it was he had. Considerable discussion ensued between his entourage and the Faculty, none of whom wanted to take the responsibility of a decision. Over this question, unspoken, hung the real issue on everyone's mind: the Sacrament. Compromise finally won the day. It was decided not to tell the King that he had smallpox lest the shock of that news seriously weaken him. On the other hand, it was agreed that no one would attempt to deceive him should he guess it himself.

Growing worse by the hour, the King was in a state of great alarm. Around him he saw the grave, anxious faces of the Faculty and sensed a constraint among them as though they were in a conspiracy to hide a piece of bad news from him. With the almost professional knowledge of diseases and symptoms which, as a life-long hypochondriac, the King had, he was very puzzled.

"Were it not that I have already had the smallpox," he cried, "that is what I should believe that I had now!" The Faculty uneasily shifted their eyes; the air of constraint grew heavier.

Sick as he was, the King still continued to give evening orders to his officers. The room was continually filled with staring courtiers, with the Princes of the Blood, and their attendants, with servants, apothecaries and doctors. It began to smell of medication, of sweat and disease. An altar was placed at the foot of the King's cot and here Mesdames heard Mass every day at noon. At least two or three Princes of the Blood were present at all times, day or night. The Duc d'Orléans, the Prince de Condé, the Duc de Penthièvre and the Comte de la Marche relieved one another at this post. In order to lessen congestion inside the King's Bedchamber it was decided to limit admission to those who had the *grande entrée*, satisfying the wounded vanity of those who only had the *entrée* by setting up a fence in the middle of the Oeil-de-Boeuf, the King's antechamber. Half of that room could be taken to represent the King's Bedchamber and those who had the *entrée* could enter it. This caused a great outcry. The sticklers for precedence were outraged and Madame Adélaïde herself finally had to settle the bickerings that were aroused by this breach of etiquette.

Madame Adélaïde and her sisters stayed with the King all day, but in the evening after they had gone downstairs to their apartments Laborde led in Madame du Barry who quietly sat by his side all night, holding his hand and talking to him. No one seems to have given her much credit for courage in the part she played. It was assumed that, like everyone else, she was doing what she could to protect her own interests. But there were no more interests to protect, as surely she must have realized while night after night she sat in that room which already reeked of putrefaction, whose air festered with virulent and deadly fumes. Surrounded by the now-undisguised hatred of the Royal Family, surrounded by the fresh intrigues which had flared up in the air of crisis, surrounded by disease and death, it must have occurred to her that she could very easily leave all this and not be much the poorer for it. D'Aiguillon, it was true, ceaselessly exhorted her to remain, but in remaining she protected his interests more than her own. She remained, in the end, because she was loyal. The tears she was seen to shed were not entirely for herself, as so naturally and ungenerously it was supposed, but, too, must have been for the abandoned and frightened old man whom she, more than anyone else at Court, knew as a man and not a King.

The quarrels that now broke loose over the dying man's head were nothing less than scandalous. The palace was in a ferment of excitement and those two factions, the Barryiens and the anti-Barryiens whose mutual hostility had more or less subsided after the dismissal of Choiseul were once again at daggers drawn. Those who were hostile to the d'Aiguillon Ministry prudently concealed their inner glee with lugubrious and melancholy expressions, while those loyal to it concealed their alarm with expressions that were falsely cheerful and full of hope. All was dissimulation. "Politics," remarked the Baron Besenval who was present during these days, "will follow Princes to their very tomb. The more virulent and hopeless the King's disease became, the more was it stressed that all went marvelously well with him."

All intrigue, effort and dissimulation centered now upon the question of the Sacrament, the anti-Barryiens doing all that was in their power to force the King into making that Confession which would spell the dismissal of the Favorite and the downfall of the Ministry, while those, in their turn, who were profiting from d'Aiguillon's Ministry were doing all that they could to prevent such a turn of events. It was a curious reversal of things indeed that found the former Choiseul party, the *philosophes* and anti-clericals who were known to view God and the Sacraments as so much superstitious twaddle, now lifting scandalized eyes toward Heaven, walking about with the solemn air of those who had a pious purpose in doing all that they could to insure the King's salvation. The Church Party, on the other hand, the very party which at this point ought to have been offering its consolation to the King with all the vigor of its convictions, was, on the contrary, doing everything in its power to prevent such a happening, minimizing his illness and insisting, with the encouragement of the Faculty, that the shock would put the King beyond all hope of recovery. When a conflict arises between his moral convictions on one hand and his private interests on the other, the experience of history testifies that a human being will usually speedily adjust such differences in favor of his own interest, thinking up all manner of good reasons—even to the point of inventing whole philosophies and political systems—for doing so. Given a normally rational mind there seems to be no reason for anyone ever to feel morally in the wrong. Somewhere there may be found an excuse for everything.

In Paris, where the decencies imposed no mask, joy was unconfined. On the streets the King's illness was spoken of openly and from the very start, such was the hope of the Parisians, it was assumed that he would die. Everyone was impatient for the beginning of a new reign. The bones of Sainte-Geneviève were exposed, but scarcely a soul came to pray. At Notre-Dame where thirty years earlier during the King's illness at Metz private individuals had ordered no less than six thousand Masses for his recovery, only three were now paid for. If they prayed for anything, the people of Paris prayed for Louis' death.

Much of this hatred, of which Louis XV, to give him credit, was not entirely deserving, owed its origin to the bitterness of the parlementarians and magistrates who execrated the name of Louis XV and had persuaded the popular mind to blame him and not themselves for the oppressive taxation under which the nation groaned. The populace of Paris, has, in any case, always been notoriously fickle. Almost forty years later when the beaten Bonaparte left the city of Paris for Elba, he was met by a screaming crowd who pelted him with stones and spat insults. Not many months later when he returned, apparently to win fresh victories, all Paris was there to greet him, throwing flowers before his feet and waving flags. A hundred days later they were all back in place again, this time to hiss and spit. Such were the loyalties of the Paris mob.

On May 1, four days after the nature of his illness had announced itself, the King's condition took such a turn for the worse that it was clear he could not hope to survive many more days. He still did not know what he had, still did not realize the gravity of his condition. Word of all this and of the scandalous intrigues that were being waged over the dying man's soul had by now reached the ears of that stern prelate Monsiegneur de Beaumont, Archbishop of Paris, who dropped a stone into this pool of pullulating pollywogs with the announcement that on Monday morning, May second, he planned to appear at Versailles and would not be deterred from visiting the King's bedside.

This announcement caused people to scatter wildly in all

directions and created the greatest consternation among the supporters of the Duc d'Aiguillon who quickly pulled themselves together to calculate their next move. They decided through the Duc d'Orléans, who was keeping an attitude of cautious neutrality in all this disorder, to appeal to Madame Adélaïde. When Orléans solicited her views on the matter, Madame Adélaïde, as it was supposed that she would, turned to the doctors for their advice. They did not hesitate to tell her that the Sacrament at this moment would be her father's death blow. Still convinced that there was hope for the King's survival, Madame Adélaïde accordingly told the Duc d'Orléans that though the Archbishop could hardly be prevented from visiting the King, he should be warned beforehand not to mention the Sacrament. In order to prevent the conversation from taking this dangerous turn, the Duc d'Orléans was to join the Archbishop at the King's bedside and never leave him for an instant during his visit there.

True to his promise, the Archbishop arrived at eleven o'clock Monday morning, rigged out in the full vestments of his high station. Followed by a crowd of gossips and curiosity seekers, the grim-jawed prelate was immediately ushered to the King's antechamber. All eyes were fixed on him as the door to the King's room flew open and that aged satyr, the Duc de Richelieu, came hurrying out to meet the Archbishop. The Duc, no doubt conscious of the probing eyes and straining ears that were fixed upon himself and Monseigneur de Beaumont, conducted the Archbishop to a corner of a side room. Seating themselves upon a bench, the two men immediately entered into a deep discussion. The Duc was observed to speak "with great vehemence and many animated gestures. Although no one could hear a word that they were saying it was not difficult to see that Richelieu was trying to dissuade the Archbishop from his purpose." So relates one witness to this scene. Another, possibly with sharper hearing, pretends to have heard the Duc say, "If it's a Confession you're after, Monseigneur, why don't you hear mine? I guarantee you'll hear some interesting things you've never heard before"—an unlikely story since no one would have dared jest with the stern and incorruptible Christophe de Beaumont who many years before had so valiantly refused Mass to the Jansenists.

The Archbishop was a man who would have sacrificed much for the Faith. It was no small sacrifice that he had dragged himself from his own deathbed—he was suffering agonies from the stone—in order to do what he conceived to be his duty by the King. As a man of principle he was now called on to make a still more troublesome sacrifice because the Duc de Richelieu, wasting no words, pulled out his trump card and put it to the Archbishop that the dismissal of Madame du Barry would meant the return of the Parlements and possibly even of Choiseul. This possibility, which apparently had not occurred to him, caused the worthy prelate to blanch. The crowd which crowded about the door to watch the tête-à-tête between the Duc and the Archbishop saw the decision which earlier had been written on the prelate's face now slacken and give way to an expression of uneasy embarrassment. Torn between his zeal for the furtherance of the Faith on one hand and his conscience on the other, the Archbishop was undergoing one of those inner battles which are the lot of those committed to conviction. At this moment the Duc d'Aumont joined the conversation and suggested that they now repair to the King's chamber. Joined by the Duc d'Orléans who had promised Madame Adélaïde that he would try to keep the Archbishop from mentioning the Sacrament, the party now entered the sickroom.

Unfortunately no one had thought to warn Madame du Barry that the Archbishop was about to enter the King's bedroom, with the result that there was a slightly disconcerting moment for everyone when the door was flung open to reveal that lady perched on the sickbed of the King. At the sight of the violet vestments of the Archbishop the Favorite hurriedly fled through a side door, but not before the Archbishop had had a look at the cause of the commotion which now raged almost as turbulently in his own soul as it did in the corridors of the palace.

The outcome, or rather the lack of one, in the ensuing interview, represented a resounding victory for the d'Aiguillon party. The two dying men, the King and the Archbishop, exchanged polite questions concerning one another's health and after a few minutes the prelate departed, remarking to Richelieu that, after all, the question of the Sacrament rested under the jurisdiction of the Cardinal de la Roche-Aymon, the Grand Almoner. "All that was now needed to complete this scandal," bitterly remarked the Baron Besenval, an observer, "was that the Archbishop instead of remaining at Versailles should calmly return to Paris—which he now did." The King, who interpreted the Archbishop's conduct as the best possible evidence that his condition was not as serious as it seemed, summoned Madame du Barry back to his side, showering her with tears of joy and many kisses.

The hopes of the anti-d'Aiguillon party now fixed themselves upon the Cardinal de la Roche-Aymon, a "sly and calculating priest." The Cardinal had little wish to become involved in the row which raged over the Sacrament. He knew very well that if he exhorted the King to Confession and the King recovered, he would be ruined. On the other hand he was put in a position of considerable embarrassment by the zealous Bishop of Carcassonne who, brandishing the pectoral Cross before him, demanded in the name of that Cross that the Cardinal propose the Sacrament to the King. The supple Cardinal wriggled his way out of this dilemma by approaching the King's bedside and speaking in so low a voice that nobody could hear what he was saying: if the King died the evidence that the Cardinal, in fact, had said nothing about the Sacrament died with him; if he recovered no harm was done.

There was such a marked improvement in the King's condition on the day that followed the Archbishop's visit that Madame du Barry's antechamber, which had been abandoned for the past few days, was suddenly crowded again with smiling friends. But during the night of May 4, the eighth day of the King's illness, the King sank so low that in their morning bulletin, much to the fury of the Duc d'Aiguillon, the doctors used the word "delirium." The Comtesse's apartments once more were hurriedly emptied and a tremor of expectation shuddered through the palace. That day, looking at his hands, the King realized that he had smallpox.

"The smallpox!" he cried in horror. No one attempted to deceive him. "I have the smallpox!" When the doctors tried to assure him he tremblingly answered: "At my age one does not recover from this disease. I must put my affairs in order."

That evening when Madame du Barry was brought to his side he said: "I realize now that I am seriously ill. The scandal of Metz must not be repeated. I owe myself to God and to my People, so we must part. Go to the Duc d'Aiguillon's château at Rueil and await my further orders there. Please believe that I shall always hold you in the most affectionate regard."

Half-fainting, the Comtesse quietly departed. The ever-watchful courtiers read her fate in her tear-filled eyes, and they could scarcely conceal their scorn for her. When she reached her room she abandoned herself to wild weeping, the culmination of the anxiety of these many days so filled with worry and physical horror. The Duc d'Aiguillon stayed with her most of the night, offering her what solace he could.

There was some consolation for the Duc, at least, in the fact that Rueil was but two leagues from Versailles. "Strict observers," commented the Duc de Croy, "found this 'exile' far too smoothly arranged. Should the King die, the Duc d'Aiguillon risked the wrath of the Royal Family. Other people said that to have refused his help to the lady at this point would have been the gravest breach of gratitude." But Monsieur d'Aiguillon full well realized that in any case he could expect little indulgence from the new Sovereign. He showed his last gallantry toward this woman who had made his fortune by the kindly and tactful manner with which he arranged her departure. Somehow he managed to make it appear as though Madame du Barry were taking a short trip to the country for a few days' rest.

At four o'clock that afternoon a carriage drove up to the north arcade of the palace and a few moments later the Comtesse du Barry, accompanied by Chon and the Duchesse d'Aiguillon quietly entered it, so stepping forever from the stage on which she had played her short rôle in history. Her carriage carried with it the last hopes of the Duc d'Aiguillon, and probably, too, the King's last real hold on life. A few hours later he impatiently asked to have her brought to him.

"She has departed, Sire."

"Where has she gone?"

"To Rueil, Sire."

"Already!" he groaned. A tear coursed down his cheek. The palace, for Louis, was now as empty as his life. "Gone," he sighed, "as we all must go."

It was expected that the King would receive Communion that very evening, but much to the disappointment of the anti-Barryiens he too clearly indicated that his wandering mind was more fixed on the subject of the absent Madame du Barry than on the Blessed Sacrament. He was heard to ask Monsieur d'Aiguillon if he had been to Rueil and evidenced great eagerness for news from that direction. The King, *dévot* though he was, obviously was hedging his bets and had no intention of taking the Sacrament until he knew for certain that there was no more hope. The anti-Barryiens were thus disappointed of a confirmation of their triumph.

That evening the Curé of Versailles took it upon himself to threaten to enter the King's bedroom and exhort him to Confession. An outrageous quarrel broke out in the antechamber, almost within hearing distance of the dying man, between the Curé and the Duc de Fronsac who threatened to throw the priest out of the window if he so much as mentioned the word "Confession" to the King. "If I am not killed I shall come right back," answered the defiant priest. Fronsac's threats eventually silenced this zealot, but not before further damage had been inflicted on the little dignity that remained to the death scene of Louis XV.

In the early hours of May 7 the King suffered a relapse and realized that the time had come. Accordingly he ordered the Duc de Duras to summon the Abbé de Maudoux to his bedside in order that he might prepare to receive the Sacrament. The Abbé, the highly respected Confessor to the Dauphine, put forth an objection to the presence of Madame du Barry at Rueil, insisting that she be removed to Richelieu's castle at Chinon in Touraine. When the Duc d'Aiguillon learned of this demand he hurried to the Abbé and, with the support of the Cardinal de la Roche-Aymon, managed to bargain the priest into permitting the lady to remain at Rueil. It was now five o'clock in the morning and the King had already issued orders to prepare for Holy Viaticum. He summoned Madame Adélaïde to his side and asked her to waken his grandchildren so that they might be present at this solemn ceremony.

By six o'clock the palace troops were under arms. The Bodyguard and the Swiss Guard had formed a long double line from the Chapel up the Stairway of the Dauphine to the door of the King's Apartment. In the courtyard outside the French Guard stood at attention while drums beat the approach of the Holy Sacrament. Preceded by the clergy of the parish of Versailles and those of the Royal Chapel, surrounded by bishops and their attendants bearing torches, the Cardinal de la Roche-Aymon, in pontifical robes, bore the Host before him. Immediately behind came the Dauphin, the Dauphine, and all the Princes and Princesses of the Blood, holding lighted tapers. The Royal Family was followed by the officers of the Crown, the Ministers of State and then the entire Court. At the foot of the stairs the Dauphin and those Princes close to the succession fell to their knees in prayer and then left the procession. Custom did not permit them to see the King who was dying of an infectious disease. At the doorway to the King's apartment the four ranking Gentlemen of the Bedchamber took the poles that held the canopy over the Host and ushered the procession into the King's presence. The dying man, his face swollen and blackened beyond recognition, lay on his bed. Weakly he tried to rise to make obeisance before the Sacrament. "If God pays the honor of a visit to such a wretch as myself, the least I can do it to receive Him with respect," he declared.

Surrounded by priests intoning Latin prayers, the King, clutching a crucifix sent him by his daughter the nun, humbly received the Host. Supine on his bed, his face motionless in the flickering candlelight, Louis appeared to be a man already dead and reposing in state. Whispering a few words to him, the Cardinal leaned over and administered the Sacrament.

Even now, even in this most holy of moments, intrigue raised its ugly head. The Abbé de Maudoux had to recall the reluctant Cardinal to his duty by a sharp tug at his robes. There was no escape for the Barryiens. The Cardinal stepped forward to the kneeling crowd at the door and said: "Gentlemen, the King has asked me to say that he begs the forgiveness of God for the scandal which he has shown his people; if God returns him to health he will devote himself to penitence and to the maintenance of religion."

These were the words for which the enemies of d'Aiguillon had been waiting. All was over. Intrigue could do no more—and so from this moment it ceased. Everybody who could properly do so fled the King's Chamber. Although the windows were flung wide open and the air fumigated with pastilles and aromatic vinegar, the terrible smell was overpowering. Louis XV was putrefying alive. But after he had taken the Sacrament he seemed to grow calmer in his mind. "Never in my life," he whispered to Madame Adélaïde, "have I felt more happy." On the following day he received Extreme Unction and shortly after began the death agony.

A candle was placed in the central window of the suite of rooms overlooking the Cour de Marbre and the main courtyard of the palace. Below, a great crowd of people waited impatiently for the news which the candle, when it was extinguished, would tell them. Shortly after three in the afternoon of May 10, 1774, an usher entered the room and the flame was put out. The reign of Louis XV was over; that of Louis XVI had begun.

Within the palace the doors of the Oeil-de-Boeuf, the room of the waiting courtiers, parted and the Duc de Bouillon entered. "Gentlemen," he announced, "the King is dead. Long live the King!" The words would never again be heard at Versailles. Immediately after they had been pronounced, Madame Campan who was in a part of the palace near the Dauphin and the Dauphine heard a strange noise that sounded to her like the roar of distant thunder. It was the sound of the courtiers running to salute the rising sun.

Louis XVI, with his Queen, Marie Antoinette, at his side, seemed dazed by the swirling tide of humanity that poured in on him.

"May God protect us," he was heard to say. "We are too young to reign."

PART II

Chapter 10

TOWARD EVENING of May 12, 1774, a curtained coach drawn by six horses, followed by a second carriage carrying two inspectors of police, arrived at the Abbey of Pont-aux-Dames in the remote countryside of Brie. With its forbidding fortifications, its dank, stony corridors, its dovecote, herb-beds, stables, and poultry yard the Abbey of Pont-aux-Dames belonged still to the life of the Middle Ages. The sweet and charming melody of the Eighteenth Century had not penetrated its grim walls. It had long been favored as a place of exile for ladies whose conduct had met with the disapproval of the King.

When she saw the place to which she had been sent, for all she knew to spend the rest of her life, Madame du Barry was heard to cry out in dismay, "So this is where they have sent me! How gloomy it is!" She was met in the reception room by the stern-faced Abbess, Madame de la Roche-Fontenille, who obliged her to wait while a room in the remotest part of the building was prepared for her. While she sat there the occupants of the convent, twenty nuns and canonesses, tiptoed shyly into the room to look at the celebrated guest whose reputation was such as to make them shudder. Not daring to look the creature full in the face, the timid sisters stole glances at her in a mirror. They were much astonished, as one of them was to relate many years later, to find themselves looking at the tear-stained but sweet and kindly face of a woman who more suggested the picture they entertained of a saint than the Devil. She had hardly been in the convent two weeks before she became a close friend to all of them. "The du Barry is very happy in her convent," it was reported. "The nuns are enchanted by her;

she gives them little presents and perhaps will end by making them very worldly."

The prisoner's conventual background stood her in good stead at Pont-aux-Dames and no one was more surprised than the Abbess suddenly to find herself a friend and even, indeed, a warm admirer of the scandalous Madame du Barry. They formed a friendship that lasted twenty years and it must have been a satisfaction to the Comtesse that during the Revolution she was able to risk her life to conceal the Abbess's nephew, the Abbé de la Roche-Fontenille. The sisters surrounded her with such kindness and affection that in after years Madame du Barry returned from time to time to find a few day's solitude among her good friends at the Abbey of Pont-aux-Dames. "They love you there for yourself," the Duc de Brissac once wrote her after a visit he had paid to Pont-aux-Dames, "because they know you so well. It would be hard not to pay tribute to the goodness, gentleness and sweetness of disposition which make your company so charming."

After the recent upheavals at Versailles the rest, regularity and quiet did her much good. Every day she went to Mass and during the day she followed the nuns in their offices. In the afternoon she would often walk in the shade of the old chestnut trees and limes, sometimes bringing a book with her which she would open beside the fountain that in after years became known as the *fontaine du Barry*, but it was noticed by the nuns that her attention would soon wander from the page. No doubt she dreamed of the past, already so far away.

Bit by bit, news began to reach her of the fate of friends and former associates. Maupeou, d'Aiguillon, Terray, one by one they had fallen into disgrace. The du Barry clan had hurriedly scattered in all directions. The wretched Roué when he learned of the King's extremity had fled to Lausanne leaving behind him a coopful of weeping women ("la Thévènet, la Dubois, la Morance and la Breda"). "Valuables and post-horses" had been the quick retort of a friend when asked by the Comte Jean what he should do. Du Barry had been wise to comply with this laconic advice because the same order for a *lettre de cachet* which consigned his sister-in-law to the Abbey of Pont-aux-Dames had him staked out for the grim fortress of Vincennes, a darker, deeper prison than the Bastille.

Neither Madame du Barry nor the Roué probably ever learned the strange truth about these *lettres de cachet:* they were ordered not by the new King, but by Louis XV! This fact is plainly apparent in the register of palace orders: the order is dated May 9, the day before he died. Louis XV had been observed speaking in low whisper to the Duc d'Aiguillon shortly after he had received Extreme Unction on that day. Apparently it was this command which he had been giving. Did it represent a last-minute sacrifice to God unto whose mercies he was about to commit himself? Or was it to steal the thunder of his successor and especially of his successor's wife, the Dauphine, and so spare Madame du Barry from a possibly worse fate? The answer went to the grave with this enigmatic prince who remained to the end of his days "the indecipherable" as Madame de Pompadour once had called him. Chon fled to the Chateau du Barry at Lévignac, the Marquis Elie changed his name, while the Vicomte Adolphe and his wife received *lettres de cachet* banishing them from Court. "All who bear this scandalous name have been driven from the Court," Marie Antoinette reported to her mother with satisfaction.

Soon after the Comtesse's arrival in the convent a Mass was celebrated in memory of the late King. Because the disease from which he had died was contagious, Louis XV's burial had been without ceremony. No one dared even to embalm him and the body had been hurriedly thrown into a double coffin lined with a chalk paste to which vinegar and brandy had been added. One or two loyal friends had followed the carriage that bore his coffin to the royal crypt at Saint-Denis. There had been no formal funeral. A few weeks after the late King's interment, Louis XVI ordered Requiem Masses to be offered for his grandfather throughout the kingdom. As she sat in the ogival chapel of the convent so far from the world of Versailles where the princes of this earth had once paid her homage, it must have been an odd experience for Madame du Barry to hear the virtues and piety of her deceased lover extolled to the rafters. No doubt the nuns stole an occasional glance at the lady dressed in simple black who dabbed at her eyes in a corner of the chapel. A moralist might have wondered at the strange ways of Fate which found one of a pair of guilty lovers weeping in her prison while she listened to praises of her deceased colleague being sung by saintly lips.

The news of d'Aiguillon's downfall brought with it a momentary pang of fear. In his retreat at Chanteloup, Choiseul was stirring himself in the expectation that his hour had come round again. Madame du Barry well understood that she could expect from Choiseul little of that charity which she had shown him. Had Marie Antoinette's ascendancy over her husband been all that it was said to be, there is no doubt that, indeed, Choiseul would have been recalled. Fortunately for Madame du Barry, Louis XVI detested Choiseul. His tutor, the Duc de la Vauguyon, "a despicable old *dévot,*" had raised him on the story that Choiseul had poisoned his father, the first Dauphin, in order to destroy the last hope of the Jesuits. Louis XVI probably no longer believed the story, but Vauguyon's particular poison had done its own mischief and the new King could not bear the sight of Monsieur de Choiseul. Marie Antoinette managed to secure a return from exile for her friend, but no more.

It must have been with a sigh of relief that Madame du Barry, in her "retreat" at Pont-aux-Dames, learned that the new Minister was to be the old Comte Maurepas. Maurepas, a half-forgotten relic from the past, who had been the bitterest of the Pompadour's enemies (she effected his downfall in 1749), was a well-intentioned, honest but superficial old man. His appointment testified to the new King's serious consideration of his subjects' welfare, and added still more to the wild acclaim which everywhere greeted the new reign. Maurepas happened to be a relative of d'Aiguillon, and slight though Madame du Barry's acquaintance with him was, she knew that the old man was well disposed toward her. She could now feel that she had at least one friend of influence at the new Court.

Of friends without influence she had plenty. The Prince de Ligne was perhaps the most loyal of these. She had known him since the days when she "did the honors" of the Roué's house. In his memoirs, written after the Revolution, this gallant of the old school who lived to see the rise and the fall of Bonaparte, who died finally from over-indulgence at the festivities of the Congress of Vienna, has nothing but good to say of Madame du Barry. No doubt in his mind he associated her with the reckless, rose-scattered past, a past that whatever its actual charms may have been, must have seemed almost poignantly lovely to one who recalled it from across the chasm of blood and violence that had rent his life asunder.

Ligne now did what little he could (he was a friend in good favor of Marie Antoinette) to help this lady in distress. Thanks in part to his intervention some of the more onerous restrictions on her liberty were gradually removed. She was allowed to see her banker, notary and steward. The King's death and the consequent suspension of all income had thrown her affairs into chaos. The jewelers, goldsmiths, dressmakers and milliners who a few months earlier had pressed a bottomless credit on her were now nervously clamoring for payment. Accordingly, she gave orders that a magnificent set of diamonds and another of rubies be put up for sale and the proceeds applied toward the satisfaction of her more urgent creditors.

As the weeks and then the months slipped by and her unclaimed possessions at Versailles and Louveciennes gathered dust, the Comtesse began to grow uneasy. The possibility that Marie Antoinette or Mesdames might persuade Louis XVI to confiscate her belongings in the name of the State filled her with great anxiety. In August, three months after the King's death, she wrote to the Duc de la Vrillière submitting a request to Louis XVI that she be released from detention on the grounds that her health was being endangered by convent life. La Vrillière, a friend, answered her request politely but he was unable to offer her any immediate hope. In November of the same year the Abbesse de la Roche-Fontenille wrote to Court and solicited the release of her "prisoner." The Abbesse's request had no more effect than had had the Comtesse's. In the meanwhile, the loyal Chon had obtained permission to join her sister-in-law in her place of retirement. A few friends such as the Prince de Ligne and the Duc de Brissac defied the anger of Marie Antoinette and paid the lady a visit, bringing with them news and gossip of the outside world.

Among those who did not call, although permission to do so had expressly been given them, were the Vicomtesse Adolphe and the Marquise Elie du Barry. Neither of these women made the slightest effort to see this fallen relative who, whatever her morals might have been, had never shown herself to be other than warmly generous toward her du Barry in-laws. The Marquise had persuaded her husband to change his name from du Barry to Hargicourt (the name of one of her uncles) while the Vicomtesse, the former Hélène de Tournon, was busily trying to ingratiate herself with the new Court by shrill denunciations of Madame du Barry. One of the debts that the Comtesse had been called upon to pay through the sale of her diamonds and rubies was the interest on her generous marriage settlement to Adolphe du Barry and his wife. Now that Hélène du Barry could count no more on the princely munificence of her fallen relative who had showered her with many presents and provided her with a rich trousseau, she quickly abandoned her. The Comtesse learned of her niece's continuing existence only on those occasions when she was overdue on her interest payments, at which times she never failed to receive a sharp reminder of her obligations.

Stimulating though she managed to make the kind nuns feel that their companionship was, the winter of 1774-75 must have seemed a long one to Madame du Barry. The adjustments that the King's death had forced her to make had been satisfactorily effected, and now in her thirty-second year she was impatient to return again to the world of the living. At last, toward the end of March, 1775, almost a year after the death of Louis XV, it was announced in a Paris journal that: "Madame du Barry has received permission to leave the convent of Pont-aux-Dames. She takes walks in the neighborhood, but returns to the Abbey to sleep. It is rumored that she is about to buy an estate. . . ."

Permission to leave the Abbey indeed had been finally granted, but with the restriction that she keep ten leagues from the Court. Therefore, Louveciennes, only a few leagues from Paris, still remained forbidden to her and she was obliged to buy another residence. On April 9 she signed papers that made her *châtelaine* of the estate of Saint-Vrain. By a curious turn of destiny's wheel Saint-Vrain had once been the château of the daughter-in-law of that Madame de la Garde, the financier's widow to whom the young Jeanne Bécu had so briefly and unsuccessfully been companion in 1760; very probably she had visited it at that time. She paid two hundred thousand livres for this property which included one hundred fifty acres of income-producing land and a sizable Sixteenth Century château which was surrounded by a moat. D'Aiguillon advanced her the money to make this purchase, but in October of the same year, the matter of her income still being unsettled, she was obliged to make a further liquidation of capital by selling her magnificent residence on the avenue de Paris at Versailles which had been completed only a few months before the death of Louis XV. It was bought by that plump and enigmatic prince, the Comte de Provence, brother to Louis XVI, who seems to have had a taste for du Barry property. Shortly after this purchase the Comte de Provence also bought the Château and County of L'Isle-Jourdain from the Roué, Jean du Barry. During the Empire when the future Louis XVIII wandered homeless but proud through the obscure provinces of Europe, biding his time for the downfall of the man he always referred to as "General Bonaparte," he assumed the title Comte de Lille, a dignity which had no relation with the town of that name but rather was a corruption of the Comte de l'Isle, a one-time appanage of the du Barry.

Through her uncertainties, the Comtesse had remained loyal to her large staff of servants, dismissing none of them and continuing to pay them throughout the period of her detention at Pont-aux-Dames. All of them, including Zamore, now joined her at Saint-Vrain. Chon arrived with the Comtesse and soon the old château sprang to life. Prudently conscious of envious eyes that might be observing her from Paris, Madame du Barry's entertainments were not on the courtly scale of yesteryear. She entertained the neighborhood gentry, invited the peasantry to dance in her park, gave tea or dinner to the occasional visitor from Paris or to companions in disfavor such as d'Aiguillon, who happened in to see her. The visits to Saint-Vrain of the Duc d'Aiguillon, who still retained his commission as Captain of the Lightguard, did not pass unnoticed at Versailles. Once, when in line of duty, d'Aiguillon was waiting for the Queen's orders, Marie Antoinette wrathfully whirled on him and said, "Go take your orders from the Comtesse du Barry at Saint-Vrain rather than from me at Versailles!"

Contemporary descriptions of the Comtesse's life at Saint-Vrain and later at Louveciennes suggest that she was a better example of the principle of *noblesse oblige* than were many of those who were to the manor born. At Saint-Vrain she acquired for herself the reputation of a Lady Bountiful, a reputation which her life at Louveciennes was greatly to enhance and which—so well established was it—would one day even succeed for a little while in deflecting the guillotine from her neck. In the eighteen sixties, Charles Vatel, one of Madame du Barry's early biographers, made a trip to Saint-Vrain where he found an old man who could recall stories told him by his mother who remembered well the brief stay of Madame du Barry in the sleepy little village:

"She made distributions of bread, meat and wine to the poor. The unfortunate all received help from her. To one she would send something for the pot; to another, if it was a woman lying-in for instance, she would send soup and linen. Her maids brought all her cast-off clothing to the village in order that they might be made over for the little girls of Saint-Vrain. Often she used to invite the villagers to dance in her park. Her departure was deeply regretted.

"As to her appearance I can tell you nothing. Everyone knows that she was a beautiful woman. I remember my mother telling me another thing. Madame du Barry kept a black parrot which always cried out, 'There goes the pretty Comtesse!' whenever she passed by."

The winter of 1775-76 was enlivened for the ladies of Saint-

Vrain by two rather seedy house guests who seemed to have settled in with them for the winter. One of these, the Marquis de Fauga, is described as a "beau" of Chon, while the other, a certain Vicomte de Langle, was apparently paying court to Madame du Barry. Whatever their purposes (or their success in the pursuit of them), they seem to have kept their hostess amused during the long winter months. Exile had not dulled Madame du Barry's insatiable appetite for gambling and the Vicomte de Langle, an adventurer who had escaped from more than one prison, was all too willing to provide her with opportunities to make a bet. Some of these games became so reckless that stories of them reached Paris and caused a mild stir.

One evening "in a fit of boredom" the Comtesse sat down to a game of bagatelle, betting the Vicomte that she could sink nine balls out of the nineteen allowed her. Each time that she failed to do so, she would renew her bet until suddenly she realized that she was in debt to him for nearly one hundred thousand dollars. The Vicomte gallantly refused to accept payment. On another evening, in order to recoup her earlier losses, she recklessly doubled her stakes until her losses reached the staggering sum of two million dollars. Once again the Vicomte played the gentleman and, significantly glancing at the fascinated bystanders, permitted the Comtesse to continue doubling her bet until, as was inevitable, she finally won it back. In Paris the Vicomte was accused of having wrung one hundred thousand dollars out of the unfortunate woman. He was also accused of betraying the secrets of her household to the Duc de Choiseul because Madame du Barry had "repulsed his overtures to her." Langle took enough offense at this malicious gossip to write and publish a *Memoir Justificatif,* declaring that his behavior toward her had been nothing but honorable—as indeed it had been if he had helped her out of a gambling debt of over two millions dollars. But gone were the days when trivia such as this could rock a ship of state!

In the early part of 1776 the specter of her former notoriety rose to disconcert the new regime and to upset the Comtesse. Another of those scurrilous publications had been printed in London and surreptitiously introduced into France where it was enjoying a brisk sale. Rightly, the Government of Louis XVI looked on it as an attack on the Monarchy as much as on Madame du Barry. The *Anecdotes About Madame du Barry*, as it was called, made spicy reading indeed for those able to believe they were being given an authentic peep into the royal boudoir. The author, Pidansat de Mairobert, was skillful enough in his craft of slander to wrap his lies and inventions about a certain body of fact. "The author has found a subject," he wrote in the preface, "which to the interest of History adds all the delights of Romance." The book has been indiscriminately used by certain of Madame du Barry's more sensational biographers and the lurid picture of her which it contains has passed into the footnotes of reputable history, where she usually makes her appearance.

Mairobert found a good part of his material in the libels published by Choiseul at the time of Madame du Barry's presentation. In this collection of "anecdotes," the author (whose purpose was not so much to blacken the character of his subject at it was, at any cost, to titillate the blasé senses of a scandal-loving public) pauses a moment and tips his hat in the direction of truth: "No one could fail to like her, and to reject the impressions that her enemies and people who were prejudiced against her had spread abroad; she was so courteous and affable and gentle. She had the virtue, rare, especially among her own sex, of never speaking ill of anyone and never permitting herself complaints and reproaches against those who envied her and those who had published abroad the not-too-creditable stories of her life, and had embroidered them with infamies and enormities."

Whatever consolation it may have been to Madame du Barry, this was the last of the libels to which she would be subjected, until the Revolution. Nothing is duller than warmed-over scandal. With the death of Louis XV she ceased to be a figure of importance and the target, therefore, of spite. The scandalmongers and the cold-blooded courtiers who made use of them had already found a new and far more exalted victim. Their eyes were now turned on Marie Antoinette who, reckless and unhappy, was drowning her thwarted maternal instincts in a round of desperate frivolity. So successfully did the disaffected courtiers and their lackeys, the gutter press, throw their mud that the character of the Queen has become as ineradicably associated with frivolity as that of Madame du Barry with vulgarity and vice.

In October of 1776 Madame du Barry finally received notice that she was free to return to Louveciennes and Paris. For this long-awaited dispensation she had the good offices of the new Minister, Maurepas, to thank. Quite as important to her as the end of her exile was the news that all her property, including a large income derived from rents on the Hôtel de Ville and the Loges de Nantes which Louis XV had given her, were to be returned intact. Upon receipt of this good news she went to Paris where she stayed a few weeks while Louveciennes was being prepared for her return. Saint-Vrain was sold without regret, and in November of 1776, Madame du Barry at last returned to the beautiful little château which she considered home and where she was to remain for the rest of her life. She had been away from it for two and one half years.

Chapter 11

"THE PRESENT FASHION in France for spending time in the country is new," wrote the English traveler Arthur Young in the latter part of the Eighteenth Century. "Everybody that have [*sic*] country seats is at them and those who have not visit others who have. This revolution in French manners is certainly one of the best features they have taken from England. Its introduction was the easier because of the magic in Rousseau's writings."

While it had been by no choice of her own that the Comtesse du Barry had left the glittering world of the Court, she seems to have taken readily to the civilized and fashionable delights of country living. She soon submerged her life in the small day-by-day preoccupations that in those days distracted the wealthy proprietor of a country estate. She set out new trees in her park; she attended to the needy of her village; she planted her garden; she made preserves; she supervised her farm. During the first few years of her retirement much of her time was given to an extensive rearrangement of the rooms and appointments of the château. What would have been fit to receive a King and his Court could hardly be suitable or comfortable for a lady living in retirement. She made the rooms more homely, arranging the château to suit her simpler circumstances.

Deliberately, she let herself be forgotten, retiring almost completely from the world of fashion where in Paris, if not at Court, she might still have played a considerable rôle. In doing so she acted wisely because Versailles with its Argus eyes, ever jealous and spiteful, lay dangerously near the Château de Louveciennes. The world to which she bade farewell could in any case have nothing further, materially speaking, to offer this woman who had been Mistress to a King of France. At thirty-four she had supped well of its pleasures and had seen everything that there was to be seen. In obliging her to retire from the scene of her triumphs at the very moment when youth was vanishing, Destiny had been kind to Madame du Barry. She was spared the terrible anxieties to which the approach of middle age had pitilessly exposed other mistresses of Louis XV. Surrounded by her accumulation of treasure, tokens of a notoriety which now belonged to history, calm with that serenity which a sense of income-producing land will often lend the most agitated heart—particularly a French one—the Comtesse, as she approached middle age, could view the future with equanimity.

She was still beautiful, in many ways more beautiful than she had been in her heyday at Court. To her native charms now was added a deepening tincture of fascination. Time and the asperities of exile had given her character. Already she had about her a quality peculiar to many who have once played a great rôle upon the stage of life. As the reign of Louis XV receded into the past and Madame du Barry grew older, she became something of a legend. Strangers would beg an introduction from her friends and the Comtesse, always warm and hospitable, would invite them to Louveciennes. Such people always departed with an impression very different from the one they had anticipated. It was difficult for them to believe that this charming, unaffected woman was the scandalous Madame du Barry. No doubt the women among them noticed with interest that this *femme fatale* used no cosmetics. Every day, winter or summer, she took a cold bath. She dressed as lightly as possible, often facing the bitterest winter weather without a wrap and nothing but a thin chemise beneath her dress. Health, not cosmetics, seems to have been the answer to the question her guests were, doubtless, too polite to ask.

Reading the accounts of those who met or knew her during her years at Louveciennes, looking at the various portraits done of her then (the best of which are by Madame Vigée-Lebrun), one cannot but feel that Louis XV was a bit cheated. The Madame du Barry of mature years seems to have been even more attractive than the Bacchante of Versailles. She was, in fact, a fascinating woman.

In May, 1777, six months after her return to Louveciennes, the Comtesse received an unexpected visitor at her château—the first, apparently, of the sight-seers and certainly the most illustrious. Disturbed by reports that she had been receiving of her daughter's restless dissipations, Maria Theresa had dispatched her eldest son and co-Sovereign, the Emperor Joseph II, to France. It was many years before Vienna was to give birth to Sigmund Freud, but the stout old Empress, full of years and common sense (and mother herself of eighteen children), did not need a psychiatrist to tell her that the unfruitful nature of Marie Antoinette's marriage was rapidly forcing her to a breaking-point. One of Joseph's major missions in France was to persuade Louis XVI to undergo the surgery which was necessary to his becoming a husband, if not a father.

An egotist whose own limited talents were obscured by the shadow of his illustrious mother, Joseph II was one of those people whom vanity, combined with a very modest intelligence, forces to be different. In order that he might be noticed he became, as he imagined it, "liberal." A curious Liberalism indeed was this which manifested itself in the use of disguises, in which, Joseph, like the Student Prince of operetta, would descend to the level of his subjects and engage them in conversation. Toward the end of these informal chats the masquerade would be dropped a trifle and the not-too-startled subject would realize that he had been talking with—his Emperor!

Joseph's arrival in France was the source of mortification to his sister. He sent word that he was not to be received as the Emperor of Austria, but rather as "Count Falkenstein." He did not lodge at the palace, where regal accommodations awaited his arrival, but in a second-class boarding house in the town of Versailles. He carefully adjusted his behavior to that of some country cousin come to visit a sister who has risen a bit precariously above her station. Knowing that he could not hope to compete on his sister's ground for the applause of that unseen audience to which he played, Joseph had recourse to the country cousin's stratagem of an excess of "folksiness," of good, solid, down-to-earth, German sense, thus mortifying his sister and at the same time winning, as he supposed, everyone's applause. He shuffled about making boorish and even rude remarks that shattered the nervous, hypersensitive atmosphere of Versailles. ("Lay it on, ma'am," he sarcastically said to his sister one morning as she addressed herself to the rouge pot. "Slap some more of it on under the eyes like that woman over there." Whereupon he pointed to one of Marie Antoinette's friends famous for her artificial complexion.)

To embarrass his sister further, and probably to pique his mother too, the one person Joseph seems carefully to have gone out of his way to visit on his trip to France was the disgraced Favorite of Louis XV. His visit was made "without affectation." It was arranged that Joseph, ostensibly out to see the hydraulic machine of Marly, an engineering wonder of its time that straddled the Seine almost directly in front of the terraces of Louveciennes, should casually encounter Madame du Barry who by a strange coincidence should be taking a stroll at this very moment. All went according to schedule and the Emperor graciously expressed a desire that the Comtesse du Barry be presented to him. His Majesty spoke in admiration of the famous pavilion which he could discern, whereupon the Comtesse took the liberty to hope that she might show it to him. Joseph accepted this invitation with alacrity. When they had toured the pavilion they moved on to the château with its masterpieces of art and its wonderful bronzes, porcelains and tapestries. Here they spent several hours in conversation—its tenor is not recorded—after which Joseph expressed a desire to be shown the gardens. As they began their tour the Emperor offered the lady his arm, whereupon, modestly, she exclaimed: "Oh, no, Sire! I am not worthy of such an honor."

"Please . . . please," responded the Emperor. "Do not protest. Beauty is always Queen."

And so, arm in arm, the peculiar twosome strolled through the gardens of Louveciennes. Joseph's little bow to the lady's beauty represented a gallant lie on his part for in truth he found her plain and reported so afterward to his friends. The refined, slightly passé beauty which was attractive to the French could hardly appeal to this Teuton whose preferences ran to the bursting bodices of the land of sausage and beer.

His visit caused considerable consternation. Marie Antoinette was angry. Maria Theresa curtly commented, "I should have been better pleased if the Emperor had abstained from seeing that despicable du Barry," and Choiseul, who of all people in France was the one the Emperor should have distinguished by a visit, was mortified and chagrined. As former leader of the pro-Austrian faction at Versailles, the one-time Minister had been counting on a visit from the Sovereign son of his friend the Empress Maria Theresa. Such a visit would have done much to lend fresh lustre to his fast-fading name. But for this honor he waited in vain. Joseph's single reference to Choiseul was a remark to the King that he was fortunate in having so sensible a Minister as Maurepas instead of that "restless and turbulent spirit," the Duc de Choiseul, who "would have plunged the kingdom into difficulty."

Shortly after her visit from the Emperor of Austria, the Comtesse had a call from the Duc de Croy, a courtier who had often observed her from afar when she was at Versailles, but who had never met her. The Duc had been in the neighborhood of Louveciennes visiting a friend. "Monsieur de la Morlière took me to see the admirable Pavilion of Louveciennes facing the hydraulic machine. As there was no polite way to see the Pavilion and its gardens without seeing the lady of the Château, I paid a call on Madame du Barry to whom I had never spoken and whom I knew only by sight. I found her still lovely and with a far finer tone than one might have expected....

"After a short visit she took me to see her Pavilion. I believe it to be one of the loveliest places imaginable and with a beautiful view. Below, the hydraulic machine appears to be a kind of windmill and the river tumbles about it like a cascade, all of which makes the richest and the most agreeable sort of vista. All that taste and money can provide has gone into this charming little Pavilion. As we stood on the balcony admiring the lovely view I spoke at some length with her about the late King. I was very much astonished to find myself there talking with her. She spoke extremely well and it was difficult to persuade oneself of her former condition in life. I saw her back to the Château, stayed a bit longer and then returned home."

In February of the following year (1778) the Comtesse paid a call of her own. Voltaire, the god, Voltaire, the incarnate genius of his century, had at last returned to France! For twenty-eight years he had traveled abroad or lived at Ferney receiving the homage of the civilized world. Now he had returned—"to be killed," as he expressed it and as, in fact, it happened, "by triumph." Like a great field of wheat moved by the wind, the entire city of Paris bent toward the earth and in a sigh of adulation approximate only to ecstasy cried, "Voltaire!" The mummified old man whose jaw thrust forward in a grimace of contempt and loathing, whose bright terrible eyes darted in a restless dance of malice was carried into Paris on a wave of tribute such as has rarely welcomed Popes, Princes and conquerors or even, indeed, the film stars of Twentieth Century America. From morning till night a steady stream of visitors poured through his antechamber in the hope of a "presentation." He was at work on the staging of his tragedy *Irène* and many of these callers were turned away.

On February 21, he had been so hard at work that he had not even troubled to dress. Shortly after lunch he was startled to learn that Madame du Barry was waiting outside in the hope of meeting him. At first he refused to see her. He was not properly dressed and his excessive vanity would not allow him to be seen by the famous courtesan at an hour of the day when he felt he did not look his best. Since the Comtesse had not come to Paris to admire his elegance, but rather to hear him talk and to behold the most famous man in the world, this was a disappointment. She begged his secretary to try again. Prompted finally by curiosity and perhaps even by gratitude (Madame du Barry had been a good customer of the watch factory at Ferney, and at one time had even tried to persuade Louis XV to permit him to return to Court), Voltaire asked that the Comtesse be admitted and he soon "repaired by the graces of his mind that which he lacked in outward elegance." When this interview had been happily concluded and the mutual curiosity of these two famous figures satisfied, the Master himself conducted his guest to the door. By a curious chance the future Revolutionist, Jacques Pierre Brissot, close friend and associate of Mirabeau, happened to be on the stairs coming up as Madame du Barry came down. Brissot, a shy and unknown intellectual, had under his arm the manuscript of a work on criminal law which he hoped to show Voltaire. On the previous day he had tried to force his way into the great man's presence, but his courage had failed him. Once again he tried. He relates the story in his *Memoirs:*

"I had almost reached the antechamber where there seemed to be less commotion than on the previous afternoon when I heard a noise and the door opened. Assailed by my foolish timidity I hurriedly ran downstairs but, ashamed of myself, I retraced my steps. A woman, whom the Master had just shown out, was at the foot of the stairs. She was beautiful and had a kind face. I did not hesitate to address her and inquired if she thought it was possible for me to be introduced to Monsieur de Voltaire, telling her frankly of the purpose of my visit. 'Monsieur Voltaire has received scarcely anyone today,' she answered kindly. 'However it is a favor which I have just obtained myself, Monsieur, and I have no doubt that you will obtain it also.' Through my embarrassed air she seemed to guess at my shyness for now she returned to the Master of the house who had just closed the door upon her and I was admitted. She answered my deep salutations with a warm smile full of kindness which seemed to recommend me....

"This amiable woman whom I met at Voltaire's door was none other than Madame du Barry. In recalling to myself her smile so full of warmth and kindness I became more indulgent toward the former Favorite; but I leave to others," adds this Girondin, "the task of excusing the weakness and infamy of Louis XV."

Some time later Brissot happened to find himself in conversation with Mirabeau and Laclos on the subject of royal mistresses. No words were sufficiently strong for them to condemn Louis XV and his women. But Brissot, recalling his casual meeting with the woman whom he had met outside

Voltaire's antechamber, spoke up in defense of Madame du Barry.

"Some indulgence should be shown her," he declared. "She is vile, it is true, but a hunderd times less odious in my eyes than her predecessors with whom she had nothing in common but a favor which she never abused. . . ."

"You are quite right," answered Mirabeau. "She never handed out *lettres de cachet* to people who questioned her virtue. She was certainly no Vestal, but 'the Fault lies with the Gods who made her so fair.' "

Whereupon the three revolutionaries agreed that Madame du Barry's dishonor was the fault of her birth, her education and those who had prostituted and debased her. Laclos and Mirabeau later published a curious portrait of Madame du Barry under the name of *Elmire*: "In quitting her humble roof for the palace of a King, Elmire had taken an enormous step, but she did not find herself out of place there. She did not become swollen with pride. She did not even hurt those people whom she could have wished destroyed. Elmire, so much kinder than her predecessor, gave the lie to those scandalous biographies, those forged or made-up letters which were published as being hers. Elmire may be sure of the kinder judgment of posterity."

Toward the end of 1778, Madame du Barry suffered a heavy blow. The Vicomte Adolphe du Barry, the young man whom she looked upon almost as her own son, was killed in a duel at Bath. The details of the tragedy cannot have offered her much consolation. Although Adolphe's wife, Hélène de Tournon, had been only too complacent in accepting the Comtesse's favors, she never tired, now that such favors were no longer to be had, of reminding her husband of their ignoble source. Adolphe was very attached to his kind-hearted aunt and this subject was the source of continual friction between them. It must have been difficult, too, for this rather moody and sensitive gentleman to realize that all that he had ever had he owed to someone else. With nothing left for him to do (a noble of the *ancien régime* could not "work" in the modern sense), stripped of his former offices, Adolphe with his wife wandered aimlessly from one European gambling resort to another.

The summer of 1778 found them at Spa where they met a young Irishman, of the name Rice, whom they took with them to Bath, where the Vicomte rented the finest mansion in the Royal Crescent. Here they opened a private gaming room and seem to have been doing very well when a sudden and violent altercation flared up between the Vicomte and Rice. The reasons for this quarrel which ended in the death of Adolphe are not known. Possibly they lay in the attention which Rice was paying the Vicomtesse while her husband, who seems to have been an even more impassioned gambler than the usual Eighteenth Century gentleman, hung over the faro table living vicariously the life of excitement which had been denied him by Court disfavor. Whatever its source, the quarrel was bitter and ended in a challenge to a duel to the death.

Followed by the Vicomtesse the two men departed for a field outside Bath, where at dawn, each armed with two pistols, they engaged in mortal combat. Du Barry fired the first shot and struck Rice in the thigh. Rice did not fall. Raising both pistols, he aimed at his adversary's heart. A moment later du Barry fell to the ground and Rice, sword unsheathed, rushed in to dispatch him. The Vicomte asked for quarter which Rice granted, but it was too late. A few minutes later Madame du Barry's nephew lay dead on the alien English ground. The Vicomtesse, for whose honor Adolphe du Barry had probably died, left her husband's body lying on the ground, exposed to the view of the curious, for a full twenty-four hours before she went to the trouble of disposing of it.

A few weeks after du Barry's death she erased his arms from her carriages and appointments, and petitioned the King for the right legally to drop her husband's name. At the same time she requested that all his property be reassigned to the arms and jurisdiction of the County of Tournon. This insult to the young man's memory caused his father, the Roué, to bring suit against her. Eager as was the Vicomtesse to drop the name du Barry, she had no intention of relinquishing the property and emoluments that went with it. The Roué lost his suit and Hélène de Tournon, a short time later, was granted permission to return to Court. A few years later she married a relative, the Marquis de Claveyron. Even as the wife of another man she continued to collect interest on the dowry which Madame du Barry had generously settled on her at the time of her marriage to Adolphe du Barry. The former Vicomtesse du Barry died in 1785, but even this did not put an end to her claims against the Comtesse. Her second husband, Monsieur de Claveyron, demanded that, as his wife's heir, the interest continue to be paid to him.

For some years after the death of Louis XV, Madame du Barry seems to have formed no serious attachments of the heart. Whether this was due to prudence, to loyalty to the memory of her lover, or to the absence of acceptable candidates one can but surmise. In or about the year 1780, however, she formed a brief, obscure but storm-tossed and passionate liaison.

Not far from the Château de Louveciennes, and clearly visible from its terrace, lay the small neighboring Château de Prunay. In 1778 this property was purchased by an Englishman, Henry Seymour, a nephew of the seventh Duke of Somerset, who having married *en seconde noces* a lady of the Norman nobility, had come to live in France. At this time he was about fifty years of age, a stout, squire-ish individual who, with the two young daughters of his first marriage and the recently born son of his second, was living at Prunay the agreeable country life of an English gentleman. Between Madame du Barry and her sister-in-law at Louveciennes and the new tenant of Prunay a pleasant friendship was soon established. Neighborly visits were exchanged; over tea or supper, affairs of the neighborhood were discussed. Sometimes of an evening Seymour would remain at Louveciennes for a game of cards or Lotto.

Evidence of what occurred between Seymour and Madame du Barry comes to us by a slender thread. Only thirteen short letters, all of them written by the Comtesse to Henry Seymour, have been published and twenty survived the upheavals of revolution and war and the accidents of time to tell us the story of this obscure love affair. All are written hurriedly and without date (although they are generally marked with the day or the hour of the day), so that it is impossible to know either the year in which they were written or the length of time that they cover. Certain references in them fix the probable date at 1779 or 1780. Neither grammatical or even—in the romantic sense—passionate, these letters are intensely immediate. They speak not only in the voice of the long-vanished woman, but in the voice, too, of her time. One reads then with a guilty sense of intrusion that is softened by a compensating sense that, like the minuet or the snuffbox, they belong to another age. "What an unlooked-for tone in this correspondence!" comment the Goncourts. "How different a du Barry is revealed to you in the shadow, behind the popular du Barry of pamphlets and romances. This is no longer the courtesan, but a woman who loves." Whatever may have been her feeling toward Louis XV, these letters leave no doubt about those she entertained for Seymour.

The first (written on a "Saturday at six o'clock") is a friendly note to Seymour saying that she and Chon, who have apparently just returned from a trip, are both sorry to learn that his daughter is ill. Madame du Barry was fond of this child and had sent her a puppy. The relationship between the *châtelaine* of Louveciennes and the squire of Prunay is that of pleasant friendship.

"I am very distressed, Monsieur," she writes, "by the cause that robs me of the pleasure of seeing you at my house, and am sorry to learn of the illness from which your daughter suffers. I imagine that you are suffering as much as she and I can sympathize with your feelings. Take courage in the doctor's assurances. If my sympathy could comfort you, you would be less distressed.

"Mademoiselle du Barry [Chon] is as much concerned as myself and asks me to assure you of this on her behalf.

"Our journey went off very well. Cornichon does not forget you and talks of you constantly. I am delighted that the little dog has given your daughter a moment's distraction.

"Accept, Monsieur, my assurances of the sentiments I have for you."

The reference to Cornichon is of some interest since it helps to place a date on this letter. Cornichon was the daughter of Madame du Barry's gardener and was born in 1775. For her to be "talking constantly" of Monsieur Seymour she would have had to have been at least three or four years old. The reference incidentally hints at the comfortable relationship between the Comtesse and her tenantry. Little Cornichon was apparently a favorite at Louveciennes and seems to have had the run of the house.

The second letter hints at a growing tenderness. The Comtesse is apparently happy to find some reason to put herself in touch with Monsieur Seymour; the pretext here is the gift of a coin or plaque which Seymour had evidently admired one evening while playing Lotto at Louveciennes. Seymour seems to have sent a little dog to Louveciennes in exchange for the one given his daughter by the Comtesse. This letter is not dated:

"It has long been said that small kindnesses are the food of friendship and Monsieur Seymour must be aware of the solicitude felt at Louveciennes in regard to what might please or satisfy him. He appears greatly to desire a coin reprehensibly used for playing Lotto; it is of the time of Louis XIV. Monsieur Seymour is a great admirer of that age, so rich in marvels. Here is a miniature of it which the ladies of Louveciennes send him: they make him a present of it with great joy because they know he will appreciate it and will realize that the ladies will sometime find more serious ways of demonstrating their friendship for him.

"There is no news here except of the little dog who is well and drinks all by himself."

Between this letter and the next, Seymour and Madame du Barry have become lovers. The next is the letter of a woman in love, addressing her lover:

"I have a thousand things to tell you, a thousand things to communicate. . . . Never have I felt so much as at this moment how necessary you are to me. It would be a happiness to be with you always. Adieu, my friend. What an age there is between now and Saturday."

The letter that follows must have been written shortly after the above. It is dated "Friday at 10 o'clock" and refers again to the rendezvous on Saturday which she so impatiently awaits.

"The assurance of your tenderness, my true friend, is the happiness of my life. Believe that my heart finds these two days very long and if it were in my power to shorten them it would cease to suffer. I await you on Saturday with all the impatience of a soul that belongs entirely to you. I mean to be rid of all my ailments by Saturday and to feel only the joy of proving to you how dear you are to me. I hope that you will want for nothing more. Au revoir. I am yours."

And then:

"My heart is entirely yours and if I have failed to keep my promises, only my fingers are to be blamed. I have been very indisposed since you left me. I have the strength only to think of you. Au revoir, my loving friend. I love you—I tell you that once more—and I think myself happy. I kiss you a thousand times and am yours. Come early."

Veiled in the obscurity of the last sentence in the following letter we detect the figure of another man, a rival who has appeared to threaten this idyll. There has been a quarrel.

"You will have only one word from me, and if my heart could reproach you, it would be one of reproach. I am so tired from four long letters I have written that I have only strength enough left to say that I love you. Tomorrow I will tell you what has prevented me from giving you any news of myself, but believe me—whatever you may say—you will be the only friend of my heart. Au revoir. I have not the strength to write more."

"Mon Dieu! my sweet friend, how melancholy are the days

which follow those that I have had the pleasure of spending with you," she assures him in her next letter. "And with what joy I see the moment approach which will bring you to me."

But the rival's shadow looms larger in this love story. He has come from Paris to see the Comtesse in her place of retreat. A storm of jealousy and reproach begins to gather.

"I shall not go to Paris today," she writes, "because the person I was to go to see there came here on Tuesday just after you left. His visit greatly embarrassed me for I believe that you were the object of it. Au revoir, I await you with all the impatience of a heart that is entirely yours and which in spite of your injustice feels that it cannot belong to another. I think of you, and I tell you and repeat it and have no regret but that I am unable to tell you so at every moment."

But Seymour cannot forgive this visit. The air grows heavy with recrimination.

"I was as much surprised as yourself by the visit, my dear friend," she answers him. "I assure you that it gave me no pleasure. I am so absorbed with you that I could not be diverted by anything that was not you. How unjust and cruel you are! Why must you torment a heart which cannot and shall not belong to anybody but you? Adieu. Do not forget your friend who loves you. I lack the strength to tell you more. I would like to flee from you, but I cannot."

But the Comtesse, too, is jealous. Seymour is married; he has a family. She cannot happily share his love with others:

"I wish it were possible for you to live only for me, just as I would live only for you; but your ties cannot be broken. Every moment of my life, even those I pass with you, is embittered by this cruel fact."

Their love has blazed suddenly and burned quickly. Too much jealousy, too many quarrels have already dampened the flames. Is it possible that the rival (whose name is never mentioned, but whose identity can be surmised in the light of approaching events in Madame du Barry's story) has already stolen the Comtesse's heart from Seymour? The answer lies in the grave with the actors in this little drama. The following note can hardly have assuaged Seymour's fear:

"I am vexed at having an engagement today," she writes. "I do not go much into society, but since we cannot pass our lives together in a tête-à-tête you will understand that I need a few diversions."

Seymour answers with a bitter letter, one of several, full of recrimination. He wishes to bring the affair to an end.

With a cry of pain Madame du Barry realizes that she cannot live without him:

"Your letter has torn my soul apart. The idea of seeing you no more completes all my sufferings. Please, dear friend, strengthen my weak heart. Only your sweet friendship can heal the throbbing wound in my soul. Come back to me, dearest friend. I cannot be happy without you."

"I am so ill I believe it would be impossible for me to live without seeing you," she cries in the next note.

But at last, after such rackings of the soul, after such tears, headaches and inner consultations as can but be imagined, the *affaire* draws to an end. The last letter is Madame du Barry's farewell, the result, apparently, of considerable reflection. It was penned "at midnight, on Wednesday."

"I need not tell you of my tenderness and feeling. You know them. But what you do not know are my sufferings. You have not condescended to reassure me about what disturbs my peace of mind. Therefore, I believe that my peace of mind and my happiness touch you but little. I speak on this matter with regret, but for the last time. My head is clear, but my heart suffers. With courage and resolution I shall succeed in taming it. The task will be hard and sorrowful, but it is necessary. It is the last sacrifice that I have left to make. My heart had made all the others. My reason must now make this. Farewell! Be assured that you alone will fill my heart."

What, one wonders, was the mysterious matter about which Seymour had not condescended to reassure her, the matter that disturbed her peace of mind, of which she speaks for the last time and with regret? One can only speculate. Apart from these letters there exists no evidence of this passage in Madame du Barry's life. It seems to have been unknown even to Madame du Barry's close friends and contemporaries. No mention of it is made by the memoir writers of the time.

The letters made their appearance long after the Revolution. Understandably reluctant to destroy these souvenirs of a departed happiness, Seymour apparently kept them under lock and key in some desk or cabinet at Prunay where he continued to live quietly until the thunderclap of August 10, 1792, when with the storming of the Tuileries, the French Revolution began in earnest. Like most of his compatriots living in France on that day, he hurriedly made his way back to England, not pausing to pack more than his clothes. His property was placed under seal by the Republic and finally sequestered. In ransacking his desks someone apparently came upon Madame du Barry's love letters and kept them. Possibly they were submitted, as they should have been, to the police, and it was between the police office and the archives that they lost their way. They appeared for the first time at a Paris auction in 1837 where they were bought by a collector named François Barrière. Barrière handed them out in reluctant dribbles to the Comtesse's early biographers, the Goncourts and Vatel. He claimed that there were only eight of them and that he had shown them all. But in 1892 thirty more came up for auction, tied in a blue ribbon and accompanied by a lock of Madame du Barry's hair. Once again they vanished and they have not been seen since. If they have somehow survived the carnage of the Twentieth Century, they remain to be discovered. It is possible that they would shed a brighter light on this remote little drama, but it is not likely that they would much change the essential story.

Chapter 12

"BE ASSURED that you alone will fill my heart," Madame du Barry had written Seymour in her farewell letter. Scarcely had the words been penned when she entered into the longest, the finest, perhaps, indeed, her only *grande passion.* Her liaison with the Duc de Brissac (unquestionably Seymour's mysterious rival) seems to have begun in the early months of 1781, soon after the end of the Seymour affair. It lasted until Brissac's murder in 1792.

Louis-Hercule-Timoléon de Cossé, Duc de Brissac, was one of the greatest nobles in France and a man, moreover, of immense wealth. At this time (1781) he was forty-six years of age, "tall, blue-eyed, and blond." Madame du Barry had known him since 1770 when he appeared at Versailles as Captain of the Hundred Swiss and occupied there a suite of rooms adjacent to her own. In those days he had been known as the Duc de Cossé (he succeeded to Brissac in 1780 upon the death of the sixth duke, his father) and had been one of those who comprised the inner circle whom the Comtesse gathered about her in the evening to play cards and amuse the King. Cossé-Brissac remained loyal to her after her disgrace, writing letters to her at the Abbey and visiting her at Saint-Vrain. For nearly twelve years they had been friends. It is possible that, suddenly aware of her attachment with Seymour, Brissac realized with a stab of jealousy the nature of his own sentiments toward her. By the year 1783 their liaison was well known to the society of that day and, although Brissac was married, it was generally viewed with sympathy. "Her love for Monsieur de Brissac," commented a contemporary, "did Madame du Barry the greatest honour and it might have been the purification of her past life had it not been, from a moral point of view, doubly adulterous." Madame du Barry was given a suite of rooms at the Hôtel de Brissac in Paris, while the Duc, when he was able to do so (he was Governor of Paris at this time and a very busy man) made himself comfortably at home at Louveciennes.

Brissac was a man of great loyalty, indeed of great bravery —as subsequent events were so tragically to prove—and in many respects he must have recalled to the Comtesse's imagination the chevalier of a bygone age, the *chevalier sans peur et sans reproche*. Honorable, compassionate, and a great gentleman, he seems unfortunately to have been a little stupid. One cannot read his letters to Madame du Barry, letters full of amorphous idealism and vague political musings based on the optimistic assumption of man's inherent goodness, without realizing with a start what a world it was that separated the cold, skeptical mind of a Richelieu or a Maupeou from that of Brissac and his generation. The years that immediately preceded the Revolution in France brought with them the curious effect of a nebulous idealism that like some unseen but intoxicating gas made rational heads so giddy. While one part of the nobility nibbled in spite at the foundation of the structure that supported it, another part, with an almost passionate idealism, embraced the phantom promise of a New Order in which all men would be equal, each generously assisting the other toward his inherent perfection. The sheep themselves knocked down the fence that protected them from the wolves. The Duc de Brissac, idealist and dreamer, was one of the sheep. Very possibly it was exactly this quality which the Comtesse, who at the Court of Louis XV had had her fill of rational and witty men, found attractive in her lover.

In 1782 the Duc took her on a trip to his estates in Normandy. At Bayeux she met her youngest brother-in-law the former Elie du Barry, who now styled himself the Marquis d'Hargicourt. The Condé Regiment was garrisoned there and the Marquis Elie was in command. A sham battle was staged and afterward a magnificent ball was given by the officers in honor of the Mistress of the late King to which everyone in the neighborhood was invited: a rather audacious courtesy to Madame du Barry since she was still very much *persona non grata* at Court.

In 1783 she had a visit from a loyal but silent admirer out of the past. Her friend Belleval, the Lightguardsman on whose behest she had intervened for the deserter some fourteen years earlier, came to call on her at Louveciennes. "I had not met her for eight years," he records, "but her beauty seemed more remarkable and perfect than ever. I had only to mention my name and she exclaimed as she used to do: 'My Lightguardsman,' but instead of the happy peal of laughter of former days, the tears sprang to her eyes. She talked much of the past, in which I saw with pity she took as much refuge as possible for it was worth more to her than the present. I must have reminded her of what was gone and of all that had been lost. When I left she gave me her hand and said 'Adieu' to me in a voice full of feeling."

The tears of which Belleval speaks were perhaps for Adolphe whose good friend Belleval had been, for, despite the Lightguardsman's impression, Madame du Barry at this time had every reason to be happy. Brissac's devotion to her grew with every day. She had friends who were full of affection for her. Her pension of fifty thousand livres which had been given her by Louis XV was called in to be exchanged for a million and a quarter livres in outright capital, a sum of money that made her a very rich woman. Under Brissac's influence she seems to have come partly out of retirement, taking a box at the Opéra, attending the theatre with her lover, though always heavily veiled and in strict incognito. Brissac was one of the most distinguished collectors of art of his day. Together they would attend exhibitions and visit galleries. But for the fact that happiness made the years fly more swiftly by, imperceptibly carrying with them the beauty of the famous courtesan, her life was full of contentment.

With the passing of time, new friends, and for this reason, loyal friends (for she now had little more than her company to offer them) were made. Among these, curiously, were the Prince and Princesse de Beauvau, cousins of the Duc de Choiseul, who once had been the bitterest of her enemies. "How is the Comtesse's lumbago?" writes the Prince in a note to her. "Is she still bothered by the smell of the river? I don't like to think of her not enjoying the charms of Louveciennes which because of its situation, has so many. How happy Madame de Beauvau and myself would be to have the honor of seeing you here soon . . ." Madame de Beauvau and the Comtesse reminisced over the past. Madame du Barry spoke of the hatred which had been felt for her. "There was none at all," replied Madame de Beauvau. "All of us only wanted your place." A sentence in one of the Prince de Beauvau's letters suggested that all did not continue well between Madame du Barry and certain fair-weather friends. "It were better," he adds at the end of an invitation, "that you did not come this week, for Madame de Mirepoix will be with us then." The old Maréchale, at odds with the new Court, rarely left Paris these days, gambling away her nights and substance with the recklessness of one who has only money to lose, but who may have a few hours amusement to gain. Madame du Barry could be of no further benefit to her and no doubt from this view there had sprung a certain coolness between them.

Another friend was the Baron de Breteuil, Minister of the King's Household and a devoted friend of the Queen. "Might I dine with you today, Comtesse?" he writes with the assurance of one who knows he will be welcome. "It would give me such pleasure to spend the day with you. . . ." Gossip had it that when Marie Antoinette wished to buy the Château de Saint-Cloud from the Duc d'Orléans, Breteuil turned to Madame du Barry to bring indirect pressure upon Orléans to lower his excessive price on that château. Madame du Barry could twist Brissac about her finger while Brissac in his turn had considerable influence over Madame de Montesson, the morganatic wife of Orléans. Orléans finally did lower his price and Marie Antoinette did finally obtain Saint-Cloud, the last of her "follies."

The Queen's feelings toward Madame du Barry, slight as they would be about a woman who no longer played a part in her life, seem to have undergone a change. Herself the victim of increasingly atrocious libels, Marie Antoinette was learning in the cruel school of adversity to temper her once impulsive judgments with wisdom and sympathy. The Crown interceded to support the Comtesse against the Roué whose incessant demands on her charity had become a genuine annoyance to her. The Comte Jean had received permission to return to France, but prudently lived in Toulouse in a condition of ever-increasing debt and extravagance. The Comtesse had not seen him since the death of Louis XV and would never see him again, but his letters and demands rained down on her right up to the Revolution. "May God preserve you, dear Sister," he concludes one such letter with a leer. "I am told He has taken care of your freshness and of all your charming forms. I am delighted to hear that. You may profit again by a few sparks from my genius. They once lighted your way very well. They can do so again." Such reminders of the past from the incorrigible old rake in Toulouse can hardly have been agreeable to Madame du Barry. It was reassuring to know that she could rely on the sympathy and help of the Crown in this matter.

"If ever you should need a knight, Comtesse," writes the Marquis d'Armaillé, an acquaintance who had been a guest at Louveciennes, "I will gladly offer my services. Until yesterday I knew but a part of your admirable qualities. It is a great deal, Comtesse, to be amiable, beautiful and genuine. Yes, *genuine!* I need not tell you that I never leave Louveciennes without regret; but one cannot command his heart. One would like to spend his life there, Comtesse. To know you and to be devoted to you are synonymous. . . ."

Light and inconsequential though they are, such graceful little notes of invitation or of gratitude bring with them a vivid glimpse of the society to which they once had meaning. The exquisite blending of a formality that belonged to a courtly past (even Brissac addresses Madame du Barry in his love letters as "Comtesse" while she addresses him as "Monsieur le Duc") with the flowery, almost Romantic compliments so reminiscent of Rousseau's pastoral idylls, convey perfectly the spirit of the *ancien régime* in France as it approached its destruction.

Another of Madame du Barry' friends was an interesting Spaniard of the name Olavidez, Count of Pilos, a refugee of the Inquisition in Spain. At his large establishment in Madrid he had had the audacity to have the plays of Voltaire performed; he was known, too, to be an admirer of Rousseau. During an epidemic he had refused to permit the ringing of bells on his estates because he felt the noise would alarm his peasants. In consequence of this bold act he was arrested and dragged before the Inquisition. He was condemned to spend eight years in a monastery at La Mancha, there to practice austerities and to dress for the rest of his days in rough, yellow cloth, which would remind him of the sulphur and stake which he had so narrowly escaped. After three years of monastic seclusion, the unfortunate man managed to escape to France where in Paris (according to the chronicler Baron Grimm), "he soon made himself at home among our theatres, our philosophers, our Aspasias and sometimes even our Phrynes." Madame du Barry became a friend and admirer of this victim of the dreaded Inquisition. Olavidez happened to mention the name of the former courtesan to a group of friends and when they learned that he knew her, they begged him to arrange a dinner at which they might meet her. The Comtesse, when she learned of their desire, was very glad to oblige her friend Olavidez. One of the guests, the Comte de Cheverny, has left this interesting account of their meeting with her in 1786:

"We were all of us longing to meet the famous Madame du Barry. Nothing could be easier. She was at the service of Count Pilos for whom she had openly expressed her respect. We finally decided on a day and the Count took it upon himself to ask her if she would dine with him on this particular day. She lived in her charming house at Louveciennes that Louis XV had given her and Louis XVI had allowed her to keep. A small party of us betook ourselves to the house of Count Olavidez. It was cold enough to freeze stones. Madame du Barry arrived alone in a carriage drawn by six horses, and entered the room with easy dignity. She was tall, beautifully built and in every respect a beautiful woman. My wife was the only other woman present. All Madame du Barry's attentions were therefore directed to her and to the master of the house; but to everyone she was amiable and gracious. At the end of a quarter of an hour she was as much at ease with us as we were with her. Président de Salaberry and the Chevalier de Pontgibault were there with several others. She bore the burden of most of the conversation, talking much about Louveciennes of which we all knew that it was a wonderful place both on account of the good taste with which it is arranged and of its splendor and luxury. She invited us all to come and see it and to dine with her.

"Her pretty face was slightly flushed. She told us that she took a cold bath every day. She showed us that under her fur pelisse she was wearing only her chemise and a thin dressing gown. Everything she wears is of superb quality, the remains of her former splendor. I have never seen finer batiste. She insisted that we should all feel her petticoat to prove to us how little she feared the cold.

"The dinner was delightful. She told us a hundred stories about Versailles, all in her own style, and she was very interesting to listen to. She noticed that the Chevalier Pontgibault (a veteran of the American Revolution) wore the Order of Cincinnatus and she told us the following story: 'When I was at Versailles I had six footmen, the finest men that anywhere could be found, but they were the most troublesome rascals in the world. The ringleader finally realized that I should be obliged to dismiss him. It was at the beginning of the war in America and he came to me asking for a recommendation which I gave. A year ago he came to see me and what do you suppose he was wearing? The Order of Cincinnatus!' Everyone laughed at this story except the Chevalier de Pontgibault.

"After dinner the conversation took a more serious turn. She spoke of the Duc de Choiseul with charming frankness, expressing regret that she had not been on friendly terms with him. She told us of all the trouble she had taken to bring about a better understanding between them and it was her opinion that if it had not been for the Duchesse de Gramont, his sister, she might have succeeded. She complained of no one and said nothing spiteful."

During these recollections the Comte de Cheverny spoke up to say that during her terms of favor he had once made an unsuccessful attempt to obtain a Court post for some friend. "But why didn't you come to me!" cried Madame du

Barry. "I wanted to oblige everyone. What a pity it was that Monsieur de Choiseul never became my friend."

"She departed," concludes Cheverny, "as quickly as she had arrived, leaving us all with the impression that she had been very wise to return to an ordinary station in life with admirable good humor. We realize that she must have been a charming mistress and were no longer astonished to recall the part she had played in the life of a blasé man of sixty-five years. Her conversation in no way disillusioned us."

Brissac, patron of the arts, was naturally anxious to have a likeness made of Madame du Barry. Accordingly, in 1786 he commissioned Madame Vigée-Lebrun, then at the peak of her success (she had recently completed her most famous portrait of Marie Antoinette) to do a portrait of the Comtesse du Barry. During the years of 1786-1789 Madame Lebrun, as charming as she was gifted, did not one portrait but three of Madame du Barry. The last of these was interrupted by the outbreak of the French Revolution and was not finished until some years after the Comtesse's death. Of these portraits the first was perhaps the most successful. Madame du Barry, dressed in a filmy peignoir, stands with her face half-turned toward the viewer. Gone are the pompadour and the hoopskirt. Her hair now falls lightly about her shoulder in girlish, countrified curls while on her head, cocked at a jaunty angle, is perched a plumed hat of straw. Her slanting, mischievous eyes, her tiny mouth, half-open to reveal a line of pretty little teeth, convey most successfully a picture of the lady (who was then forty-three years old) as she must have appeared in the style of 1786. One is given the impression that she has just come in from or is about to depart on a country walk—not the insipid exercise it had been at Versailles, but a good brisk stroll. "She was growing stout," Madame Lebrun recalls of this first sitting with the Comtesse, "and her throat was a trifle thick, but she was very beautiful. Her face with its regular features and its sweetness of expression was still charming. Her hair was ash colored and fell in ringlets like that of a child; only her complexion had begun to spoil. . . ."

In the next few years Madame Lebrun was a frequent guest at Louveciennes. In her *Memoirs* she recalls with pleasure the many agreeable hours she had spent there. "Every day after dinner we would have our coffee in the pavilion that was so celebrated for the taste and magnificence of its decoration. The drawing room was an enchantment; it had the loveliest view imaginable and the chimney pieces and doors were most beautifully worked. The locks were masterpieces of goldsmith work while the richness and beauty of the furniture surpassed all description." When he was staying at Louveciennes, Brissac would repair with the ladies to the pavilion, but directly after coffee he would retire to the smaller salon where he would stretch out on a sofa and take a nap. But "nothing in his manner or that of Madame du Barry would have caused anyone to suppose that he was anything other than a good friend of the mistress of the château."

Madame Lebrun enjoyed the excitements of society and she found the life at Louveciennes a little too sleepy for her own taste. In the evening the two women would sit by the fire and talk. The artist, hopeful of hearing something interesting about the Court of Louis XV, was rather disappointed. Madame du Barry always referred to Louis XV with the greatest respect while she spoke very cautiously about his Court. Madame Lebrun, in fact, received the impression that Madame du Barry did not care to talk about the past and the subject was tactfully avoided. Like all who met her, Madame Vigée-Lebrun was struck by the Comtesse's kindness: "She showed herself to be as good in deed as she was in intention. She did a great many kindnesses in the neighborhood of Louveciennes where the poor could always count on her for help. Together we often visited the unfortunate of the neighborhood and to this day I can remember her anger when she visited a woman who had just given birth and who had nothing in the house. 'What!' she cried. 'You have neither linen nor soup nor wine?'

" 'Alas, nothing, Madame.'

"As soon as we had returned to the château Madame du Barry summoned her housekeeper and other servants who had not obeyed her orders. I can't describe to you the indignation she was in. She had them make up a parcel of linen on the spot and bring it at once to the poor woman, along with soup and Bordeaux wine."

The splendor of the château with its dazzling objects of art contrasted strangely with the simplicity of its owner's way of life. Madame Lebrun noted that in winter as in summer the Comtesse wore only white muslin or thin cambric peignoirs. Every day, no matter what the weather, she walked in the park or beyond it, thus keeping herself in excellent physical condition. Her old friend the Comte d'Espinchal confirms Madame Lebrun's picture of the Comtesse: "She had become a little stout," he recalled, "and her face was a bit pitted when I last saw her in 1789, but she was still wonderfully attractive. She owed her charm largely to the most scrupulous attention to cleanliness and to her habit of taking a daily cold bath, whatever the season or the weather."

Madame Lebrun happened to be at Louveciennes in 1788 when Madame du Barry was the recipient of a curious visit. The Sultan of Mysore, Tipoo-Sahib, had sent envoys to France to secure French support against the English in his principality. The Sultan appears to have been behind in his news for among the first people his envoys visited, obviously in the hope of enlisting the sympathy of this Sultana, was Madame du Barry. They brought with them rich gifts from the East which they laid at her feet. Madame du Barry and her guest were considerably amused by this episode. The Comtesse gave Madame Lebrun a bolt of "exquisite muslin whose golden colors were a marvel of subtlety" which had been among Tipoo-Sahib's gifts to her. When, with the storming of the Bastille, Madame Lebrun fled France in the following year, she took this souvenir of Louveciennes along with her. The precious material followed her in her wanderings through Italy, Spain and Russia. When, under the Consulate, she finally returned to France—a France she scarcely recognized so completely had the Old Order been swept away—she happened one evening to be invited to a reception for which she had no proper dress. After some reflection on this matter she suddenly remembered Madame du Barry's muslin. With a few adjustments from her resourceful hands she soon fashioned a brilliant, sari-like garment (thanks to Bonaparte's Egyptian campaign the "mysterious East" had become the rage) that was the sensation of the evening. Some of the effect no doubt owed itself to the story behind the cloth, evoking as it did a world immeasurably distant from the Consulate.

In 1812 Madame Vigée-Lebrun purchased a small country house near the village of Louveciennes. Curiosity prompted her to visit the château where she had bade farewell to Madame du Barry twenty-three years earlier. "I hastened to visit the villa which I had seen in all its loveliness in 1789. All the furniture was gone and every one of the decorations. Not only had all the statuary and busts been taken, but the very bronzes of the chimney pieces and the exquisite doorlocks that had been like goldsmith's work." All was desolation and decay. Madame Lebrun's mind must have filled with many recollections of Louveciennes as she had known it and of its warmhearted hostess whose body had long been moldering in an unmarked grave.

The uneventful years sped swiftly by and the fatal year 1789 opened without portent. Dividing her time between the Hôtel de Brissac in Paris and her château at Louveciennes, the Comtesse's life continued in its placid course. A few new friends appeared that year at Louveciennes, among them the Abbé Billiardi, the economist, who was introduced to her by the Abbé de la Roche-Fontenille, the nephew of her good friend and one-time jailer, the Abbess of Pont-aux-Dames. "Not certain that I shall find you home on Friday," the Abbé de la Roche-Fontenille had written, "I beg you to let me know if I might come visit you. The Abbé Billiardi, intimate friend of Monsieur de Choiseul and of Monsieur and Madame du Châtelet, has been pestering me for ages to be presented to you. If you care to meet him I should like to know on what day and at what hour it would be convenient for you to receive him. He is a most delightful man and is excellent company. . . ."

Billiardi soon became one of the most devoted friends of Madame du Barry and the Duc de Brissac. He was a man of liberal ideas and a friend of the controversial Minister of Finance, Necker. For hours Brissac and Billiardi and their little circle of friends, all civilized people of the world, all products of the oldest and most cultivated soil in Europe, would happily discuss the approaching dissolution of the feudal system and the Golden Age of freedom and equality that lay ahead. Fired by Brissac's idealistic enthusiasm, Madame du Barry took up the study of political science and of economics. In a country such as France the intellect is as much at the mercy of fashion as are hats and dresses. The provincial, the foreigner or the boor betrays his origins as much in conversation as in dress. Whereas in the seventeen-sixties chemistry had been the rage and fashionable ladies kept laboratories in their houses, chattering among themselves about such things as mercury and oxygen, in the seventeen-eighties political philosophy had become the vogue. Everybody talked of constitutions and contracts; of Rousseau and d'Alembert. All supported reform; few realized that France stood on the threshold of Revolution. Mankind being better educated (and consequently—such was the curious conclusion—more enlightened), the excesses of the past could not possibly be repeated. When, in 1788, Louis XVI made the momentous decision to convoke the States-General, a decision that gave the Third Estate, the "people", an opportunity to assemble as a national power, he was warned of the possible consequences by his wise friend and advisor, Malesherbes: "They will try to wrest from you by degrees many of your prerogatives," said Malesherbes, and then in an ominous comparison that was not lost on Louis XVI, who was one of the best read men of his time, Malesherbes reminded him of what had happened to Charles I in a similar situation. "But, of course," his advisor hastened to assure him in a classic of complacency, "the softer manners of today assure us against the violence of those far-off times."

Complacency, optimism and a conviction that he lived in the best of all possible worlds, at the best of all possible times, were the marks of an educated Frenchman in 1789. "We were proud of being Frenchmen," recalled one of them after the Revolution. "Still more were we proud of being Frenchmen in the Eighteenth Century. Without regard for the past, without disquiet for the future, we walked gayly on a carpet of flowers which concealed from us the abyss." It never occurred to Brissac, to Liancourt, to Clermont-Tonnerre and the dozens of noble-minded aristocrats who so gracefully and wittily discussed the philosophy of Equality, that the bourgeois banker or silk merchant and beneath him the energetic, anonymous soldiers of fortune, the provincial politicians, the men of shrewd wit and resource, all longed for equality too—so that they themselves might attain to power. The Revolutionist Cambacérès who, ordering Louis XVI to his execution, addressed him as "Louis Capet," not many years hence, as a Prince of the Empire, would be confidentially informing his friends that "in public you must address me as Your Highness although among ourselves Monseigneur will be quite sufficient." The murderer of Lyons, Fouché, whose boast it was that he had had two thousand men shot, the most savage enemy of wealth and privilege in France, would not many years later be the multi-millionaire Duc d'Otrante.

On May 4, 1789, at Versailles the antiquated machine, the fourteen-centuries-old French Monarchy creaked at last to a halt. Bereft of competent Ministers, abandoned by his Court, torn in all directions by selfish and conflicting counsel, the disheartened King—who, with a little more will power and at any other time in his country's history, might have become the most revered of his dynasty—had decided to place the insoluble problem of the national debt before the recommendations of the nation. Debt and debt alone inspired Louis' fatal decision to assemble the States-General. The most frugal of men personally, he was the helpless victim of a system of interlocking interests as dark, complicated and crooked as the streets of some medieval village. "Twenty-five million united egotists," wrote the Prussian Ambassador from France in 1788. "Vain of their union, despising all other nations. They end up in arms if the slightest attempt is made to destroy abuses or to remedy evil." From the ladies-in-waiting at Versailles, who since 1670 had had the privilege of selling the candles from the queen's apartments (replaced daily whether they had been lighted or not), down to the provincial police officers who were given their share of the tariff on local grain manipulations, everybody had an interest of his own to guard. All were eager for reform; none was willing to sacrifice for it.

France might well have staggered forward under its accumulating burden of debt—it was, so to speak, a fixed expense—had not Louis made the fatal error of supporting America in its War of Independence. In terms of money the cost to France of this folly is incalculable: it went into many millions of today's dollars. In order to maintain its armies after the war, the American Government persistently asked for and frequently received large loans of cash at a time when the French Treasury was already bled white by its initial support of the Americans. For this act of generosity, foolish as it was, France neither received nor hoped to receive anything in return. ("Your Sovereign apparently can afford to speak the language of Idealism," was Frederick the Great's dry comment on the matter to the French Ambassador in Berlin.) The unfortunate Louis XVI has been given little credit by the country indebted to him. Recently studied documents leave no doubt that the decision financially to support the American cause was the King's own and not that of his Ministers. It was a decision that looms large in the chain of events that brought Louis XVI's head to the scaffold.

Although no one can have foreseen its far-reaching consequences, the convocation of the States-General was the occasion of immense excitement throughout the kingdom. It is probable that Madame du Barry was among the thousand of sight-seers who poured into the town of Versailles to watch the historic procession of the Three Orders, as they marched to the Church of Saint-Louis. She would no doubt have observed the Royal Family with particular interest, as one by one, its members filed forward—the King, so conspicuously unregal for all the splendor of his robes, as awkward as he had been when she had known him as Dauphin. The crowd broke into spontaneous applause when the King passed. He had always been liked; almost to the end of his life Louis XVI occupied a place of affection in his subjects' hearts. It was the Queen, the proud foreigner, whom they hated. A stony silence broken only by an occasional hiss or insult greeted Marie Antoinette on whose heart lay a far heavier sorrow than the hatred of the Court or mob. Her eldest son, the eleven-year-old Dauphin, was dying. That he might see his mother and father pass in their robes of state he had been carried to a window. Only once in the grim parade did Marie Antoinette's face change expression. She looked up at the window from which her son was watching and smiled.

The cold silence which greeted the Queen was made more insulting and significant by the great wave of applause which greeted her implacable enemy, the Duc d'Orléans. Orléans' sympathies were already boastfully with the Third Estate. Insanely ambitious and vengeful, he had long been scheming the overthrow of the Bourbons in order that the Orléans branch might sit on the throne of France. The Comtesse's eyes would not have lingered long on the soberly dressed representatives of the Third Estate, already rent among themselves with squabbles and conflicting ambitions as intense as any among the representatives of the Court. No one would have distinguished among them a prim little lawyer from Arras of the name Robespierre whose lips prissed disapprovingly and on whose nose was perched a pair of green-tinted spectacles. But in a matter of weeks the Third Estate was to declare itself the National Assembly, an act that was followed by a wave of anarchy throughout the country: châteaux were burned, municipal records were destroyed and there was rioting in the cities. An air of tense expectancy settled over France. Paris was like some city that has felt the first warning tremor of an earthquake and uneasily awaits the second.

The "disturbances," as euphemistically they were called even in the bloody days of the Terror, did little to upset the day by day life of Madame du Barry and her friends. They continued to go to the theatre, they visited friends and received guests. A charming letter from Madame d'Angivillier, wife of the Director of Monuments at Versailles, gives us a little glimpse into that lady's concerns on the day of June 12, 1789: "How many thanks we send you, dear Comtesse, for your kind thoughts. This lovely weather reminds us how sweet it would be to stroll in your beautiful woods and how pleasant it would be to have you beside us. But we are upset *(contrariés)* by a previous engagement on Saturday which we cannot beg off of without offending the Deputies. If it is not inconvenient to you we will arrive Tuesday next at about three. Do let us know if this is convenient. We will then have the pleasure of rectifying our involuntary mistake and enjoy that perfection of art and nature which is to be found at Louveciennes. Convey our warm regards to the fair enchantress [Madame Lebrun] who has no need of her art to make her picture of you full of charm. Excuse all the spots of water on the paper. They will inform you that I am in my bath and that the desire to answer you as soon as possible kept me from waiting until I came out of this damp compartment where I spend my days."

During that same month Madame du Barry, unknown to herself, was observed by another of those sight-seers who often came to see the famous pavilion, probably hoping at the same time to catch a glimpse of its owner, "the most curious relic of the former reign." "This afternoon," noted the American Minister to France, Gouverneur Morris, in his journal, "we visit the pavilion of Madame du Barry. This temple is consecrated to the concupiscence of Louis XV. It is in fine taste and the finish is exquisite. The view most delightful and yet very extensive; in returning from thence we see Madame. She is long past the day of beauty and is accompanied by an old coxcomb, Flesselles, the Provost of Merchandise. They head their course toward the pavilion, perhaps to worship on those altars which the Sovereign raised. From the pavilion we ascend the hill and go between the house and fishpond, which stinks abominably, to watch the villagers dance." Gouverneur Morris, who appears to have been trespassing, was scarcely in a position to tighten his lips over the "concupiscence" of Louis XV for his own life in Paris at this time was something less than edifying. Neither Morris nor Madame du Barry could have imagined that in less than a month's time her companion, Flesselles, would be dead—his head carried through the streets on the end of a pike.

During the spring and early summer months of that year Madame Lebrun worked on her third portrait of Madame du Barry. Sitting in the gardens of Louveciennes the two women gazed toward the distant spires of the city whose streets were soon to run with blood. In July the far-off rumble of cannon fire became almost continual and Madame Lebrun, taking alarm, returned to Paris. The Bastille had been taken. Drunk with its sense of power, the populace marched about the streets carrying human heads and hearts at the end of pikes. Terrified, Vigée-Lebrun did not return to Louveciennes as she had planned. Disguising herself as a peasant, she left Paris as quickly as she was able. Only when she had crossed the Italian frontier did this sensible woman breathe a sigh of relief. In all directions a long line of humble carts and simple carriages bearing "peasant women" with delicate hands and "farmers" with plump, dainty little feet poured out of Paris in the direction of Switzerland or Italy. A week after the taking of the Bastille, Versailles was as empty as a great hotel toward the end of its season.

The French Revolution had begun.

Chapter 13

WHEN THE NEWS of the provincial insurrections reached him, Brissac—an exemplary landlord—departed immediately for his estates near Angers in Anjou. Scarcely had he arrived in the district than he was arrested on the pretext of "being under suspicion." The matter was quickly referred to the Government in Paris and Brissac was soon released, but the event grimly foreshadowed the terrible end that awaited him three years later. During the ensuing months the Duc remained at his estates. A few of his letters written to Madame du Barry at this time have survived and they make interesting reading. Brissac's overly optimistic estimate of human nature seems to have been undergoing trial:

"There are three or four people here at Angers who disturb the peace that otherwise would reign over this neighborhood," he writes. "The fact of their existence must be borne with patience for Liberty is far too precious a thing to be sacrificed for the sake of a little ease. Whether we shall be any better for it perhaps is doubtful. But happier we should certainly be. Equality, moderation and simplicity conduce to the growth of a tranquility that ought to promote humane and polished feeling. Yesterday my birthday was celebrated here with much noise and martial display. I felt that my fellow citizens put their heart into this demonstration. The feudal system has been destroyed, but this should not deprive us of respect and love. . . ."

A few weeks later, in a letter dated August 29 (1789), he writes her: "What a wise and philosophic letter, Comtesse, is yours of the twenty-second. Yes, it is necessary to speak of hope and philosophy and of patience when the States-General work so slowly on the important matters which all France awaits and which ought to calm her. They say that Paris is not at peace. . . . How I wish that I could share with you some of the wonderful fruit that the Angevin Ceres has given us this year, but it would be neither wise nor possible to try to send you anything at this time. Adieu, adieu, Comtesse. It is nearly noon and I am to dine at Brissac. My happiness is in hearing from you, is in the thought of you and in the everlasting affection which I have for you."

On the fifth of September of that year he writes her a letter that again suggests his disappointment in human nature and speaks of his discouragement. "Yes," he writes, "the future is as disheartening as the present. Of men who work for the good of the nation, of men who agree to arrangements that are to the advantage of all, how many have we? Very few, or else they are not heard or they do not speak or they do not exist. What melancholy feelings such thoughts inspire!" This gentleman of the Old Regime is more at home in matters of love, of art and of music than those of political philosophy. "By the way," he continues, brightening as he discusses the latest exhibition in Paris, "I hear that Vien's canvas 'Love Fleeing from Slavery' has been unfavorably criticized for being cold and correct, but unattractive. To some extent I agree with the critics, but the detail and finish of the picture as well as its coloring are good and will always ensure its having charm. No woman will apply to herself the insults offered the sex by Love or rather by the painter who, when you consider his age, has every right to be cold. I suppose that there were few portraits hanging except by Madame Lebrun who painted the one of the Duchesse d'Orléans [wife of the future Revolutionary]. But Madame Lebrun is made for the esteem and love of all and may appear in public at any time. Is the Salon beautiful this year?"

As the skies grew darker and the future more uncertain the man and his mistress drew closer, finding in each other's company the solace and assurance which love alone can bring. There is something touching about Brissac's next letter written from Paris in November after the Royal Family had been removed from Versailles to the Tuileries. With its down-to-earth reference to a cold in the head it seems closer to us than do many of the florid and more studied love letters of the later romantics: "I am going to bed, dear heart, so that tomorrow I may be less stopped-up than I am now and so be better company for you than I should be if I were as ill as I am now. This cold is a humor and the result of stagnating so long in Paris to which I am not accustomed. It will either end in killing me or driving me mad if my stay here doesn't come to an end. I hope that soon it may but will not speak of this for fear that premature rejoicing might defer it. Farewell, sweetest friend. I love you and kiss you a thousand times with all the tenderness of our hearts. I meant to say *my* heart, but will not cross out what my pen has written, for I like to think that our hearts are forever one. Adieu, until tomorrow. I will try to spit and sweat. . . .

Everything that happens seems to me to be mysterious and mad and the only wisdom is for us to be together. Adieu, beloved friend; adieu, dear heart. . . ."

The world they knew was crumbling fast about them. On October 5, 1789, a mob of "women" (a number of whom were observed to have suspiciously hairy arms and legs) marched from Paris to Versailles demanding bread. The fact that at that time there was more bread than usual in Paris and that, despite the Crown's orders that it be released, it was not distributed is but one of the many mysteries that cloak the machinations of the Revolutionary *agents-provocateurs*. Through that afternoon and evening the mob milled restlessly before the palace gates. Assured by Lafayette, Commander of the National Guard, that there was no danger, the Royal Family went to bed. During the small hours of October 6, a side entrance to the palace was quietly opened and the mob streamed in. Bearing pikes and axes it howled through the golden halls, screaming for the head of the Queen. Many people later claimed to have seen the Duc d'Orléans, disguised as a washerwoman, standing at the head of the Queen's Stairway pointing the way with wild gestures of his arms. The courageous Palace Guard stood bravely at their posts, but they were quickly cut down and hacked to bits; their heads were mounted on pikes and borne triumphantly forward. Thanks to the two sentinels who stood guard in front of her apartment the Queen was given the few minutes she needed to make her escape. She fled through a secret passage connecting her chambers with those of the King. Daybreak brought with it the decision by Louis XVI to comply with the demands of the mob and to move the Court from Versailles to the Tuileries in Paris.

In the courtyard below a sea of people howled its victory. They demanded to see their King and Queen. Together, Louis XVI and Marie Antoinette stepped onto the balcony overlooking the Cour de Marbre (the same balcony from which Louis XV had watched the funeral procession of Madame de Pompadour). The mob then demanded to see the Queen alone. With her two children at her side Marie Antoinette faced the turbulent sea of hatred below her. "Take away the children!" someone cried. "Stand alone!" The children were sent inside and for a long menacing moment the Queen stood on the balcony alone, a target for every assassin's gun. Not a sound was heard; mollified by this example of courage the fickle crowd suddenly burst into applause. As soon as he heard the applause, Lafayette, who had been standing safely inside, hurried out on the balcony and falling to his knees before the Queen, kissed her hand. Thus was enacted the Monarchy's last drama at Versailles. A few hours later the beautiful palace, theatre of so much vanity, was empty.

The events at Versailles were not without echo at nearby Louveciennes. Two of the wounded guard who managed to escape were advised by someone, perhaps Brissac, to take refuge with Madame du Barry at Louveciennes. Laffont d'Aussonne, an early biographer of Marie Antoinette, tells the following story in his book, *Mémoires de la Reine de France:* "The *gardes-du-corps* who escaped the massacre of October 6 dragged themselves from Versailles to Louveciennes and the Comtesse du Barry nursed them at her château as their families would have done. The Queen, informed in Paris of this generous conduct on the part of the Comtesse, charged certain nobles who were in her confidence to go to Louveciennes and carry thither her sincere thanks. Madame du Barry then wrote the following letter to the Queen:

> Madame: the young men who were wounded only regret that they did not die with their companions for a Princesse so completely and entirely worthy of such sacrifice as Your Majesty. What I can do here for these brave chevaliers is much less than they deserve. If I were here without servants and handmaidens I would wait upon your guards myself. I comfort them and honor their wounds when I reflect that but for their willingness to die and their wounds Your Majesty might no longer be alive.
>
> Louveciennes is at your disposal, Madame. Is it not to your favor and kindness that I owe it? Everything I possess I owe to the Royal Family. I have too good a heart and too much gratitude to forget that. The late King, by a sort of presentiment, made me accept a number of valuable presents before sending me from his person. I have already had the honor of offering you these treasures at the time of the Assembly of Notables. I offer it you again, Madame. You have so much expenditure to meet. . . . permit me, I beg you, to render back to Caesar the things that are Caesar's.
>
> Your Majesty's faithful subject and servant,
>
> COMTESSE DU BARRY

This is evidently not the exact wording of the letter sent by Madame du Barry to the Queen, but rather is a paraphrase of the original which has been lost. Marie Antoinette would certainly have conveyed to the Comtesse her thanks for this act of charity, in sheltering the two of the *gardes-du-corps* (their names were Barghon-Monteuil and Lubersac), and the Comtesse, in turn, would have certainly acknowledged the Queen's gratitude. D'Aussonne claimed to have had the wording of the original from one who had read it. The reference to the offer of her valuables made at the time of the Assembly of Notables (held in 1787, a feeble preview of the States-General) is interesting. Outside this letter no record of such an offer by Madame du Barry at that time exists. However, it is known that in November of 1789 she negotiated the sale of 133,000 livres worth of diamonds in Amsterdam, and again in 1793 transmitted to the Duc de Rohan and the Archbishop of Rouen sums amounting to more than two hundred thousand livres, transactions she would have cause bitterly to regret when she appeared before the Revolutionary Tribunal.

There can be no doubt that from the beginning of the Revolution she recklessly placed much of her fortune at the disposal of the Royalists and the *émigrés,* the expatriates so bitterly hated by the Revolution. Evidence of her many acts of generosity was for the most part carefully destroyed but such acts were well known to the nobility who were active in the Royalist cause. A cryptic note from her friend the Comte d'Espinchal, who was then in Turin with the King's brother, the Comte d'Artois, hints almost openly at some large sum donated by the Comtesse: "After eighteen months of absence and silence," he writes, "would you permit an expatriate to recall himself to your memory? Nothing has diminished my attachment, *but many things have greatly heightened my esteem.* It is enough for me to say that although I have not written, I have none the less had you very much in mind, having learned of certain actions of which all who know you realize *that you are well capable but which in these days are very admirable.* To spare your modesty I shall say no more. It should be sufficient for you to know that your grandchild [the Comte d'Artois] has been informed of your act, as have all who share his troubles whom I have followed here. . . ."

In his journal Espinchal wrote more explicitly: "I must speak of what Monsieur Prioreau [one of Artois' attachés just returned from France] has told us respecting the Comtesse du Barry. This lady, a recluse at Louveciennes, has from the beginning of the Revolution shown the most loyally Royalist sympathies. It is known that through the sale of certain valuables she has raised the sum of five hundred thousand livres which she has placed at the disposal of the King and Queen whenever they may have need of it. This should serve to make her better understood and cause people to judge less severely a person who has been cruelly calumnied."

For Madame du Barry the year 1790, critical for France, passed without event. Brissac, loyal to the King, remained with the Royal Family in Paris while Madame du Barry continued to live quietly at Louveciennes. Although Brissac was frequently and ominously a target for the hatred of the hysterical Revolutionary press, his mistress remained unnoticed. It is possible that she might have remained in the safety of her obscurity throughout the Revolution had there not occurred during the night of January 10, 1791, an event that inadvertently brought her name back before the public and which, in the end, was to bring her head beneath the guillotine.

On January tenth, the Duc de Brissac gave a large lunch at his house in Paris. After the reception the Duc urged his mistress to spend the night with him in Paris rather than to return to Louveciennes that evening as she had planned. This the Comtesse did, secure no doubt, in the knowledge that there was a guard on duty at the gates of her château and that she had instructed the gardener to sleep in the small antechamber leading to her bedroom where she kept her jewelry, should she not return to Louveciennes that night.

Early on the following morning a messenger arrived in great haste from Louveciennes to announce that during the night thieves had entered her bedroom and made off with almost all her jewelry, a vast treasure that represented a good part of her entire wealth. It was a bold and extraordinary robbery. The thieves had drugged the sentry, while the gardener, believing that all was secure as usual, had abandoned his post and gone home. Upon receipt of the news, Madame du Barry at once departed for Louveciennes and when she had reported the theft to the local authorities, she put herself in touch with her jeweler, Rouen, who immediately and most unwisely published a handbill of which he posted and distributed a great many copies throughout Paris. "TWO THOUSAND LOUIS REWARD!" read this indiscreet announcement, "And a recompense commensurate with the value of the articles. . . . During the night of January 10-11, 1791, there were stolen from the château of Madame du Barry at Louveciennes near Marly diamonds and jewelry as listed: a ring set with a white oblong diamond weighing about 35 grains; a green rosette box containing twenty-five rings of which one is set with a very large emerald, one is in onyx supporting a portrait of Louis XII whose hair is done in sardonyx, one is of Caesar in two colors surrounded by diamonds, one of Bacchus cut in cornelian, one of yellow sardonyx representing Louis XIV, one a large heart-shaped sapphire surrounded by diamonds; two very large diamond earrings; a rose-cut diamond clip surrounded by 258 small white diamonds the central stone of which weights almost 28 grains; a pair of shoe buckles set with 84 diamonds; a magnificent pair of diamond pendants valued at 120,000 livres; a double rope of large pearls with pendants composed of 200 pearls each weighing 4-5 grains, holding at the top a large white diamond weighing 26 grains and at the bottom a tassel of knotted pearls; a pair of pearl bracelets of six strands each, the clasp of these bracelets being an emerald on which is mounted the diamond-studded monogram of L. and D.B. A crucifix with sixteen diamonds; a pair of sleeve buttons consisting of an emerald, a sapphire, a yellow diamond and a ruby, the whole encircled by rose diamonds, weighing 36 to 40 grains; a small golden reliquary enameled in black and white, a box of rock crystal containing . . ."

On and on went the inventory. To print it in its entirety would take several pages. It was one of the most famous private collections of jewelry in Eighteenth Century Europe. The effect of such a sensational list of valuables on a city in the throes of revolution may be imagined. Instantly Madame du Barry became the target of a press ever eager to pounce on injustices, real or imagined. She was spoken of as "that women still proud of having been the ranking strumpet of the land." Her jewelry was compared to the treasure hoard of Golconda. Marat himself wrote an angry article on the affair.

From the start curious rumors and suspicions surrounded the story of this robbery, lending to it an air of mystery that continues to surround it today. It was said in Paris that the jewels had not been stolen at all, but rather had been removed and hidden so that Madame du Barry could claim that she was poverty-stricken. In the neighborhood of Louveciennes the impression was firm that there was something "fishy" about the whole affair, an impression that eventually fixed itself upon the notice of the Committee of Public Safety one of whose accusations against Madame du Barry at the time of her trial would be that her jewelry had been stolen "by arrangement." A month after the robbery the jewels turned up in England, headquarters of Royalist, counter-Revolutionary activity, thus providing this "notorious enemy of the people" with a good excuse and a valid passport to travel back and forth between France and England at a time when very few people could legitimately do so.

As it stood, such an accusation was ridiculous. There cannot be the slightest doubt that Madame du Barry was the victim of an audacious robbery. But in charging her with acting as an agent or as a courier between the Royalists in England and those in France, the Revolutionary Tribunal, for once, may have come close to the truth. Although little evidence exists either to support this charge or to refute it (evidence in those times meant death and it was carefully destroyed), certain letters and certain curious associations help nourish the suspicion that Madame du Barry might indeed have been playing some undercover rôle in her ensuing trips to and from England.

One of the most suggestive facts is the appearance in her life of a shadowy individual of the name Nathaniel Parker Forth, a private detective, an adventurer and a notorious spy. Forth was hired to recover her jewelry, but it is curious that this man, who was known to be in the pay of Prime Minister Pitt and who, indeed, was denounced as an *agent-provocateur* by the French Ambassador in London, should be the person to act as the Comtesse's detective. The mysterious activities in Revolutionary Paris of English agents, some hired by the French Royalists, some by the English Government, some by the French Jacobins, all willing to betray one party to another, is fit material indeed for the writer of historical fiction. Time has long since obliterated their footprints and their very names are for the most part obscured by the double or triple identities which they assumed. Through that dark and dangerous city, rife with plot and intrigue, they moved in pursuit of their various purposes, some of them, it is said, even attaining to positions of authority in the dreaded Committee of Public Safety. The most famous, and little enough is known about her, is the curious "Mrs. Atkyns" an Englishwoman who, dressed as a sailor, rescued many aristocrats who faced death under the Terror. More mysterious is the Nathaniel Parker Forth whose path now crossed that of Madame du Barry, and who was soon directing her every movement, placing himself at her disposal both in London and in Paris and who traveled with her back and forth between England and France in such a way that it is impossible to tell when he may have been acting for her or when pursuing his other business as secret agent for the British Government. "This mysterious jewel robbery gave her an opportunity to make frequent trips to London," pronounced another Englishman, George Greive, the man who was to bring Madame du Barry to the guillotine, "and the two Courts took advantage of her situation to pass information between themselves. Such craft and prescience are worthy of the school of that Machiavellian monster, Forth."

On February fifteenth, over a month after the theft, Madame du Barry was informed that her jewelry had been recovered in England. The culprits, three Germans, a Frenchman and an Englishman named Harris, made the mistake of trying to sell their loot, at one-sixth its value, to an honest jeweler, one Simon. His suspicions aroused, Simon alerted the British police and the thieves were apprehended. The Comtesse immediately departed for London. She was accompanied by the Chevalier d'Escourre (equerry to Brissac), by a lady's maid, two valets and her jeweler, Rouen. At Calais she was met by the ubiquitous Forth and crossed the Channel during the night of February 19. She took rooms at Grenier's Hotel in Jermyn Street, a center for many French *émigrés,* and here she stayed until March 1, going through the legal formalities of identifying and recovering her jewelry. During this first trip she seems to have remained in seclusion. Unknown to herself her movements were closely observed by an agent of the Revolutionary Government stationed in London, a man named Blache. Blache noted that Forth scarcely left her side and that she was frequently in the company of Madame de Calonne, wife of Louis XVI's one-time Finance Minister and the man who, with the Prince de Condé, now headed a kind of government-in-exile in London.

Safe in England, Belgium and Germany from the dangers that existed in France the *émigrés* with their threats and projects of violence were becoming an increasing embarrassment to the Royalists who remained in France beside the King and Queen. When warned, indeed when actually ordered, to act with more caution, the unofficial government of the *émigrés* had the answer that the King and Queen were being held under duress and that their orders could no longer be considered valid. Louis XVI had to cope not only with a revolution among his subjects in France but with an equally sinister revolt within his nobility. Liaison between the Court at Paris and those of his subjects in exile who had cast their lot with his brother, the Comte d'Artois, was a matter of exceeding importance to Louis XVI and if Madame du Barry were acting as an unofficial agent of the Royalists the messages she carried back and forth across the Channel would certainly have related to this delicate and dangerous matter. That is why her frequent association with Madame de Calonne was carefully noted by the spy Blache and filed away for future reference.

Madame du Barry identified her jewelry and on March first (still accompanied by Forth) set sail for France. The expenses of this trip to England were defrayed by the Duc de Brissac who reproached himself for being the inadvertent cause of the robbery. She remained at Louveciennes for a month, and on April fourth again departed for England to face a snarl of legal difficulties which had arisen to prevent her from reclaiming her jewelry. She arrived in London on the eighth. "The Comtesse du Barry arrived in London early yesterday morning," reported the *London Chronicle* on April 9. "She left Paris Monday morning at an early hour and embarked from Calais on Wednesday. Her passage was a very difficult one and she did not land at Dover till twelve o'clock in the evening. The Comtesse is returned to attend the Sessions and hopes to recover her diamonds which cost her near 2,000,000 livres."

On her second visit Madame du Barry arrived in London with a letter of credit from her Paris bankers, the Vandenyvers, on their London correspondent, Simmonds and Hankey. The Revolutionary court later became very interested indeed in the Comtesse's accounting of the large sums she withdrew from Simmonds and Hankey while in London on this and on subsequent trips. She seems to have been warmly welcomed in high circles of English society during this trip and through her old friend the Duke of Queensbury whom she had known in Paris some twenty-five years before when "doing the honors of his house" for Jean du Barry, she was introduced to the Prince of Wales. She remained in England until the middle of the following month, arriving back in Louveciennes on May 21. Two days later, during the night of May twenty-third, a courier arrived in hot haste to inform her that her presence was again urgently needed in London, and on the following day she departed on her third trip to England where she was to remain for three months.

During her third visit to London Madame du Barry rented a house in Margaret Street, near Oxford Circus, and did a great deal of entertaining. The gay and frivolous French aristocracy, incorrigible even in poverty and exile, gathered like butterflies about honey in the salon of Madame du Barry, squabbling wittily and venomously among themselves as though they were back again in the halls of Versailles. Among them she was able to renew many old friendships. Every day brought with it the arrival in London of some new noble whose title was great in the history of France. She moved freely in English circles as well. Horace Walpole met her at a reception at Queensbury House. "I had a good deal of frank conversation with her about Monsieur de Choiseul," he reported, "having been in Paris at the end of his reign and the beginning of hers and of which I knew so much through my intimacy with the Duchesse de Choiseul." Mrs. Hobart, the future Countess of Buckingham, gave a lunch to her at Sans-Souci. She made the acquaintance of Lord Hawkesbury who later placed his services at her disposal in the litigation of her case. She did "the sights," visiting the Tower (somber building for a Frenchman of those times to contemplate), dancing at Vauxhall and going to Ranelagh. She gave away large sums in charity and seems, too, to have gone on something of a shopping spree: she bought some books for her former enemy the Prince de Beauvau, a set of Shakespeare for herself and several large portraits in oil, one of the Prince of Wales and another of the Duchess of Rutland.

During this visit to England Madame du Barry sat to the English painter Cosway, who made the last likeness done of her, a fascinating picture of a fascinating woman which survives in an engraving done of it by the artist Condé. Her head, surmounted by curious, serpentine curls, is thrown back to expose an expanse of white throat about which hangs a necklace of pink pearls. Half-closed, as always, her eyes seem to be laughing at some inner reflection: a smile flickers about one corner of her mouth. In the words of the Goncourts: "One seems to see here the portrait of all the voluptuousness of the Eighteeenth Century: it is the picture of a Bacchante by Greuze." It is difficult to believe that this is the portrait of a woman forty-nine years old.

For all the pleasant distractions and the safety which England had to offer, Madame du Barry was constantly homesick for France and for Brissac: "I am miserable in being so far from home," she wrote her steward at Louveciennes. "Whatever people may say this country cannot compare with France as it was before the disturbances. I approve of Morin's plan to put my things in safety. But he should ask the Duc's advice and do so carefully so that no one may suspect. . . ." She goes on to ask for "orange-flower water and some of my pots of preserves that were put up last year, if there are any left."

In August the English court finally came to the decision that since the theft had not taken place on English soil, it would be necessary for the Comtesse to obtain the condemnation of the thieves from the French courts and an official declaration from the French authorities that the property was hers. Until such claim was produced her jewelry was placed under seal with the bank Ransom and Morland in London. She set sail for France soon after this decision and, on August 25, 1791, with Forth at her side, arrived back in Louveciennes where she was to remain for more than a year. Events full of terror and sorrow were at hand.

Chapter 14

MANY SINISTER and significant changes had taken place in France during Madame du Barry's three months' absence in England. On the night of June 20-21st, 1791, the King and Queen, their two children and the King's sister, the Princesse Élisabeth, managed to leave the Tuileries and, traveling as "the Baroness de Korff and family," make their way toward the frontier at Metz. At Varennes, painfully close to their destination and to safety, they were recognized and arrested. Whatever lingering pretense of sovereignty may until then have attached to the Crown, it vanished completely from the moment of the ignominious return of the Royal Family from Varennes. The King and Queen were virtually prisoners. The King's Bodyguard was disbanded and in its place was substituted a Constitutional Guard, all members of which were required to give "proofs of good citizenship." It was left to the King, however, to choose a commander and Louis immediately offered this dangerous and prominent post to the Duc de Brissac. Soldier and gentleman that he was, the Duc did not hesitate to accept this last honor that his King was able to bestow. But it was, and perhaps Brissac knew it, his death warrant.

In the face of fast-thickening clouds of trouble, Madame du Barry continued her customary way of life at Louveciennes. Her return from England brought many of the nobility remaining in France to her door, eager for news of friends or relatives who were abroad. She still maintained a large staff of servants and somewhat defiantly kept flying the banners of a dying way of life. A letter to her from Brissac, dated the third of October, 1791, evokes something of the spirit by which they lived. Its pettiness is not that of the mindless *émigrés,* frivolous in the face of disaster, but rather, with its reference to a scheduled dinner party, an anchor in the familiar to two souls in a storm-tossed sea. He writes from the Tuileries in Paris: "My little Dauphin has gone out. I am without my glasses so I shall write you only one thought which encompasses all: I love you and will do so all my life. I dine with you tomorrow and will bring Madame de Bainville, the Abbé Billiardi and Monsieur le Goust. We rode eight leagues today and the King killed three pheasants so that my breakfast turned out to be a good dinner. I love you, my dear, and kiss you with all my heart. I have just made a blot for which I beg your pardon. There is no news."

Almost from the moment of its institution the Constitutional Guard became suspect in the eyes of the Assembly. It was denounced for its Royalist propensities. A steady stream of complaints, both anonymous and signed, poured in on the Assembly and these were quickly taken up by the rabid press. The principal victim of these attacks was the Duc de Brissac. During the evening of May 30, 1792, the Assembly convoked in an emergency session and it was unanimously decided to disband the Guard. At the same time a warrant was issued ordering the arrest of its commander, Brissac, who was to be taken before the high court, then sitting at Orléans, and tried for treason. At one o'clock in the morning Gabriel, Duc de Choiseul, nephew and heir of Madame du Barry's old enemy, hastened to inform the King of this ominous news. "The King and Queen had retired," Gabriel de Choiseul wrote of the event. "They sent me to the apartment of the Duc de Brissac with the order to advise him to flee. He was in bed; I delivered their message to him. I told him that in a matter of two hours the decree of arrest would be put into effect and implored him to take advantage of the time remaining. His age and the conviction he had of his innocence argued against me. The only matter that now occupied his attention was to write a long letter to Madame du Barry which he dispatched to Louveciennes by his aide-de-camp, young Maussabré. His only thought, his only care was for Madame du Barry."

At six o'clock that morning Brissac was arrested and, under heavy guard (which was more to protect him from an enraged populace than to prevent him from making his escape), sent to the prison of the Minimes, eighty miles away at Orléans, there to await his trial. At Louveciennes that morning, Madame du Barry was awakened by the arrival of Maussabré who delivered the Duc's letter to her. The immediate hazards of the journey to Orléans filled her with more alarm than did the thought of the Duc's eventual trial. For two days she waited in despair for news of his safe arrival. At last, on June 3 Maussabré brought her a letter announcing that Brissac had arrived at Orléans "without the smallest incident." This announcement must have been a great relief to her, for up to this point in the Revolution a declared public enemy was far safer behind the walls of a prison than exposed to the rage of the madmen who roamed the streets of Paris like wolf packs.

News of the Duc's arrest soon reached his daughter, the Duchesse Pauline de Mortemart who had emigrated with her husband at the beginning of the Revolution and was taking the waters at Aix-la-Chapelle. She immediately dispatched a letter to Madame du Barry, the woman closest to her father. Pauline de Mortemart had always looked with approval on her father's mistress. Anxiety now drew the two women into a closer friendship.

"Will you recognize my handwriting, Madame?" she wrote to Madame du Barry. "It is three years since you saw it and at a sad moment. This is a sadder one still for your affection and mine. What I have suffered these last few days! His courage, his strength, his innocence—nothing can calm my mind. Monsieur de . . . [*the name is erased*] and myself wanted to set out the day before yesterday; but several powerful persons dissuaded us from doing so, pointing out that it would be dangerous for my husband and of no help to my father, adding my husband's being an *émigré* would only injure him. But could not I, Madame, be of some help to him? Could not I see him? Can it be a crime that a woman in delicate health should go abroad to take the waters and must my father suffer for this? I cannot believe so. If you think I could be of any service to him either at Paris or Orléans have the kindness to let me know and I will hurry home. Is there any way I might hear from him or communicate with him? Send me word, I implore you, and I will hasten to take advantage of it. Through a man who is perhaps unknown to you I learn you have gone to Orléans. Such a token as this of your attachment to one who is dear to me gives you an eternal claim on my gratitude. Accept, I beg of you, the assurance of the affection which I will have for you for life.

"Permit me to omit the usual compliments at the end of letter and give me the same mark of your friendship. I am sending this letter through a reliable person in Paris who I hope will be able to forward it to you without difficulty. Excuse this scribble."

Brissac was examined on June 15 and made no attempt to defend himself. He remained in prison through the months of June and July, still awaiting trial. In Paris the atmosphere daily grew more explosive, culminating on August 10 in the sack of the Tuileries and the downfall of the Monarchy. On August 13 the Royal Family was removed to the prison of the Temple Tower. To Brissac the news could only mean his own end and on that very day he wrote his last will. He appointed Pauline de Mortemart his residuary legatee. At the end of his will he added this note and codicil:

"I recommend to my daughter a person who is very dear to me and who may be placed in a situation of the greatest distress by the upheaval of the times. To Madame du Barry of Louveciennes I give and bequeath above and beyond what I owe her, a yearly income for life of 24,000 livres, free from all conditions; or again the use for life of my estate at La Rambaudière and La Graffinière in Poitou and all the furniture belonging to it; or yet again a lump sum of 300,000 livres payable in cash, whichever she may prefer. When she has accepted one of these three legacies mentioned the other two shall be considered void. I beg her to accept this small token of my gratitude, I being so much more her debtor in that I was the involuntary cause of the loss of her diamonds. If ever she succeeds in regaining them from England those which will be lost, added to the expenses incurred in various journeys which their recovery has rendered necessary, will amount to a total equivalent to the value of this legacy. I request my daughter to prevail upon her to accept it. My knowledge of my daughter's heart assures me that she will punctually disburse whatever sums she may be called upon to pay in order to fulfill my will. It is my wish that no other legacy be paid until this one has been discharged in full."

Soon after he had written his will, Brissac penned the following note to Madame du Barry (it is dated Saturday, August 11, at six in the evening): "I received this morning the dearest of letters and one which has made me happier than any I have received for a long while. I kiss you a thousand times. Yes, you will be my last thought. We are ignorant of all the details [of the storming of the Tuileries]. I groan and shudder. Ah! dear heart! Why can't I be alone with you in some desert! But I am only in Orléans where it is most unpleasant to be. I kiss you a thousand, thousand times. Farewell, dear heart! The city is very quiet at the moment."

If Orléans was quiet, Paris was not. Bands of "citizens" searched the city for aristocrats and such of the Swiss Guard as had escaped the massacre in the Tuileries. One of those who had been in the palace on August 10 and who had taken part in its defense was young Maussabré, Brissac's aide. Wounded, he made his way to Louveciennes where the Comtesse concealed him in a room of the pavilion. When a band of Jacobins forced their way into Louveciennes, Maussabré was discovered and dragged back to Paris where he was thrown into prison to await a terrible end.

Three weeks after the storming of the Tuileries it was falsely announced in the press that Madame du Barry had been arrested. The *Courrier Français* carried this article: "Madame du Barry has been arrested at Louveciennes and has been taken to Paris. It is known that the old heroine of the late Government was constantly sending emissaries to Orléans. Monsieur de Brissac's aide-de-camp was arrested at her house. It is thought that her frequent messages to Orléans had some other purpose than love which Madame du Barry must now forget. As the mistress of the Duc de Brissac she shared his wealth and his pleasures. Who can say that she did not share his anti-Revolutionary sentiments at the same time?"

Whatever pang of anxiety Madame du Barry may have felt on reading this sinister notice was probably drowned in the wave of horror that broke over Paris on the same day, September 2, in which it appeared. The September Massacres which began on September 2, 1792, and ended on September 7, may be placed high on the list of blood baths in which throughout history man has, from time to time, orgiastically immersed himself. The spark that in this case ignited the explosion was the Manifesto of the Duke of Brunswick who, on July 25, 1792, speaking as the head of an army raised by the sovereigns of Europe, uttered dire threats against the Revolution and all who participated in it. Too late had the sovereigns realized that the "disturbances" in France which they had been hopefully inciting represented as much a threat to their own crowns as they did to that of the unfortunate Louis XVI.

As the army of the Duke of Brunswick marched into France, having reached Verdun at the end of August, hysteria gripped the already tense city. A rumor that there was to be a general massacre of aristocrats and priests swept through Paris with the speed of wind. Armed with hatchets and knives a mob marched on the prison of the Abbaye where twenty-five priests were torn from their cells and butchered. Like sharks crazed by the sight of blood the mob roared on to the Carmelite convent where a hundred and fifty more priests were imprisoned. When these had been brutally dispatched, the horde of murderers returned to the Abbaye where there still remained many prisoners. A tribunal, presided over by a homicidal maniac of the name Maillard, was set up in the vestibule and the terror-stricken prisoners were dragged before it, thence, almost without exception, to be handed over to the "justice of the people." In the courtyard of the prison where "the people" awaited him a frightful scene greeted the eyes of the prisoner about to meet his own fate. Armed like butchers with meat cleavers and axes and spattered with the blood of earlier victims, the mob, mingling its howls of blood-lust with the screams of the dying, frenziedly hacked off the heads, the arms, the legs of those delivered to its mercy. Piles of corpses stacked about the floor were from time to time carted away to make room for more. Night and day, for six days the butchery continued throughout the prisons of Paris. In that time one thousand four hundred people lost their lives, among them Maussabré, Brissac's young aide-de-camp, who tried to escape his pursuers by crawling up a chimney in his cell. He struck his head against a grating to which he desperately clung while the prison guards shot at him from below. Even with one arm shattered by a bullet, Maussabré refused to fall. Damp straw was lit in the fireplace, filling the chimney with a suffocating blanket of smoke. At last the unfortunate man released his grip on life. He fell and was instantly set upon by the warders who stabbed him to death with their bayonets, stamping insanely on his body until it was smashed beyond recognition.

The most illustrious victim of the September Massacres was the Princesse de Lamballe, Marie Antoinette's "dearest heart," a timid but loyal soul who left the security of England to be by the side of the Royal Family in its hour of trouble. Madame de Lamballe was dragged from her cell before the tribunal where she refused to swear her hatred of the King and Queen. She was delivered to the mob. Her arms and legs were hacked from her body and shot through cannon. Her heart was roasted and eaten. Her head was put on a pike and escorted by a mob of women with streaming hair and men with blood-soaked arms through the streets of Paris to the prison of the Temple Tower to be shown to Marie Antoinette.

In the midst of these horrors, word reached Madame du Barry of the fact that Brissac and the other prisoners awaiting trial at Orléans were being moved to Paris. Such a move at such a time was tantamount to the sentence of death. Under the command of a notorious and bloodthirsty Jacobin named Fournier, an escort of one thousand eight hundred National Guard was dispatched to Orléans with orders from the National Assembly to take the prisoners to the safety of the Château de Saumur. Deliberately misunderstanding this order (as it was no doubt intended that he should), Fournier set out not for Saumur but for Paris. Shackled together like beasts, the fifty-three prisoners, stripped of their possessions, were thrown into ten carts lined with straw. Brissac, dressed in a blue uniform with gold buttons, was in the third cart, conspicuous because of his height and the calm dignity of his bearing. Along the road he was everywhere singled out for the attention of the roadside crowds who cried, "Give us Brissac!" and "Death to Brissac!"

On September 6, Madame du Barry received a letter from the Chevalier d'Escourre informing her that Brissac and his fellow prisoners were due to arrive at Versailles on the following day: "The Orléans prisoners will arrive tomorrow at Versailles. Two representatives of the Commune have been sent ahead to warn the National Guard that it has already broken the law in removing the prisoners to Paris and that it will be held responsible for anything that might befall the prisoners. It is to be hoped that they will arrive safe and sound and that by gaining time their lives will be saved. The Assembly is tired of so much bloodshed and proposes a general amnesty. Not a very great sacrifice since none of them is guilty....

"I am sick at heart. I shall only be easy when I know that the Duc has reached Versailles. If I cannot go there myself I shall send someone. You, too, should send someone but be very careful and avoid taking any steps that might be made public and be injurious to both of you."

As the ten carts and their escort approached Paris, the crowds that surrounded the cortege grew thicker and the cries of hatred louder and more menacing. The convoy reached the gates of Versailles at about one o'clock in the afternoon of the ninth, two days later than scheduled. Seized by the convulsion of blood-lust which had gripped Paris, the rabble of Versailles turned out in surging droves to greet the prisoners of Orléans. Their number was swelled by many of the butchers from Paris, who, still spattered with the blood of their earlier victims, hurried out to Versailles in search of more. The prisons of Paris had now been nearly emptied and the news that the fifty-three prisoners of Orléans were arriving at Versailles caused many of these madmen to sharpen their knives and hatchets. The name of Brissac and the fact that he was among the lot arriving in Versailles was well known to them. Brissac along with Lessart, a former Minister of Foreign Affairs, were the principal objects of the rabble's murderous hatred. Terrified by the ominous rumbling of this fast-gathering horde, the Commune of

Versailles sent orders that the prisoners were not to be conducted through the central part of the town, but rather were to be locked up for the night in the cages of the former zoo. "Feelings of hatred will be lessened by arousing those of contempt" was the logic that inspired this decision.

As the procession moved down the rue de l'Orangerie someone in the mob went ahead and locked the Orangerie Gate, so blocking the exit. The procession was obliged to turn around and make its way back up the now dangerously crowded rue de l'Orangerie. Brandishing knives and pikes, the crowd howled, "Give us Brissac at least!" The tumbrels pushed slowly forward, but suddenly at a point near the Fontaine des Quatre-Bornes, almost opposite to the former Hôtel de Brissac, the mob lurched forward, broke through the escort and fell upon the helpless prisoners.

Brissac, "with terrible wounds on his nose, mouth and forehead," bravely defended himself with a knife which he had snatched from one of the mob; but the force of numbers was too great for him and in a short while he was torn from the cart, dragged to the ground and there, along with forty-five others of the Orléans prisoners, brutally murdered. The madmen mutilated his body with homicidal fury, hacking off chunks of flesh which they passed among themselves and ate. His head was cut from his body and a label bearing his name pasted on the forehead. Carrying this gruesome trophy on the end of a pike and screaming obscenities, the crowd set out for Louveciennes where it was known that Madame du Barry was awaiting news of her lover.

The Comtesse had taken the advice of Brissac's loyal friend and equerry, the Chevalier d'Escourre, and had sent agents to Versailles. These men were supposed to keep her posted on the events of the day. Twilight was now falling at Louveciennes and still she had received no word. It was a warm, humid evening, and the windows of the château were open. Her anxiety was increasing by the minute when all at once the evening stillness was broken by the sound of shouting and the strains of the bloodthirsty song, the *"Ça Ira."* Terrified, she gave orders that the gates to the château be secured. The mob quickly broke through the gilded railing. Bearing the bloody head before it and shouting triumphantly, the ragged crowd made its way to the open windows of Madame du Barry's salon. The head was removed from the pike and tossed through a window. It rolled across the parqueted floor and came to rest almost at the feet of Madame du Barry. A moment later the unfortunate woman realized that it was a human head, and then—whose head it was. She fell to the floor, unconscious.

It was only some days later that she was able to write a letter. She wrote first to the Duchesse de Mortemart: "No one has felt more than I the great loss which you have just suffered. I hope you will understand the reason for my delay in mingling my own tears with yours. The fear of adding to your grief prevents me from speaking to you of it. Mine is complete. A life which ought to have been so splendid and glorious! My God, what an end!

"The last wish of your father was that I should love you as a sister. This wish is very close to my own heart. Never doubt the love which will attach me to you for the rest of my life."

Pauline de Mortemart answered her in a letter dated September 30, 1792. "Your letter reached me this morning. You have lessened my anguish and brought tears to my eyes. I have been meaning to write you and speak of my grief; my heart is torn and broken. I have been suffering ever since that day when my father was taken from Paris. I still suffer more than I am able to say, but I felt it wiser to wait until I could have a grip on some of my feelings. I must open my heart to you. Only you can understand my grief. I am eager to fulfill the last wish of him whom I shall mourn forever. I will indeed love you as a sister. The smallest of my father's wishes is a sacred command to me. Excuse this scrawl. My head is aching so that I can scarcely see. . . ."

Soon after she had written Pauline de Mortemart, Madame du Barry wrote to another friend: "I am in a state of suffering that you will easily understand. It is consummated, this ghastly crime that will leave me in eternal sorrow. In the midst of the horrors and outrages that surround me my health remains good. One does not die of grief. Your kindness touches me deeply. It would soften my grief if I did not feel it every minute." One does not die of grief . . . the sentiment belongs among the convictions of an expiring culture. In the approaching century it would be supposed that if one did not actually die of grief, one at least would like to. Such a notion would have appeared false to Madame du Barry and the heirs of French Rationalism, a generation who were more likely to die of gout and syphilis than of consumption and brain fever. A solid streak of coarse, common sense still bound the Eighteenth Century Frenchman to life and its ephemeral pleasures.

On October 14, scarcely more than a month after the murder of her lover, Madame du Barry set sail on the fourth and last of her trips to England. The ostensible motive of this trip was the recovery of her jewelry which was still being held under seal in London. Some months earlier a new difficulty had arisen over the matter of a reward. The English jeweler, Simon, who had caused the thieves to be apprehended demanded additional "recompense commensurate with the value of the articles" as promised in Rouen's sensational handbill, and had brought his claim into an English court. It was a matter that probably could have been settled for the Comtesse by her solicitors in England and did not, as she represented to the Convention in her application for a passport, "urgently require her presence in London." In any case it is not difficult to perceive other motives in this trip to England, the foremost of which was probably the opportunity it offered to talk with Brissac's daughter, the Duchesse de Mortemart, who was herself on her way to England. Surely, too, Madame du Barry would have been glad to put behind her the scene of so much recent horror.

Once again one is brought to face with the question: Was Madame du Barry an agent or courier for the Royalists? In this instance the mystery does not so much arise with her motives for going to England on this fourth trip, but rather in a consideration of those reasons which, five months later, caused her to leave the safety of England and return to Revolutionary France.

Nothing more evokes the atmosphere of those far-off Revolutionary times than the sense of mystery which one is given while attempting to trace, as did the police of the Revolution, the movements and motives of those who may have played some part in that upheaval. The yellowing letters with the names of certain people and places reduced to their initials or hurriedly erased, the cryptic diaries with their prudent, elliptical references, the memoirs so full of rumor or cautious reticence; all convey an atmosphere of fear and danger which is so strong as to be almost immediate. To pursue a particular contention or thesis through those thickets of obscurity is to chase shadows. It is enough that one should be left with this sense of mystery which allows that it is very possible that Madame du Barry may have been playing some rôle for some party in her trips back and forth from England.

The Comtesse this time obtained permission to leave France with the greatest difficulty. Her passport was dated September 21, 1792, the day of the formal abolition of the French Monarchy. She took care to procure a visa both from the administration of her Department as well as from the

Government office at Versailles. At the same time she left a written promise with the President of the Convention, Thuriot, to the effect that she would return to France immediately upon conclusion of her business in England. The passport, a precious article which every day was growing more rare, was valid for only six weeks. She set out for Calais in an ordinary diligence and was accompanied by the Duchesse de Brancas and her old friend the Duchesse d'Aiguillon, widow of the one-time Minister. Madame d'Aiguillon was without passport and traveled with Madame du Barry disguised as her lady's maid, an ill-advised piece of kindness on the part of the Comtesse which soon became known in London to the busy spies of the Revolutionary Government.

In London Madame du Barry and the Duchesse de Brancas rented a furnished house in Bruton Street, Berkeley Square. The Duchesse de Mortemart soon joined them and here, in the ensuing months, Madame du Barry put herself in close association with most of the distinguished *émigrés* living in England. The Princesse d'Henin, Monsieur de Breteuil, the Prince de Poix, Talleyrand, Narbonne and persons distinguished either by their rank or the part they had played in the fallen Government were among those observed by the Jacobin spies to have been entertained by or to have received the Comtesse du Barry. Poverty, in many cases even starvation, now stalked the steps of these once-pampered people. Duchesses and princesses were forced to beg their bread from strangers. The lot of the priests was especially tragic and it was with gratitude that the Archbishop of Rouen, Cardinal de la Rochefoucauld, accepted from Madame du Barry the princely gift of two hundred thousand livres for relief of the worst distress among them.

English society, whose doors were rudely closed to all but *émigrés* of the highest distinction, welcomed the Comtesse du Barry with warmth. Her friend the Duke of Queensbury took her to Windsor where she was presented to George III. She met Pitt the Younger, bitter enemy of the Revolution. One evening at a dinner party she found herself seated next to the young Duc de Choiseul. "I was placed next her at table," Gabriel de Choiseul recalled some years later. "During dinner she endeavored to be most amiable, speaking to me at some length about my uncle, deploring the counsels she had followed and giving me to understand that she had had a genuine affection for him, but that she always found him cold and reserved."

The Marquis de Bouillé, soldier and courtier, and one of the most distinguished of the *émigrés* in London at that time, has left a description of Madame du Barry in his readable and reputable memoirs. "During the time in London when I used to dine with the mistress of the Prince of Wales, I used to see much of a lady who herself had once been honored with royal favors. She had come to London to follow a lawsuit over the theft of her diamonds which had been occupying her for several years, and to flee the bloody scene where her lover the Duc de Brissac had some months earlier been murdered almost in front of her eyes, a scene to which she had the temerity and misfortune to return shortly after and where she herself suffered a fate no less cruel than his. She lived in London with the Duchesse de Mortemart, daughter of Monsieur de Brissac; *her fatal devotion to Madame de Mortemart's interests enticed her back to France.* [Author's italics.] Madame du Barry was then about forty-seven years old [she was in fact fifty]. Although the freshness and first bloom of her charms had long since vanished, enough remained for one easily to imagine how lovely they must once have been. She had blue eyes with an expression of the greatest sweetness, her hair was chestnut colored. Her elegant and noble figure, despite a tendency to *embonpoint,* had about it much suppleness and grace. Her clothing, especially that which she wore in the morning, could not conceal her still-voluptuous form. There was nothing at all common about her, still less was there anything vulgar. We were all of us deeply concerned over the situation of the King and Queen, and I was much surprised and touched to find that this lady whom they had treated so harshly upon their succession to the Throne could now think of little but their sufferings. The tears she shed for them were as sincere as they were constant."

Because she was in mourning for the Duc de Brissac, Madame du Barry's excursions into society on her fourth trip to England were for the most part limited to those which might in some way serve the cause to which she was wholeheartedly devoted. Agent she may or may not have been, but there is no doubt about the direction of her sympathies nor of the other complicities into which her loyalty to the Royalist cause led her. To cap the gift of two hundred thousand livres to the Archbishop of Rouen, the Comtesse in January, 1793, advanced an equal sum to the Duc de Rohan-Chabot. Rohan-Chabot was then in France, and the size of the "loan" coincident with the time at which it was given him suggest that it may have been put to use in the Royalist uprisings in the western provinces and the Vendée. Such at least was the interpretation placed on the matter by the Revolutionary

Tribunal who soon enough had evidence of this dangerous transaction in hand. The money was advanced to Rohan-Chabot through the Comtesse's bankers in Paris, the Vandenyvers, a fatal indiscretion which the Vandenyvers and Madame du Barry believed could be corrected by the explanation that the money had merely been a loan to Rohan-Chabot and a good investment for the Comtesse since, in exchange, she had been given a duly executed mortgage on certain of the Rohan properties in Brittany. This, at least, was the defense offered by Madame du Barry and the Vandenyvers at their trial.

The degree to which Madame du Barry was guilty of anti-Revolutionary activity through other loans and other gifts more successfully concealed from the prying eyes of the Committee of Public Safety can only be surmised. It is a curious fact that up to the year 1833 Madame du Barry's heirs (the Bécu family) continued a fruitless search for what they estimated to be a fortune in jewelry which the Comtesse had left in England. The respectable London banking house of Ransom and Morland with whom the jewels were presumably in deposit put them up for auction in 1795 in order to pay the expense of litigation and administration. Their sale realized nothing like the sum which this "treasure trove of Golconda" should have fetched and it becomes evident that between the time of deposit (1791) and the time of sale (1795) the jewelry of Madame du Barry, which contained some of the most valuable diamonds privately owned in Europe, had diminished to a value of less than $20,000. An act of embezzlement by the bank of Ransom and Morland is almost beyond the range of possibility.

A more satisfactory solution to the mystery is offered in a letter from the French Consul in England to the high court at Versailles which is dated July 24, 1829: "I answer your letter respecting the theft of Madame du Barry's diamonds. The heirs of this lady have been concerning themselves with this matter for some time, contending that the thieves were arrested in London where they were tried and that the jewelry had been sold and the proceeds from the sale had been deposited either with Ransom, the Bank of England or the Chancellery. I am very much surprised that their claim has no other basis than the alleged trial of the thieves in London and the sequester of her jewelry which was the consequence of this trial. A trial of this sort could not have taken place in England at that time (allowing that the theft had been committed in France) and the jurisdiction of English law was limited to crimes committed on the soil of Great

Britain. Therefore if there was no prosecution of the alleged thieves, there could have been neither sequester nor deposit of the diamonds. . . ." In other words, all the time that she was in England, Madame du Barry may have been quite free to sell or otherwise dispose of her jewelry. If such actually had been the case it provided her with an excellent screen behind which she might have given clandestine aid to her friends and explains very simply why it was that, after the Revolution, her heirs found the value of her estate in England so strangely diminished.

On January 21, 1793, Louis XVI, a man whose virtues were his ruin, mounted the scaffold and was executed. The news reached London in the evening of the following day and electrified the English capital. Plays were stopped in mid-performance, the audience in many cases rising spontaneously to its feet to sing "God Save the King" and afterward filing silently into the street. The French colony living in London was momentarily united by a common sense of shock and perhaps of guilt. In its disaffection at Court and disobedience abroad, the *émigré* nobility was almost as responsible for the death of Louis XVI as were the Jacobins in Paris. Court mourning was worn by all Frenchmen living in London and Requiem Masses were celebrated in all the Catholic embassies in London. Dressed in black, Madame du Barry attended the services held in the Spanish Embassy where she was duly observed by Jacobin spies and denounced in a report sent back to Paris.

On February 1, 1793, the war began that was to last for over twenty years and was to see the rise and fall of Napoleon Bonaparte. The French Ambassador at London was handed his passport by the British Government and Pitt formed the First Coalition against France, which was now convulsed with Revolution in Paris and counter-Revolution in the Vendée and many of the provinces. On February 27 the English court gave a verdict in favor of Simon for one thousand louis. Despite the sinister news from France, Madame du Barry was now determined to return home. Her motives for doing so can only remain mysterious. Certain of her biographers have explained this rash decision by the argument that she was ignorant of the dangers that awaited her in France. She of all people, who had seen the head of her lover on a pike, who had been in France during the September Massacres, would have been most aware of the murderous violence of the Revolutionary mobs. She knew very well indeed, and by experience, the dangers that lay in wait for her. Others have argued that the urge to protect her possessions at Louveciennes overcame prudence, a not-too-plausible explanation since she had always shown herself to be the least possessive of people and had indeed disbursed a sum of at least four hundred thousand livres while in England, a sum which, with that realized by the sale of her jewelry, might have supported her luxuriously in London throughout the Revolution. Homesickness probably explains her return, but another explanation is hinted at in the sentence in Bouillé's memoirs: "Her fatal devotion to Madame de Mortemart's interests enticed her back to France." It is known that a Madame de Mortemart, possibly the Duchesse but more probably her sister-in-law, was in France at that time, living in Calais under the name Mortimer. Did her presence there have any connection with Madame du Barry's return to France or with Bouillé's reference to "Madame de Mortemart's interests?" Like so much that has to do with these trips to and from England, the answer will probably never be known.

Whatever her reasons may have been for returning to France, they must have been compelling. If she herself had not known the dangers which lay ahead of her, her friends, both English and French would have hastened to explain them to her, imploring her to remain in England. In fact, Pitt himself is said to have urged her not to go back to France, where, he warned her, "she would meet the fate of Regulus." To these well-intentioned entreaties Madame du Barry turned a deaf ear. She set sail on March 1, 1793, and landed in Calais on the following day. Here she was obliged to stay for two weeks, waiting for a new passport that would permit her to cross the many barriers that now lay between the coast and Paris, and which, one by one, like the doors of a maze or a trap, closed behind her when she had passed them.

She reached Louveciennes on March 19 where she received a rude jolt. Her property had been placed under seal and she herself declared an outlaw. It was now that she learned for the first time of the existence of the sinister man whose energies were soon to be devoted to the single-minded purpose of bringing her head under the guillotine.

Chapter 15

SINCE THE BEGINNING of the Revolution the village of Louveciennes had remained, for the most part, a little island of peace and contentment in the turbulent waters of revolt which surged on all sides of it. Thanks possibly to the many tactful acts of charity of their kindhearted *châtelaine*, the citizens of Louveciennes had shown little enthusiasm for the excesses of Jacobin patriotism which convulsed others towns proximate to Versailles and Paris. They were content to leave well enough alone, and might indeed have happily slept through the entire Revolution had there not appeared among them, one day soon after Madame du Barry's departure for her last trip to England, an individual of the name George Greive.

This Greive was an agitator of English birth who called himself "a Revolutionary and anarchist of the first order, overthrower of despotism in both hemispheres and friend of Franklin and Marat"—one of those fanatics who are not in the least concerned with the larger vistas of political theory or with the improvement of man's lot, but who readily attach themselves to any cause or movement that promises violence, murder and destruction, and an unleashing on society of their own pent-up hatreds and resentments. Malformed psychically as he was physically, Greive by all accounts seems to have been a Revolutionary of the most mean-minded sort, one of those persons who bring discredit on any cause, Royalist or Revolutionary, Communist, Republican or Fascist, with which they ally themselves.

At Louveciennes his eye soon fell on the lovely château and its famous pavilion, hateful reminder of someone's enjoyment of a life from which circumstances had forever excluded him. Since such people as Greive are more concerned with the eradication of the rich than they are with the elimination of the poor, the sight of Madame du Barry's well-manicured property must have filled him with rage. He took lodgings in the village of Louveciennes and devoted his energies to the seizure of this arrogant property from its absent owner. Within a few months he had transformed the once-peaceful village into a hornets' nest of Jacobinism.

By bribes, by threats, by the shrewd use of psychology, he managed to enlist in his cause a good many of the townspeople and two of Madame du Barry's servants: Salanave, her cook, and Zamore, her Bengalese page on whom with ill-judgment she and the late King had lavished so many favors. The adder of resentment must long since have sunk its fangs into Zamore's inscrutable heart. It is as difficult for those of a certain psychology to accept kindness as it is for those of another to offer it. In the coming months Zamore proved himself to be the bitterest and most implacable of Madame du Barry's enemies. Through her disloyal servants, Greive was soon able to learn many of the secrets of Madame du Barry's household, bits of stray information which he distorted and twisted to fit his purpose. A Jacobin club was formed and meetings were audaciously held in the very salon of its intended victim.

Strutting through the rooms of the beautiful château, which mirrored all the refinements of French luxury, Greive seems to have conceived a homicidal lust for its absent owner whose portraits gazed down on him from every wall. Little else can explain the passion with which from this moment he mercilessly hounded the helpless woman to the steps of the guillotine.

During the Terror it was Greive's boast that he alone had caused sixteen people to lose their heads. It seems probable that he suffered some obscure psychosis of a Sadic nature. Many Terrorists of the same stripe (such as the loathsome Hébert and Chaumette) made a brief, bloody appearance during the French Revolution. Like the bacilli of disease which are latent in every body and which appear with virulence when the resistance of that body has been lowered, so does the social order apparently support its host of psychopaths and sadists, which remain more or less quiet in ordinary times but emerge in times of revolution or violence, committing with impunity crimes that are hidden under the cloak of "patriotism." Thus during the Terror it was not an unusual occurrence—it happened indeed at the execution of Jean du Barry, the Roué, in Toulouse—to have some screaming madman rush forward at the instant a head had tumbled into the wicker basket and, putting a cup in front of the bleeding stump, drink from it to the wild applause of the assembled mob. His almost-insane persecution of Madame du Barry suggests that Greive may have been a man of this order.

In his interesting book, *Vieilles maisons, vieux papiers,* G. Lenôtre suggests that more rational motives may be detected in Greive's persecution of Madame du Barry. It is Lenôtre's conjecture that Greive may possibly have been at Louveciennes on the night of January 10, 1791, when the jewel robbery occurred. Along with Blache, the Jacobin spy who dogged Madame du Barry's footsteps in London, and a third individual named Rotondo, a thief and convicted murderer, Greive, in the opinion of Lenôtre, may have planned and executed the theft of Madame du Barry's jewels. The men arrested in London were but the agents of this sinister trio who lived in fear that their complicity in the affair might be discovered. Greive's object became the destruction of all those who might hold some clue to this fact and his first target was naturally the Comtesse herself. Greive it was, in Monsieur Lenôtre's view, who spread the rumors that no robbery actually had occured, who attacked her in the newspapers with articles demanding her arrest, who with unremitting energy compiled a dossier which, when submitted to the Public Accuser, could not fail to destroy her. Lenôtre's theory is of interest, but it is based on evidence so slight or circumstantial that it merely succeeds in adding further mystery to the already obscure affair of the jewel robbery.

One fact, however, is certain. After Madame du Barry's arrest Greive took entire possession of the Château de Louveciennes and remained there alone for more than six months. His solitude was guarded by five men posted outside the walls and on the château gates a large sign was fixed which prohibited all entrance. Assisted by Zamore, Greive went to work digging up quantities of buried treasure: a bag filled with rubies, a solid gold dinner service, chests filled with coin and plate. All who remained loyal to the Comtesse or who might have known the true extent of her possessions were silenced by the guillotine: Morin, her steward, and his wife, her bankers the Vandenyvers, the Chevalier d'Escourre and his nephew Labondie. The once-peaceful village of Louveciennes was gripped by fear as, one by one, the local peasantry were brought before the new resident of the château and met with threats and warnings. Behind locked doors Greive gathered together the buried pieces of an incredible treasure. "What became of all this wealth," states Lenôtre, "is a mystery. It is said that Greive drew up inventory after inventory and bills announcing approaching sales were posted. But time passed and nothing was done. Nowhere can we find a reference either to regular confiscation or to an honestly conducted sale. The larger pieces of furniture remained at

Louveciennes and long after the Revolution fragments of this mighty wreck were to be found in the villagers' homes."

Whatever else he may have been, it would appear that this "friend of Franklin and Marat," this patriot who described himself as being "ever true to the dear principles of Equality," was incidentally a common thief.

So does it often seem to be with those who most aggressively talk of Patriotism and Democracy, who salute flags and who march in parades. While applauding the community patriot, a wise man will do well to keep an eye turned on the cash register when the patriot is near it. Many reasons have been given for the French Revolution, but not the least of them was the opportunity it offered dishonest people to steal with impunity. The genial Danton best expressed it when in an expansive moment he confided to a friend: "Well, the wheel has turned and it is our turn now to enjoy life. Delicate food, exquisite wine, women one dreams of, all this is the prize of our power! We are the strongest and now it all belongs to us."

Whatever may have been his motive Greive worked at Madame du Barry's destruction with wolfish ferocity. On February 16, 1793, a month before her return to Louveciennes, he succeeded in persuading the authorities of the Seine-et-Oise that she should be declared an *émigré* and her property placed under seal. On reaching home, Madame du Barry was greeted with the disagreeable news that she was no longer in possession of her château. She immediately dispatched a letter to the Director of the District of Versailles reminding him of the reason that had obliged her to leave France. "The Citizeness Du Barry is very astonished. . . . Before her departure she communicated to you the declaration that she had also made to her municipality. It is in your office. She hopes that you will be willing to remove the seals which have been put on her house. All France knows of the robbery which occurred on the night of January 10-11, 1792, that the thieves were apprehended in London and that a trial followed in which the final decision was not arrived at until February 28, 1793, as the enclosed certificate bears witness."

Her letter had the desired effect and the seals were soon removed. A considerable correspondence between Madame du Barry and the authorities of the Department of the Seine-et-Oise appears to have ensued over the various certificates and identity cards which are the symptom of a country at war or in chaos. During the course of her petition for a Certificate of Residence she made the acquaintance of a Revolutionist named Lavallery, vice-president of the Department of the Seine-et-Oise. The charms of the fifty-year-old courtesan had not entirely faded, nor had the principles of Equality and Fraternity driven from all men's hearts the regard which a civilized man has for an attractive woman. "I will attend to your request as soon as possible," Lavallery wrote her on May 17. "In view of the well-known motive for your absences there should be no great difficulty, particularly if you attach certified copies of your passports, certificates, etc. Your sex gives you the right to wish for peace while your kindness—well, a thousand pardons, Citizeness. A Republican and one who does not know you must limit his enthusiasm to the language of officialdom. . . ." In her approaching battle with Greive, Lavallery (whom some have said was in love with Madame du Barry) was to prove a valuable ally.

On losing his first skirmish, Greive sullenly retired to prepare for the next. He summoned to his side the spy Blache (who seems to have returned from London at about the same time as the Comtesse du Barry) and her two treacherous servants, Salanave and Zamore. Shortly after her return from England she had caught Salanave stealing some porcelains and dismissed him, but she was not yet aware of Zamore's treachery. In spite of the menaces which surrounded her, Madame du Barry continued to entertain her friends, most of whom bore the forbidden titles of Marquis, Baron, Prince or Comte. "A chain of aristocrats of both sexes exists along the banks of the Seine," wrote Greive in one of his denunciations, "holding hands from Mantes to Reuil." Many of these, the Princesse Lubomirska, the Prince and Princesse de Rohan-Rochefort, the Chevalier d'Escourre, the Abbés Billiardi and Fontenille, gathered at Louveciennes where they were entertained in the dignified and graceful style of the past. At Louveciennes they addressed one another by title and were addressed so by the servants. In their conversation they no doubt regretted the past as much as they deplored the present. All this was observed by Zamore and was duly reported to Greive.

Some time during these somber days Madame du Barry began her last liaison. The identity of the man who loved her cannot be established with certainty for he did not sign his name to the single letter which has survived to tell us of his love for her. That he was one of the Rohans is certain and it is the opinion of most people that he was the Duc de Rohan-Chabot, a man nearly thirty years younger than the Comtesse and the same to whom she had advanced the indiscreet "loan" while in London. The letter was found among the papers she did not succeed in destroying at the time of her arrest. It is dated September 7, 1793, and deals in its opening paragraph with the effects of the Duc de Brissac:

> Dear and affectionate friend: Here is the picture you wished for, sad present. In a situation such as ours, with so many subjects of pain and grief, we need food for our melancholy. I have sent for the three portraits of you which were at his house. They are here with me. The large one by Madame Lebrun is delicious and is a ravishing likeness. It is a speaking portrait and infinitely pleasing. . . . With regard to your large portrait and to the one which I am keeping, tell me, dear friend, if you wish me to send them to you or if I ought to have them taken back to where they came from. In short, what do you wish done with them?
>
> Come then, dear love, to spend a few days here. Give me a few moments of happiness for I have none but with you. Come to see him who loves you above and beyond all things and who will love you to the last moment of his life. I kiss a thousand times the loveliest of all women in the world, the woman whose sweet and noble heart deserves eternal fidelity.

Madame du Barry has been reproached for this, her last attachment, and because of it many have considered her faithless to the memory of Brissac. But she herself has best answered such criticism with the words she wrote directly after Brissac's death: "One does not die of grief." For her to live meant that she should love. All about her were swirling the forces of hatred and destruction. What could be more natural than that this child of nature, this woman of essentially sound emotion, should instinctively seek to right the balance of things through the oblivion of love, man's one triumphant assertion over the chaos which threatens to engulf him? "Everything that happens seems to me to be mysterious and mad," Brissac had once written her, "and the only wisdom is for us to be together." Such love affairs, many of them noble and passionate, were common in that dark night of a world's downfall. Under the very shadow of the guillotine many men and women found in each other's person a final confirmation of the joyous life principle and so triumphed over the contemptible malice of a Greive, the loathsome sadism of a Hébert, the cold and virginal primness of a Robespierre who planned his loveless, lifeless Utopia with the dryness of a professor of economics and the precision of an operating surgeon. At what date Madame du Barry's liaison with her last lover began and when it ended is not known, but it is probable that it started soon after her return from London in March, 1793, and no doubt ended only with her arrest in September of that year, a few weeks after this letter was penned.

In the early part of June, soon after the terrible decree of June 2, 1793, which permitted the authorities throughout the Republic of France to place under arrest all persons suspected of "a notorious lack of patriotism or aristocratic tendencies" (which, in other words, gave such authorities carte blanche to arrest whom they chose), Greive launched his second attack on Madame du Barry. Armed with an inflammatory address which had been signed by thirty-six of the villagers of Louveciennes who demanded the arrest of "many aristocrats" living among them, Greive marched to the officials of the Department of the Siene-et-Oise and insisted that the decree of June 2 be put into immediate effect. Accordingly he was ordered to submit a list of the "suspects" at Louveciennes which he proceeded to do, putting at the top of the list the name of Madame du Barry and beneath hers the names of the three servants who remained loyal to her. Triumphant, he immediately set out for the Château de Louveciennes with the intention of arresting her.

The Comtesse, in the meanwhile, had been warned of Greive's latest machinations and wasting no time had sent her steward, Morin, and her friend young Labondie, nephew of the Chevalier d'Escourre, to the headquarters of the administration to plead her cause and to seek the protection of her guardian angel Lavallery. The outcome of this mission was that when Greive gloatingly arrived at Louveciennes to make his arrest, he was met by several superior members of the administration and severely rebuked for abusing a law which was intended to apply only to "notorious" cases and to be applied only in times of emergency. Transported with rage at seeing his victim once more escape, Greive slunk back to his lair to plan the next attack.

On July 3, 1793, having denounced Lavallery to the Committee of General Security, Greive made an appearance before the Convention in Paris. He was accompanied by a band of the "*sans-culottes* of Louveciennes" in whose name he now spoke. He delivered a fiery denunciation of the woman whose head he was determined to see fall: "Despite her notoriously unpatriotic associations, she has managed by her wealth and her caresses to evade the spirit of the Declaration of the Rights of Man. It was she who was on the closest and most constant terms of intimacy with Forth, the notorious English spy. It was she who, intoxicated by her title of Comtesse, complacently received homage as such and defying all decrees gave those of Prince, Baron, Comte, and such like to the aristocrats who frequented her château. By her luxury she has insulted the sufferings of the unhappy people whose husbands, brothers, fathers and sons are shedding blood for the cause of Equality . . ." Greive's declamation was signed by some thirty "patriots of Louveciennes."

Thuriot, President of the Convention, answered Greive's attack with the ominous words: "The deeds you have been denouncing are grave indeed. Rest assured that if they are proved against her, her head will fall on the scaffold." Orders were issued for the house arrest of Madame du Barry and an investigation into her alleged lack of patriotism was immediately undertaken by the Department of the Seine-et-Oise. Alarmed by this news her friends Labondie, Rohan and d'Escourre rushed to her aid and brought to bear what influence they could upon the officials of the Department. One friend, the beautiful Princesse Lubomirska, was so rash as to send the Comtesse a note of sympathy expressing her indignation at Madame du Barry's arrest and nobly offered to join her at Louveciennes for its duration. In the confusion that followed her final arrest Madame du Barry unfortunately forgot to burn this letter. It was found by Greive and for this "crime" the Princesse Lubomirska was denounced and soon after guillotined.

More helpful than the efforts of well-intentioned friends was the sudden appearance of many brave and grateful people among the poor and nameless of Louveciennes. Nothing more eloquently attests to Madame du Barry's unforgotten deeds of kindness in her community than the fact that at this moment, in the face of great danger to themselves, fifty-nine citizens of Louveciennes drew up their own petition declaring that Madame du Barry had always been and still remained their benefactress: "We have seen her in every kind of weather come to the help of the sick and poor. Since the Revolution we have also seen her conform to every law, making financial contributions either obligatory or voluntary. She has even offered rooms in her house for the use of local meetings, a mark of patriotism that cannot be questioned." Their petition concluded with the statement that "our village had never known the disturbances which trouble the peace of respectable citizens until six months ago when certain persons arrived here, established themselves in our midst and began to disturb the harmony and good feeling which have always existed among us . . ." an obvious reference to Greive and his sinister colleague and informer, Blache.

Not only did these brave villagers volunteer their defense of Madame du Barry, but many of those who had signed Greive's angry petition now withdrew their original support of it, thus tacitly admitting that they had been coerced by bribes and threats into signing it in the first place. Provided with this good proof of the Comtesse's "patriotism," the gallant Lavallery was once more able to come to her rescue. The malignant Greive was again routed. On August 13 a decree was issued restoring Citizeness du Barry her liberty. Her first act was to request the liberation of her servants who had been arrested and taken to Paris; her request was granted.

Infuriated by this new frustration, Greive set to work preparing a pamphlet entitled: *Sham Equality or a Short Account of the Protection given to the Du Barry woman, former Mistress of the Tyrant Louis XV, with documents attached to serve as examples to those ardent patriots who would save the Republic and those Moderates who marvelously well understand how to ruin it.* The pamphlet was not only an attack on Madame du Barry (it concluded with a demand for the head of the "rose- and ivy-crowned Bacchante, the Courtesan of Louveciennes"), but was also an attack on those officials who thus far had been willing to defend her, the most prominent of whom was her admirer Lavallery. Zamore, the treacherous page, supplied Greive with many of the domestic details which were included in this denunciation. When she read it, Madame du Barry, with a shock, at last realized his duplicity. Zamore was dismissed on the spot and from that moment he openly joined Greive in his campaign and became the most dangerous of her enemies.

Alarmed by the persistence and intensity of Greive's attacks, Madame du Barry again solicited the protection of the Department of the Seine-et-Oise. Lavallery, very indiscreetly, came personally to Louveciennes to advise her to move to Versailles where she would be nearer the authority of the officials who could help her. His visit to Louveciennes was, of course, observed and duly reported. Probably because she had secreted large quantities of treasure about the grounds of her château—some of these hiding places would have been known to the wretched Zamore and the thieving Salanave—Madame du Barry decided to remain at Louveciennes and take her chances. But it is unlikely, as events were about to demonstrate, that a change of residence to Versailles might now have saved her.

In the early part of June there had occurred one of those political cataclysms on which depended the lives and destinies of so many obscure Frenchmen. The Girondins, the party of moderation, idealistic men for the most part, met the sanguinary party of the Jacobins in mortal debate and lost. Not only was the fate of the Girondins sealed (all who could be arrested were sent to the guillotine), but the fate of many thousands of people who knew little about factional disputes within the Convention and who only wished to live out their lives in peace was written in this event. The way was now paved for the Terror and the Reign of Robespierre. Among the many who, unknown to themselves, were doomed by the fall of the Girondin party, was Madame du Barry.

The first effects of this upheaval were felt in September when several moderate members of the Committee of General Security retired and were replaced by three bloodthirsty representatives of the Jacobin party, Amor, Vadier and Panis. Greive, elated by this turn of events, immediately presented himself before the new committee with a written demand for the arrest of Madame du Barry. The times were at last with him and on September 21, 1793, the Committee of General Safety endorsed a warrant for her arrest.

"The Committee decrees," read this document, "that the woman named Dubarry, residing at Louveciennes, shall be arrested and taken to the prison of Sainte-Pélagie and detained there as a person suspected of incivism and aristocratic leanings. Seals are to be placed on her effects and her papers are to be sequestered. Those which appear suspicious will be brought to the Committee of General Security. The Committee delegates the Citizen Greive to execute the decree and authorizes him to requisition such armed forces as may be needed. . . ."

On the twenty-second, accompanied by the Mayor of Louveciennes, two gendarmes and several municipal officers, Greive triumphantly entered the portals of the Château de Louveciennes and pre-emptorily ordered its mistress to enter a carriage and depart with him for Paris. It was a coincidence that on that very day and almost indeed at that very hour the civic authorities in far-off Toulouse entered the palatial Hôtel du Barry and arrested the *"ci-devant* Comte Jean du Barry," also on grounds of incivism.

Madame du Barry herself has left a brief description of the brutal manner in which Greive seized her person and property. Soon after the gates of the prison of Sainte-Pélagie closed behind her, she wrote a letter to the authorities of the Department of the Seine-et-Oise complaining of the treatment she had received at the hands of Greive, and defended once again her innocence which had already been twice established by the Department. The poor woman must either have been ignorant of the turn of political events throughout France or else have nourished in her bosom some faint hope that law, logic or charity still held a place in the hearts of all good Frenchmen. Unknown to her surely was the fact that on the day she wrote this letter the body of the gallant Lavallery was fished out of the Seine. A warrant for his arrest had been issued soon after the warrant for the arrest of Madame du Barry. Unable to face death on the scaffold, Lavallery had taken his own life.

In her letter to the Department Madame du Barry wrote that Greive "violated every form. He began by assaulting the person of the accused. *My pen refuses to describe the horrors and outrages which he perpetrated.* . . . He smashed doors and opened cabinets without evidencing his credentials. To such arbitrary acts, contrary to the spirit of the law, Citizen Greive added the cruelty of taking all her money from the accused and refusing her the right to take with her any of the linen of her house or the food of her larder."

At her trial it was brought out that the defendant, upon apprehending the purpose of Greive's visit, had hurried to her bedroom where frantically she began to destroy papers. Dogging her footsteps like a hound in pursuit of a frightened rabbit, Greive followed her to the bedroom where a scuffle ensued. Seizing her, he flung her onto the bed. Was it then that occurred those "horrors and outrages" to which she alluded and which her pen refused to describe? Or was it later when she and Greive made the long trip into Paris?

As she was being conducted from the château by Greive and the gendarmes, the Chevalier d'Escourre unsuspectingly turned his little *cabriolet à deux* up the drive. One look at the ill-assorted party leaving the château was enough to tell the sad story to d'Escourre and hastily he turned the cabriolet around and drove off in the opposite direction. But Greive's malign eye had already spotted this new victim and at his orders two gendarmes were sent in hot pursuit after him. The Chevalier was arrested at the foot of the Bougival hill, a short distance from the Château de Louveciennes. D'Escourre was ordered to relinquish his cabriolet and under guard he was taken to Paris in the carriage that originally had been intended for Madame du Barry. Greive took the reins of d'Escourre's little cabriolet and, unescorted and without guard, himself drove Madame du Barry into Paris. What occurred in these hours when Greive and his victim met face to face? Of what did they talk? Silence shrouds this meeting, but many writers have supposed that Greive offered her her life—on certain terms. Repelled by his proposition, Madame du Barry recoiled in disgust and so signed her death warrant.

Whatever actually took place between them, there is no doubt that after Madame du Barry's arrest and imprisonment, Greive's persecution of her became more implacably pitiless, more inexplicably malignant than before. His hatred of this helpless and gentle woman is so out of proportion to any "crime" she may have committed that once again one is left to find an explanation somewhere in the dark forces of lust and perversion.

Greive and his captive reached Paris and the prison of Sainte-Pélagie toward evening. At the time of Madame du Barry's imprisonment, Madame Roland (most famous of the fallen Girondins) was also in the prison of Sainte-Pélagie awaiting trial. Madame Roland has left this description of the place: "The women's part of the prison is divided into long and very narrow corridors on each side of which are tiny cells. Each cell is closed by an enormous lock which a turnkey opens each morning; the prisoners then gather in the corridors, on the staircases, in the little courtyard or in the dank and stinking commons room." The Comtesse's fellow prisoners in this antechamber to death were characteristic of the ill-assorted gatherings thrown together in Revolutionary prisons: duchesses and prostitutes, actresses and politicians: the Duchesse de Créquy-Montmorency and Madame Roland; Madame du Barry and Madame Brissot; the random debris of a sunken ship thrown together for a moment by the tide of fortune and a moment later violently dispersed. All of them were already ghosts, standing on the shoreline of the last limits of life, waiting their turn for Charon and his grim tumbrel to ferry them across the Styx.

Chapter 16

FEW PERSONS EVER LEFT the prisons of Jacobin Paris alive, for few eluded the deadly jaws of the Public Accuser, the horrible Fouquier-Tinville who in his brief term of office sent over three thousand people to the guillotine. Prim and austere in his private life and—like so many of the bloodier Terrorists—an exemplary husband and father, the terrible Fouquier, archetype of all public accusers who are employed by convulsed and ailing states, enjoyed to excess only one pleasure: sending his fellow humans to their death. Condemning them in lots of as many as sixty or seventy at a time, Fouquier would often hurry from the courtroom to the scene of their suffering where, concealed, he would watch his victims line up at the foot of the guillotine and one by one mount the blood-soaked scaffold to one side of which the bodies rose in stacks "like cordwood" and on the other side of which the heads were tossed helter-skelter into a large leather bag. Skidding on the blood of those who had gone before them, husbands followed wives, brothers followed sisters, mothers followed sons and daughters in a long, single line. Such was the man who presided over justice during the Reign of Terror and before whom Madame du Barry was doomed to plead her case.

Unaware of the extremity of her danger, the *ci-devant* Comtesse faced the future with the courage of one who believes herself innocent of crime and the equanimity of one who is of sound soul and body and cannot, therefore, realize the possibility of death. Madame Roland and the other wives of the fallen Girondins who were in prison with her failed to inspire her with their philosophic stoicism. The last dramatic gesture, the splendid, mournful posture so redolent of the dramas of ancient Rome, then in great popularity, held no charm for this creature attached by every fiber of her being to the delights of a—to her—warm and loving world. Just as those who by nature or accident have been thwarted of all love will grow bitter and pessimistic, seeing dangers and evils where they do not exist, so will those who have been able to love deeply and joyfully often be so optimistic as to be blind to dangers which are actual and evils which are immediate. Such persons are themselves so little capable of hatred and malice that often they are unable to perceive it in others. The day after her arrest Madame du Barry sent a little note to one of her maids, Henriette Roussel. "I am sending a line of news to my Henriette. I am fine. I have everything I need here and am sharing a room with a very nice person. Send me a cambric cap, the chemises with the small colored stripes and some kerchiefs. Give me news of home and those who remain there. Let me know if seals have been put everywhere and if the villagers have got up a petition to have me released."

Incredible to relate the villagers really had got up a petition in favor of their Comtesse. So alarming was this news to Greive that, as a move toward strengthening his case against his victim, he had her bankers, the Vandenyvers, arrested—a step that must have given even the optimistic Comtesse a considerable shock. In the meanwhile Greive had installed himself behind locked doors in the Château de Louveciennes where piece by relentless piece he fitted Madame du Barry's papers together to build a case against her. He flung himself into this work with a fervor that was almost passionate. Nothing escaped his all-seeing eye, nothing that could be fitted or twisted into the shape of his purpose escaped his malicious intelligence. These papers exist today, annotated in the tiny precise hand of Greive, evidence still of a hatred so malign as to be almost inexplicable. On a letter in which appears the name of Brissac's friend, the Abbé Billiardi, he wrote: "This Abbé Billiardi was one of her most frequent visitors after the Revolution, as was the Abbé de Fontenille, former vicar of Agen, who was guillotined a few days ago in Paris. Billiardi is dead. These Abbés were intimate friends and Billiardi was an anti-Revolutionist. Such are the friends of the Dubarry!" On a letter from Madame Vigée-Lebrun, written from Naples he wrote: "Letter from the Lebrun woman, painter and mistress of Calonne."

"He forces the letters to say what they do not say," observed the Goncourts, "he connects certain passages with events with which they have no connection. He imagines, he supposes, he lies, he tortures in order to extract from certain phrases or words material which will further his schemes and his hatred." Using the reports of Blache who had had the Comtesse under observation in London, using the word of witnesses who had been bribed or terrified, Greive accumulated and put into shape a dossier that was deadly. To this, as added evidence, he attached Madame du Barry's letters and papers with his annotations written on the margins. So thorough was his work that one-half of what it contained would have been enough to send Robespierre himself to the guillotine. So thorough was it indeed, that even today, for all its obvious distortions and specious logic, one is left after reading it with the conviction that Madame du Barry—to her honor—was unquestionably guilty of "anti-Revolutionary sentiments" and very probably guilty of actual conspiracy against the Revolution. Greive drew up his case in a neat and orderly style, first stating the accusation, then adjoining the proof. The final document reads, in part, as follows:

ACCUSATIONS AGAINST THE DUBARRY

1. She enjoyed great favor from the Crown of France even after her alleged disgrace, and she has been associated with those who are today our most dangerous enemies.

Proof: The letters of Villedeuil, de Durvey, Court banker, and others . . .

2. She has continued to associate with these people after the Revolution.

Proof: Her correspondence and intimacy with Brissac and his daughter the *ci-devant* Duchesse de Mortemart, a fact which her letters prove beyond doubt and to which Citizen Blache, an eye-witness, can testify. Her intimacy with the *ci-devant* Chevalier de Coigny whose commission with the Coalition on behalf of the tyrant has been established . . . with the Brunoy woman, *émigrée*, with the Brancas woman, *émigrée*, with the *ci-devant* Marquis de Nesle, *émigré*, with the Abbé de Fontenille, guillotined on the Place de la Revolution a month ago . . . with the Halevey woman, today called Calonne, with the Aiguillon woman and her son (Blache can prove this) . . . with Forth, the notorious English spy, who so skillfully put the real or alleged theft of her diamonds to good use in the plots hatched out between the Court of the Tuileries and London (take a look at her letters, her instructions from Brissac, the frequent trips between London and Paris taken by herself, her courier and her valet; examine Forth's letter the signature to which she tore off). Consider her friendship with Berthier the former *intendant* of Paris who took refuge at her house . . . with the former Chevalier d'Escourre, presently imprisoned at La Force, who was intermediary in the loans she gave to the Bishop of Rouen and to Rohan-Chabot (apart from the loans that the Dubarry made to the Bishop of Rouen, the books of the Vandenyvers indicate that she disbursed many other sums of a considerable size at this time). Consider her friendship with the *ci-devant* Princesse de Rohan-Rochefort . . . with the scoundrel Lavallery, the administrator of the Seine-et-Oise who recently committed suicide. . . .

3. She maintained a correspondence with the *émigrés*. . . .

Proof: Various letters found in her house . . . her correspondence with the Mortemart woman, the fact that she spent the night of Brissac's death burning letters (we have witnesses of this from Louveciennes). Consider among the documents in the attached envelope, a small note dated from Brussels which bears the ducal arms of the *ci-devant* Prince de Ligne . . .

4. She has given money to the counter-Revolution. . . .

Proof: The order on her banker (dated January, 1793) to pay within a week's notice the sum of 200,000 livres to the Bishop of Rouen. This draft was drawn in London at the time when Pitt was preparing war against us and, despite her alleged affection for France, she lived in the greatest intimacy with the Duke of Queensbury, Lord Hawkesbury, Lord Lonsborough the chancellor, and Lord Pembroke who today commands England's cavalry against us in the Netherlands.

5. She has always acted against the Revolution. . . .

6. In London, she wore mourning for the tyrant while frequenting the society of *émigrés* and the enemies of France.

7. She wasted the treasures of the State.

8. Whatever the truth behind it may have been, the mysterious theft of her jewelry offered her a pretext to make various trips to London from which circumstance it would appear that the two Courts benefited by passing information between themselves . . .

"What privilege then is it," concludes this document, "that permits the Dubarry to live thus, unpunished by the law?" To complete his dossier Greive added a list of twenty-seven persons who could be relied upon to act as witnesses against Madame du Barry. He then forwarded his material to Fouquier-Tinville, a tailor-made case that must have delighted that estimable gentleman as though it were a gift. To make absolutely certain that his prey should not escape and to prove his zeal to the Republican cause, Greive handed the Committee of Public Safety twenty-six of the letters he had found at Louveciennes.

During the early part of October the attention of France had been fixed on the approaching trial of its former Queen, Marie Antoinette, who in the Conciergerie was wearing the Crown of Sorrow with much more dignity than she had that of France. On October sixteenth she went to her death. In her cell at Sainte-Pélagie the news must have given Madame du Barry food for much recollection. The curve of destiny had brought the one-time enemies together again at the end of their lives. They had entered history within a year of one another; they were to die upon the same scaffold within a few months. Musing on the past, as surely she must have done, the gilded halls of Versailles and the sun-dappled lawns of Trianon must have seemed to Madame du Barry to be far away indeed in that autumn of 1793.

Scarcely had Marie Antoinette gone to the guillotine than one by one in a grim line the Girondins stepped up to their deaths. On November 8, lugubrious and Roman to the end, Madame Roland died ("O, Liberty, what crimes are committed in thy name," she is said to have reproached a statue of the goddess of Liberty placed beside the scaffold). The public's appetite was whetted. It demanded famous heads. The Public Accuser grew busier.

On October 30, the Committee of General Security sent two officials to Sainte-Pélagie to make a preliminary interrogation of Madame du Barry. The nature of the inquiry makes clear that they were not so much interested in establishing the guilt of the former Comtesse (she was already doomed), as they were in trapping her into an incrimination of other victims. The questions put to her had the double purpose of making her confess that she knew and wrote to certain aristocrats and of uncovering the addresses and other interesting particulars concerning these correspondents, thus collecting evidence which would incriminate them. Her interpreters had in hand the letters which Greive had given them.

"From whom is this letter which was written to you on the fifth of June?"

"It is from Madame de Mortemart who wrote me from Aix-la-Chapelle on that day."

"Who is this gentleman whose name is left blank on that letter?"

"The husband of Madame de Mortemart."

"Whose name has been erased on the back of the letter? Did you erase it?"

"I do not know whose name it was. I did not erase it."

"Who is the 'safe person' in Paris through whose hands the letter came and how did it reach you?"

"I do not know through whose hands the letter passed."

Skillfully the prisoner avoided implicating those of her correspondents and friends who were still in France or those who might be put in danger by an indiscreet answer from her. One of the cruelest of the many false stories about Madame du Barry which sensational or irresponsible historians have passed on to one another is that which claims that in a vain attempt to save her own life she recklessly denounced many of her friends. The historian Louis Blanc went so far as to place the number of these imagined victims of her cowardice at two hundred and forty! On the contrary every answer of this woman, who must have been both frightened and exhausted at the time of her interrogation, bespeaks a reticence and caution which is astonishing. Her Polish friend, the Princesse Lubomirska, might be called a "victim" were it not for the fact that Madame du Barry well knew that the Princesse's signature stood at the bottom of her indiscreet note, clearly attesting to the identity of the writer. It would have done the Princesse no good for the Comtesse to be caught in an obvious lie in her favor. She contented herself with evasions:

"Who is the person who wrote you this letter dated 'Sunday evening'?"

"A Polish princesse named Lubomirska who wrote to me, I believe, in August of this year."

"Has she been long in France? Where is she to be found now?"

"I don't know when she came to France. I have no idea where she now lives."

"Can you explain the meaning of her letter?"

"Since I did not write it," answered Madame du Barry with an irony that was no doubt lost on her inquisitors, "I can give you no explanation. Had I written it, no doubt I should be better able to explain its meaning."

The interrogation now turned to the matter of the jewel robbery.

"Was the list of the jewels which were stolen from you correct? Does it not contain a description of other jewels besides those stolen?"

"The description was perfectly correct with the exception of a chain of emeralds and diamonds which were stolen and which was brought to Monsieur de Brissac during my third visit to England. Monsieur de Brissac gave a hundred louis to the person who returned it."

"Did you ever entertain the idea of selling your diamonds and did you not take steps for that purpose and send them abroad? If so, when?"

"In 1789 or 1790. I applied to Vandenyver who sent part of them to Holland; but the price was not sufficiently high so I withdrew the jewels from Vandenyver who gave me a receipt canceling the one he had already given me."

The last question put to her referred to the shelter she had given her friend the Abbé de la Roche-Fontenille.

"Do you know an Abbé de la Roche?"

"I know an Abbé Fontenille who came many times to my house and frequently stayed there. I had given him a room there as a return for the kindness his aunt showed me when I was in exile at Pont-aux-Dames, but I have not seen him since early September and I do not know what has become of him."

This last statement no doubt gave her inquisitors a certain wry amusement for the Abbé de Fontenille had already been guillotined.

A few days after the interrogation of Madame du Barry, the senior Vandenyver was questioned at the prison of La Force. Despite an excess of prudence, the banker was unable to conceal certain movements of money. He admitted paying the sum of two hundred thousand livres to the Archbishop of Rouen (Madame du Barry had flatly denied any transaction), or at least to a "person who had called at the bank for the money." He could not state positively that this sum was intended for the Archbishop. The cautious scruples of a dry and elderly banker were of no interest to the Committee of General Security. It was enough for them that the sum of two hundred thousand livres was disbursed to a mysterious figure who apparently had been an intermediary for the Archbishop of Rouen. One more nail was hammered into Madame du Barry's coffin and on November 19, the Committee issued a decree ordering that "the woman Dubarry shall be transferred to the Revolutionary court, there to be prosecuted and judged by the Public Accuser." Preliminary to her trial she was once again subjected to a long interrogation, this time at the Palais de Justice before the brutal Dumas, vice-president of the Revolutionary court. In the shadows sat Fouquier-Tinville with a court clerk, taking notes and observing his victim.

The better part of this second interrogation dealt with the great days of Madame du Barry's past, with the time when she had been Mistress to Louis XV. A strong current of Puritanism ran beneath the surface of the Revolution. The men of the Jacobin party who had attained to positions of power were for the most part men of stern morals. In the cold Utopia which he planned, Robespierre (who was never known to have had a relation of any intimacy with a woman) was determined to see men's hearts more inflamed by a love of Liberty—a Liberty administered by himself—than by a love of women. Those who found it difficult to adjust to this new condition of things could expiate their weakness on the scaffold and thus contribute toward that "cleansing bath of blood" of which Robespierre, as he rose in power, so often spoke. Women in general he disliked; women of easy virtue or light heart he abhorred (it was only by a matter of a few days that one such, a languid Creole of the name Joséphine de Beauharnais, escaped the "National Razor").

In the eyes of the Jacobins her past alone was enough to condemn Madame du Barry. "Messalina of the people" . . . "dissipated Lais" . . . "instrument of a tyrant's debaucheries" . . . "Aspasia" . . . so was she later described to the courtroom by the Public Accuser. During the interrogation at the Palais de Justice Madame du Barry, with taste and dignity, made no attempt to excuse her past as she might, to her advantage, have done. Instead of referring to herself as an innocent child of the people seduced by the bribes and threats of a lecherous tyrant, she calmly admitted her guilt. On the other hand, when the questioning turned to the matter of conspiracy against the Revolution she firmly denied the charge, admitting nothing and denying all. Immediately after the interrogation, when she was returned to prison, she wrote a letter to Fouquier-Tinville, appealing to his "justice":

> Citizen Public Accuser: In the impartial examination of this unfortunate affair and of the charges that Greive and his colleagues have made against me, I hope that you will see that I am the victim of a plot to ruin me. I have never emigrated and I have never intended to. I

have never furnished money to the *émigrés* and I have never carried on any criminal correspondence with them. If circumstances compelled me to see either at London or in France certain courtiers or persons who perhaps were not in sympathy with the Revolution, I hope, Citizen Public Accuser, that in the justice and equity of your heart you will appreciate my conduct under such circumstances. . . . I rely on your justice and you can rely on the eternal gratitude of your fellow citizen.

(signed) VAUBERNIER DU BARRY.

The only effect this letter had on the Public Accuser was to make him hurry on his case against her. He took ten days to prepare his accusation. On December 4, Madame du Barry was transferred from Sainte-Pélagie to the grim prison of the Conciergerie, "the vestibule of the scaffold" over whose portals might have been written those words from the *Inferno:* "Abandon hope all ye who enter here." Few survived to describe their incarceration in the Conciergerie, but among those who claimed he did was Comte Beugnot whose sensational memoirs suggest that his imprisonment may have been as much a figment of his imagination as were certain of the events and scenes he so colorfully describes. Among other things he claims to have seen Madame Roland and Madame du Barry there together. He scornfully compares the Catoesque dignity of Madame Roland with the whimpering cowardice of the parvenu Comtesse. Unfortunately for his story, Madame Roland was guillotined on November 8, while Madame du Barry did not arrive at the Conciergerie until December 4. The two women did happen to be together briefly in the women's prison of Sainte-Pélagie where the Comte Beugnot could not possibly have seen them. Du Barry is not the only victim of his imagination. The book is full of interviews with people he never saw and of conversations he never heard.

Another anecdote, told by Dutens in his *Memoirs d'un voyageur qui se repose,* does Madame du Barry more credit. "Shortly before the Comtesse du Barry was guillotined," he relates, "an Irish priest found a means to enter her cell and to offer to save her if she could provide the money to bribe her jailers and pay the expenses of the trip. She asked him if it were possible to save two persons. He replied that his plan would only permit him to save one. 'In that case,' said Madame du Barry, 'I will give you an order on my banker for the necessary sum of money, but I would rather that you save the Duchesse de Mortemart than myself. She is hiding in an attic in Calais; here is an order on my banker. Fly to her help.' The priest begged her to allow him to rescue her from the prison, but on perceiving that she was resolved to save the Duchesse, took the order, obtained the money, went to Calais and brought the Duchesse out of her hiding place. Then, having disguised her as a woman of the people, he gave her his arm and traveled with her on foot, saying that he was a good constitutional priest and married to this woman; everyone cried, 'Bravo!' And they were permitted to pass. In this way he crossed the French lines at Ostend and embarked for England where I have since seen Madame de Mortemart."

It is a fact that a Madame de Mortemart (probably not the Duchesse, but her sister-in-law) was in Calais at this time. Madame du Barry had seen her there some seven months earlier upon her return from England. But it is difficult to believe that the Comtesse could have given the priest an order on her bankers since these bankers, the Vandenyvers, were in prison and like herself awaiting trial. Whatever help she may or may not have given to one of the family of her friend Pauline de Mortemart, during the long weeks of her imprisonment Madame du Barry's thoughts must often have gone to the daughter of the Duc de Brissac.

Transference to the Conciergerie meant an immediate trial; it was but a stopping-place between prison and the guillotine, convenient because it was adjacent to the Revolutionary court. Two days after her arrival there, on December 6 at nine o'clock in the morning, Madame du Barry and the three Vandenyvers, surrounded by gendarmes, were brought to trial. The courtroom was crowded with spectators eager to have a glimpse of this woman whose name already seemed to belong as much to legend as to history. Many of these curiosity-seekers must have been surprised to see a stout, matronly woman, kindly of face but disheveled and pale from an imprisonment of over two months and looking all of her fifty years, ushered before the Tribunal. It must have been difficult for them to believe that this woman was the "Messalina," the "Aspasia of the French Sardanapolis," the rose-crowned and giddy Madame du Barry to whom Fouquier-Tinville in scathing adjectives referred.

In her turn, Madame du Barry no doubt scanned the crowd for familiar faces. What must she have thought when she saw those who were to testify against her, to so many of whom she had offered nothing but kindness in the days when kindness had been hers to offer: Zamore whom she had raised as a child; Salanave to whom for twenty years she had been a thoughtful and generous employer; her maid, Henriette Couture, who blushed guiltily when called upon to give evidence? Among them, too, she saw many of the villagers of Louveciennes, women to whom she had brought soup and linen in time of need, and men she had so often helped by gifts of money and words of encouragement and kindness. Headed by the triumphant Greive they were now lined up against her: her accusers. Somewhere in the court she may have seen some person whom Rohan-Chabot, the last of her lovers, had sent to give her silent strength in the final hours of her life. Exhausted though she was by two long months of imprisonment, Madame du Barry behaved with perfect composure throughout her trial. After the jury had been sworn in, the President turned to the accused and asked them to state their names, ages, professions and their places of birth and residence. At the very portals of the tomb (a fact which even at this point she does not seem to have comprehended) the once-beautiful courtesan could not resist a final touch of coquetry. She subtracted eight years from the truth and blandly stated her age to be forty-two! The three Vandenyvers, Jean, Edmé and Antoine, gave their ages respectively as sixty-six, twenty-nine and thirty-two.

The indictment was then read and Fouquier-Tinville rose to make his attack. Opening with a highly spiced account of Madame du Barry's career at the Court of Louis XV, Fouquier went on to state that this "Aspasia" had remained the friend and protector of the former aristocracy (as an instance of this fact he pointed out the shelter she had offered the recently guillotined Abbé de la Roche-Fontenille) and indeed had become an agent of the *émigrés.* He declared that during the night of January 10-11, 1791, she had invented a robbery of her diamonds which gave her a pretext to journey back and forth to London in the company of one Forth, a notorious anti-Revolutionary and colleague of the "infamous Pitt, implacable enemy of the human race." He spoke of the large sums of money she had advanced to the Archbishop of Rouen and to the Duc de Rohan; of the company she had been seen to frequent in London: Calonne, Coigny, Narbonne, Mortemart and others. He referred to the fact that she had attended a memorial service held in London for the late "tyrant" and had been seen there wearing mourning for the monster. One by one he repeated the charges which had been put in his hand by Greive, though not in detail, for detail was not necessary to accomplish his purpose.

Turning briefly to the Vandenyvers, he accused them of having acted as agents in Madame du Barry's loans to the anti-Revolutionary cause and declared that at all times they had been "enemies of France." He then called his witnesses.

Greive, who was called first, gave evidence concerning the papers found at Louveciennes. He stated that a quantity of buried treasure had been unearthed on the grounds of Louveciennes among which were portraits of Louis XV, dressed as a Carmelite friar, of Anne of Austria, and a medal bearing the likeness of Pitt. He stated that it was "the general opinion of the village" that the robbery of her jewels had never actually occurred and that Madame du Barry had obtained passports to travel to London under false pretenses. The spy Blache gave testimony after Greive. He stated that in London he had observed the accused in the company of notorious *émigrés* and that he had seen her wearing mourning at a memorial service for "Louis Capet." One Xavier Audoin was next called. He informed the court that on August 10, 1792, while patrolling the environs of Louveciennes with a band of patriots, a rumor reached him that the Château de Louveciennes was filled with former noblemen of the Court. He immediately repaired thither where the mistress of the house offered him refreshments and assured him that there was no one concealed on the premises. Her manner appeared to him to be suspicious so he broke into a room which she told him was only a linen closet and found Maussabré concealed there, aide-de-camp to Brissac, whom he placed under arrest and removed to prison.

One by one her treacherous servants and neighbors gave their testimony. Zamore, "native of Bengal," stated that he had been brought up by the accused since the age of eleven, that since the Revolution her house had been continuously frequented by aristocrats who openly rejoiced over the checks which the armies of the Republic had suffered. He declared that he had frequently rebuked the accused on the folly and wickedness of her conduct, but that she had not deigned to reply. He went on to add that he had always regarded the robbery of her diamonds as "an idea" [*sic*] and did not believe that it was real. On hearing of his association with Greive and other patriots the accused had "informed him in an imperious tone of voice that she gave him three days to leave her house." Salanave declared that he had been dismissed from the accused's service because he was a patriot.

When asked if she had anything to say to this testimony, Madame du Barry coolly informed the court that the dismissal of Salanave had not been due to his political views but rather to the fact that he had been caught stealing her porcelain which "disappeared daily."

Henriette Couture, the Comtesse's chambermaid, declared that on the night of Brissac's arrest the accused had burned many papers. "Augustin Devrey, surgeon" stated that he had once heard the "Widow Collet" say that Madame du Barry had been seen burning papers on that night. Jean Thenot, schoolmaster at Louveciennes, formerly in the service of Madame du Barry, deposed that in 1789 he had once heard the accused declare that the people were "a pack of wretches and villains." The accused here interrupted the witness with some warmth.

"Where did you ever hear me make a remark such as that?" she demanded.

"I heard you make it one day when you were going to your melon house."

"The charge is absolutely false; it is an atrocious lie!"

Earlier in the day her old friend the Chevalier d'Escourre had been brought from the prison of La Force to testify in the matter of the loan to the Duc de Rohan-Chabot. Courageously he attempted to take the blame for this error upon himself, stating that he had recommended a mortgage on Rohan's estate as a good investment for Madame du Barry's money. The loan had been made to Rohan at an annual interest of one and one-half percent and was a business transaction and nothing more. Scarcely had d'Escourre finished his testimony than Fouquier-Tinville rose and demanded that he be immediately transferred to the Conciergerie and brought to trial as "an accomplice in criminal and counter-Revolutionary plots." Fouquier's request was granted and a few days later the unfortunate d'Escourre was guillotined.

The purpose of most of the "trials" held in the early days of Jacobin rule was not so much to condemn the accused as it was to trap a few innocent people into giving testimony for the defense. In the following year the State finally did away with the time-wasting formality of a trial, eliminating ali witnesses for either the defense or the prosecution. The accused merely stated their names, the accusation was read and sentence immediately pronounced. In this way the Public Accuser could condemn whole batches of people in a matter of minutes, emptying the prisons almost as fast as they were being filled.

The fate of d'Escourre terrified two other witnesses brave enough to volunteeer to appear in Madame du Barry's defense. When the court convened again on the following day, the seventh, both of these gentlemen were confined to their beds with severe illnesses and unable to appear, as they had earlier planned. No one but d'Escourre, therefore, gave evidence in Madame du Barry's defense. Her lawyer was Lafleurtrie who, supported by Chaveau-Lagarde, the brave advocate who had defended the Queen a few months earlier, now rose to give his case for the defense. Chaveau-Lagarde spoke for the Vandenyvers. When the defense had finished its feeble argument, Fouquier-Tinville stepped forward to reply. A few paragraphs of his lengthy speech convey an adequate sense of the whole. This weird concoction of political jargon, of hollow solemnity, of vitriolic generalities, all mixed together with pompous Roman overtones is typical of what in those times passed for "eloquence." To the reader of the mid-Twentieth Century, familiar with the prose of dictatorship, it has about it a curiously modern ring.

"Citizen jurors!" declaimed Fouquier. "You have recently pronounced judgment upon the treason of the wife of the last of the French tyrants. You are now about to judge the courtesan of his infamous predecessor. You see before you this Lais, scandalous for her dissipated life and her debauchery whom lewdness alone enabled to share the destinies of the despot who sacrificed the blood and treasure of the people to his shameful pleasure. You must decide whether this Messalina of the people . . . is guilty of conspiring against the liberty and sovereignty of the people, if, after being the accomplice of the debauchery of kings, she has become the agent of tyrants, nobles and priests who work against the Republic. . . .

"The evil which covered so many of her iniquities has been lifted—one may say that today it has been rent asunder—and nothing remains for these conspirators except disgrace and punishment. Yes, Frenchmen, we swear it: the traitors shall perish and Liberty alone survive! The vile conspiratress who stands before you today was able to live in the lap of luxury acquired by shameless debauchery in the midst of a country which seemed to have buried the remembrance of her prostitution and the scandal of her elevation. The Liberty of the people was a crime in her eyes. She required the people to be enslaved, to cringe before its masters. . . . This example, joined to many others, proves more and more that lewdness and evil morals are the greatest enemies of Liberty and the happiness of the people. In striking with the sword of the Law a Messalina guilty of conspiracy against her country you will not only avenge the Republic, but you will uproot a public scandal and strengthen the empire of Morality and Decency which is the chief foundation of the liberty of peoples."

At a quarter to ten in the evening the jury retired to consider its verdict. An hour and fifteen minutes later it returned and pronounced an affirmative answer to all counts of the indictment against Madame du Barry and the three Vandenyvers. A few minutes later, having reread the charges and confirmed the guilt, the court pronounced sentence and condemned "the aforementioned Jeanne Vaubernier, the woman Dubarry, the aforementioned J. B. Vandenyver, E. J. B. Vandenyver and A. Vandenyver to the penalty of death, ordering that this sentence be executed within twenty-four hours on the Place de la Révolution of this city."

When she heard these words—among the most terrible the human ear can hear—the unhappy woman rose from her chair and uttered a cry of despair. She was supported back to her cell on the arms of two gendarmes.

The executions were ordered to take place at eleven o'clock the following morning.

Chapter 17

LIKE SO MANY who had gone before her and so many more who were to follow, Madame du Barry, back in her cell at the Conciergerie, must have suffered a hundred times over the death that awaited her in the morning. Fastidious of person, ever clean and neatly dressed, the thought of decapitation must have gripped her imagination and filled her with horror. The body that now was warm to the touch and filled with sensation would in a few hours' time be tossed upon a carrion heap, a mutilated trunk from which still oozed the blood of life. Somewhere, perhaps into another pit, the head that had been adored by a King and painted by Drouais would be carelessly thrown. Alone in the cold final hours of her life, weakened by long imprisonment and anxiety, fear suddenly took complete possession of her soul.

Shortly before the executioner arrived at eight in the morning to cut her hair, tie her hands and prepare her for her execution, she informed the prison officials that she had important information to reveal to the Committee of General Security. Two representatives of that Committee were accordingly dispatched by Fouquier-Tinville to talk with her. She informed them that if they would give her her life she would reveal to them the various hiding-places of a considerable treasure which she had concealed about the grounds at Louveciennes. After what appeared to be a consultation with the Committee the officials returned with the promise that her life would be spared if she would give them this information. Wild with relief, clutching at life with the groping, desperate fingers of a drowning man who seizes some bit of flotsam or jetsam in an engulfing ocean, the deluded woman talked for three hours without interruption, listing with an extraordinary precision of memory a whole inventory of jewelry, plate and coin, and the place where each article had been concealed; a clerk copied down the words as they came from her mouth.

The minutes ticked away and each minute was a minute more of life. The fatal hour of eleven passed and she was still alive. The minutes became hours and at last she came to the end of her list. That she doubted the good faith of the Committee of General Security is proven in her concluding statement: she offered to write to London for the return of her jewelry which was impounded there as she "could without difficulty recover the property of which she had been robbed upon payment of the cost of the action." This would take time, many weeks, perhaps even months. It was her last straw. Supposing that her offer would at least be brought before the Committee, thus adding a day or two to her life, she probably affixed her signature to the bottom of the statement with a certain sense of relief. But whatever fresh hopes she may have entertained were soon rudely shattered. Scarcely was the ink dry on her signature when the executioner entered to cut her hair and bind her hands behind her back. She was informed that the tumbrel was already waiting for her at the prison gate.

To a natural dread of decapitation was now added the suspicion that a terrible mistake had been made. Obviously her final offer had not been brought before the Committee of General Security. Perhaps the Committee had not even been informed of what she fondly believed to be her bargain with them. The two officials and the clerk to whom she had divulged the hiding-place of her jewelry were apparently thieves who had extorted information from her by a promise that it had not been in their power to give. Death would soon seal her lips. The thieves could recover her jewelry at their leisure and no one would know the truth. She had been robbed not of her jewels but of her life! This suspicion as much as fear explains the unfortunate scene that now occurred. The fact that Madame du Barry behaved with cowardice before the guillotine has been remembered where so much else has long been interred with her bones. Her "undignified screams and futile struggles" never fail to be compared with relish to the icy disdain shown to the mob by the aristocracy.

The popular picture of a degenerate aristocracy expiating its crimes on the scaffold with dignity and courage was one dear to the heart of the Victorian historian and his middle-class English reader. It eliminated that most detestable of individuals, the arrogant, foreign aristocrat, but did so in such a way as reminded the working orders that "blood will out." The precepts of morality seemed for once to have conspired with the events of history. For the Nineteenth Century Frenchman the events of the Terror spelt a handsome increase in tourist revenue, an additional attraction in an already-rich history of violence on which the guides could so dramatically expound. The cell of Marie Antoinette at the Conciergerie was enlarged, redecorated, and embellished with an altar; the walls of the Conciergerie were whitewashed and its corridors restored. A stream of memoirs and tawdry historical writing gushed from the French presses. In France as in England all which did not conform to events as they ought to have been was either eliminated or distorted to fit the popular, sentimental picture. The blunt fact that of the thousands who went to the guillotine during the Revolution few were "aristocrats" (the wasps and trouble-makers among them had long since fled to the safety of Austria or England; only the more responsible and "liberal" of their kind, such as Brissac, remained in France) is in consequence not generally known.

Apart from politicians, the principal victims of the Terror were anonymous little wigmakers, chandlers or shopkeepers whose names survive only in the yellowing pages of contemporary news sheets where they appeared, usually misspelled, in the daily lists of the condemned. Their comportment before the guillotine seems by every record to have in no way differed from that of their social betters. Rich and poor, noble and wigmaker, all appear to have been so dazed by their sentence and the swift execution of it as to lapse into a trance-like condition of shock which in the case of a blue-blooded Noailles or a Tremouïlle might be interpreted as "icy disdain." "The mute heroism with which they met their fate was often but a semi-comatose condition induced by hopeless despair," writes R. B. Douglas, " a moral syncope which beneficently paralyzed all mental and bodily effects." There is no evidence that the upper classes were more heroic than the common people who perished with them.

Madame du Barry's final struggle for life did not, therefore, reveal her mean origins, they revealed instead a too-tenacious grip on life and the despair of one who a moment before had believed herself saved. The merciful drug of resignation did not have time to paralyze her senses. Neither emotionally nor physically did she go to the guillotine a dying woman. To the last moment she was alive and like a trapped animal every instinct caused her to struggle for life. Accounts of what occurred vary widely and for the most part are unreliable.

It was close to four in the afternoon when the gates of the Conciergerie swung open and Madame du Barry along with the three Vandenyvers and Jean Noël, a deputy from the Vosges condemned to death for his opposition to the Terrorists, were helped into a tumbrel by the executioner's assistant. Their hands were already tied behind their backs and they mounted the rough, wooden cart with difficulty.

The news that Madame du Barry was to be executed that morning had spread about Paris the night before. The delay caused by her prolonged "confession" had cheated many out of an anticipated diversion. The wintry dusk of a December evening was already falling when the tumbrel crossed over the bridge and turned into the rue Saint-Honoré. As usual a small crowd had gathered at the Conciergerie to watch the victims mount the tumbrel, among them, on this occasion, Greive, who that evening boasted to his acquaintances: "Never have I laughed so hard as I did today when I saw the grimaces that beauty made when she was facing death." The crowd that gathered at the gates of the Conciergerie, having seen the expressions on the victims' faces, would then usually hurry ahead of the tumbrel to be present at the place of execution.

The guillotine stood in the square that is today called the Place de la Concorde not far from the Obelisk. The present rue de Rivoli did not exist at that time so the route taken by the tumbrels was along the rue Saint-Honoré as far as the rue Royale where they turned into the Place de la Révolution. The Ministry of the Marine and the present Hôtel Crillon stood then, as they do now, on either side of the rue Royale where it enters the Place de la Concorde.

This roundabout route to the Place de la Concorde meant a long and agonizing trip to those who sat in the tumbrels. The cart often lurched on the rough cobbles and the wretched passengers were exposed to the curious stares and insults of those whom they passed on the rue Saint-Honoré. In the somewhat sensational biography of Madame du Barry written by the Goncourts much drama is made of her last trip down the rue Saint-Honoré, a street that, of course, was well known to this Parisienne. They speak of heartrending cries, of violent struggles, of a turning in the street where she looked up to see the girls of Maison Labille, the millinery shop where once she had worked, standing on a balcony to watch their most illustrious apprentice go to her death. The later detail is particularly cherished and has been recounted many times. Unfortunatelly, Labille's shop was not located on the rue Saint-Honoré, but on the rue Neuve-des-Petits-Champs. The story, like most of the Goncourts' juicy description of Madame du Barry's trip to the guillotine, is consequently apocryphal. Most contemporary accounts speak of her as "cowering" against the back of the cart and shuddering convulsively. Once or twice the elder Vandenyver appears to have turned and said something to her, presumably words exhorting her to the final, necessary strength.

When at last the cart turned into the rue Royale and she saw ahead of her, on a platform, the grim instrument that was to take away her life, courage failed her entirely. Half-fainting, half-struggling, the terrified woman had to be carried down from the cart and helped up the steps to the scaffold. Because of her almost-hysterical condition it was decided that she should be the first to be executed.

Despite the cold and gathering darkness a sizeable crowd had gathered about the scaffold, among them no doubt Greive, Zamore and Salanave. In the terror of her last minutes she probably did not see them. If she saw anything it would have been the gardens of the Tuileries or perhaps the dim outlines of the Louvre, visible above the bare trees of the park. When the executioner and his assistant seized her in order that she might be bound to the fatal plank she was heard to cry out (the words were heard by several independent witnesses and they have about them a terrible ring of authenticity): *"Vous allez me faire du mal! Oh, ne me faites pas du mal!"*—"You are going to hurt me! Oh, please don't hurt me!" To silence her cries and put an end to her struggles the plank was hurriedly tipped forward, the wooden collar clamped over her nape, and an instant later the great blade smashed through her neck. Her bleeding trunk was unbound and thrown to one side of the platform. One by one the Vandenyvers stepped forward....

So came to its end the life of Madame du Barry, last of the line of the Royal Mistresses of France. Summoned before the judgment of posterity and the application of the cold letter of moral law, she again must stand convicted. She was incontinent and unrepentant. She sold virtue for gold and that gold she spent on pleasures and vanities. Condemned in the court of morals, she faces a sentence yet more implacable before another tribunal. For the stern moralist of yesteryear is the grim economic theorist, the stolid sociologist of today, and the position occupied by Madame du Barry in a "socio-economic" order so outrageous as to be almost unmentionable, places her as much beneath the contempt of the former as beyond the understanding of the latter.

Her advocate can only hope for the mercy of those who believe that a fellow being is not always cut of one piece of cloth, good or bad, and that in vice as well as in virtue there are generally degrees. His plea would best be a simple one, resting on a recommendation so modest and homely that in the sonorous list of man's virtues it too often lies forgotten or overlooked: she was kind.

Bibliography

Books and periodicals consulted include:

Memoirs of the Marquis d'Argenson
Memoirs of Cardinal de Bernis
Memoirs of Baron de Besenval
Memoirs of the Duc de Choiseul
Memoirs of the Duc de Croy
Memoirs of Madame du Hausset
Memoirs of the Comte de Saint Priest
Memoirs of Prince Talleyrand
Memoirs of Madame Vigée-Lebrun
J. G. Alger: "An English Lover of Madame Dubarry" [Henry Seymour], *Westminster Review*, January, 1897
Mouffle d'Angerville: *La vie privée de Louis XV*
Octave Aubry: *The French Revolution*
Joseph Aulneau: *La Comtesse du Barry et la fin de l'ancien régime*
Belleval: *Souvenirs d'un chevau-léger*
Col. Bingham: *Marriages of the Bourbons*
Louis-J. de Bouillé: *Souvenirs et fragments*
Jacques Pierre Brissot: *Memoires de Brissot*
Madame Campan: *La vie privée de Marie Antoinette*
J. B. Capefigue: *Louis XV et la société du 18è siècle*
Dufort de Cheverny: *Souvenirs et mémoires*
Louis Dutens: *Mémoires d'un voyageur qui se répose*
R. B. Douglas: *The Life and Times of Madame du Barry*
Philippe Erlanger: *"Realités,"* 1957
J. T. d'Espinchal: *Revue retrospective*, Paris, 1887 (Vol. 6)
Fauchier-Magnan: *Les Dubarry: histoire d'une famille du 18è siècle*
Flammermont: *Le chancelier Maupeou et les parlements*
Flammermont: *Correspondances des agents diplomatiques étrangers en France*
Funk-Brentano: *L'ancien régime en France*
Pierre Gaxotte: *Le siècle de Louis XV*
E. and J. de Goncourt: *La duchesse de Châteauroux et ses soeurs*
Les maîtresses de Louis XV
G. Gooch: *Louis XV: The Monarchy in Decline*
Sara Goudard: *Remarques sur les anecdotes de Madame la comtesse du Barry*

S. P. Hardy: *Journal*
E. d'Hauterive: *Souvenirs du comte d'Espinchal*
A. Jabez: *La France sous Louis XV*
Fiske Kimball: *The Creation of the Rococo*
G. Kunstler: *La vie quotidienne sous Louis XV*
Charles de Lacretelle: *Histoire de France pendant le 18è siècle*
Georges Lemaître: *Beaumarchais*
G. Lenôtre: *The Tribunal of Terror*
Vieilles maisons, vieux papiers
The September Massacres
A. Leroy: *Madame du Barry et son temps*
Ch. de Ligne: *Mémoires*
Louis Madelin: *The French Revolution*
La France de Louis XV
Pidansat de Mairobert: *Anecdotes sur Madame du Barry*
Gaston Maugras: *Le duc et la duchesse de Choiseul*
La disgrace du duc et de la duchesse de Choiseul
Sénac de Meilhan: *Portraits et Caractères*
Gouverneur Morris: *A Diary of the French Revolution 1789-93*
Pierre de Nolhac: *Marie Antoînette, dauphine*
Madame de Pompadour
Louis XV et Marie Leczinska
Le château de Versailles sous Louis XV
J. B. Perkins: *France under Louis XV*
Imbert de St. Amand: *The Court of Louis XV*
The Last Years of Louis XV
Claude St.-André: *Madame du Barry*
Kurt von Schumacher: *The Du Barry*
Sainte-Beuve: *Portraits Litteraires* (Vol. 3)
Marquis de Ségur: *Au couchant de la monarchie*
Helen Simpson: *The Waiting City* (from Mercier: *Le tableau de Paris)*
D. M. Smyth: *Madame de Pompadour*
Casimir Strienski: *Mesdames de France*
The Eighteenth Century
Taine: *L'ancien régime*
C. Vatel: *Histoire de Madame du Barry*
Walpole-Du Deffand: *Correspondence* (Yale edition)
Nesta Webster: *Louis XV and Marie Antoinette before the Revolution*
The French Revolution
H. Noel Williams: *Madame du Barry*
The Duc de Richelieu
Arthur Young: *Travels in France and Italy*
Stefan Zweig: *Marie Antoinette*
Correspondance secrete de Mercy-Argenteau avec l'Empereur Joseph II et le Prince de Kaunitz (Arneth-Flammermont)
Kaunitz (Arneth-Flammermont)
Correspondance secrete de l'Impératrice Marie-Thérèse avec Marie-Antoinette et Mercy-Argenteau (Arneth-Geoffroy)

Notes

Chapter 1

Hausset: *Mémoires*
Nolhac: *Madame de Pompadour*
Smyth: *Madame de Pompadour*
Perkins: *France under Louis XV*
Goncourt: *La duchesse de Châteauroux*
Gooch: *Louis XV*
St.-Amand: *The Court of Louis XV*
Nolhac: *Louis XV et Marie Leczinska*

Chapter 2

Simpson: *The Waiting City*
Fauchier-Magnan: *Les Dubarry*
Mairobert: *Anecdotes sur Madame du Barry*
Maugras: *Le duc et la duchesse de Choiseul*
Gooch: *Louis XV*
Goncourt: *Les maîtresses de Louis XV*
Duc de Croy: *Mémoires*
Walpole-Du Deffand: *Correspondence*

Chapter 3

Fauchier-Magnan: *Les Dubarry*
Flammermont: *Le chancelier Maupeou*
Walpole-du Deffand: *Correspondence*
Correspondance secrete de Mercy-Argenteau
Strienski: *Mesdames de France*
Williams: *The Duc de Richelieu*
Maugras: *Le duc et la duchesse de Choiseul*
Duc de Croy: *Mémoires*
Goncourt: *Les maîtresses de Louis XV*

Chapter 4

Espinchal: *Revue Retrospective*, Paris, 1887 (Vol. 6)
Hauterive: *Souvenirs du comte d'Espinchal*
Belleval: *Souvenirs d'un chevau-léger*

Walpole-du Deffand: *Correspondence*
Flammermont: *Le chancelier Maupeou*

Chapter 5

Mouffle d'Angerville: *The Private Life of Louis XV*
Walpole-du Deffand: *Correspondence*
Mercy-Argenteau: *Correspondance secrete*
Flammermont: *Le chancelier Maupeou*
Maugras: *La disgrace du duc et de la duchesse de Choiseul*
Madelin: *La France de Louis XV*
Gaxotte: *La siècle de Louis XV*
Perkins: *France under Louis XV*
Talleyrand: *Mémoires*
Choiseul: *Mémoires*

Chapter 6

Nolhac: *Marie Antoinette, dauphine*
Zweig: *Marie Antoinette*
Correspondance secrete de l'Impératrice Marie-Thérèse
Mercy-Argenteau: *Correspondance secrete*
St. Amand: *The Last Years of Louis XV*
Nolhac: *Le Versailles de Louis XV*

Chapter 7

Goncourt: *Les maîtresses de Louis XV*
Fiske Kimball: *The Creation of the Rococo*
Nolhac: *Le château de Versailles sous Louis XV*

Chapter 8

Fauchier-Magnan: *Les Dubarry*
Strienski: *Mesdames de France*
Lemaître: *Beaumarchais*

Chapter 9

Mercy-Argenteau: *Correspondance*
Mouffle d'Angerville: *Private Life of Louis XV*
Baron Besenval: *Memoirs*
Nolhac: *Marie Antoinette, dauphine*
Sainte-Beuve: *Portraits Litteraires* (Vol. 3)

Chapter 10

Fauchier-Magnan: *Les Dubarry*
Goncourt: *Les maîtresses de Louis XV*
Mairobert: *Anecdotes sur Mme. du Barry*
Prince de Ligne: *Memoirs*

Chapter 11

Gooch: *Maria Theresa*
Duc de Croy: *Mémoires*
Alger: *Westminster Review*, January, 1897
Young: *Travels*
Dutens: *Mémoires d'un voyageur qui se répose*

Chapter 12

Cheverny: *Souvenirs et mémoires*
Vigée-Lebrun: *Mémoires*
Belleval: *Souvenirs d'un chevau-léger*
Ségur: *Au couchant de la monarchie*
Erlanger: *Realités*, 1957
Morris: *Diary of the French Revolution*
Madelin: *The French Revolution*

Chapter 13

Campan: *La vie privée de Marie Antoinette*
Espinchal: *Souvenirs*
Walpole-du Deffand: *Correspondence*
Goncourt: *Les maîtresses de Louis XV*
Madelin: *The French Revolution*
Aubry: *The French Revolution*

Chapter 14

Lenôtre: *The September Massacres*
Bouillé: *Souvenirs et fragments*
Madelin: *The French Revolution*
Gabriel de Choiseul: *Memoires*
Aulneau: *La Comtesse du Barry*

Chapter 15

Lenôtre: *Vieilles maisons, vieux papiers*
Fauchier-Magnan: *Les Dubarry*
Webster: *The French Revolution*
Madame Roland: *Mémoires*
Madelin: *The French Revolution*

Chapter 16

Lenôtre: *The Tribunal of Terror*
Dutens: *Mémoires d'un voyageur qui se répose*
Dossier du Barry, Tribunaux revolutionnaires, National Archives (as given by C. Vatel, Goncourt and C. St.-Andre)

Chapter 17

Dossier du Barry, *ibid.*
Lenôtre: *Vieilles maisons, vieux papiers*
Douglas: *Life and Times of Madame du Barry*

Index